Sometimes I get pretty homesick but I guess everyone does.
If we didn't what the hell would our home mean to us if we didn't
miss it and the people we hold dear to us. — Willie, July 1945

Dear to Us

A Tug Hill Family's
World War II Story in Letters

Compiled and Edited by

JILL S. MARKHAM

Dedicated to my grandmother,
Evelyn Wasmuth Markham

The editor with her grandmother, 1953

ISBN-10: 0692051007
ISBN-13: 978-0692051009

Book design by Veronica Seyd
Cover design by Jill S. Markham
Photo collages on pages ii, 2,
and back cover by Glenn Gaston

Contents

Introduction

In the spring of his 90th year, my dad, retired Air Force Reserve Major Theodore W. Markham, did an unplanned vault from the back of his tractor while working on his Christmas tree farm in Steuben County, New York. The resulting broken leg called for some live-in help, and I spent most of that summer with my parents at their home on their tree farm in Bath.

Here was the opportunity to do some routine housekeeping and re-organization of my parents' house, necessitated by virtue of their living in the same place for 35 years. The office was the place to start. I organized its books, tidied its desk, discarded its collection of junk mail, and in a final purge of its built-in cupboard, unearthed a dented, round, tin can, once a safe storage place for biscuits or some other food stuff. Inside the shabby tin was a collection of over 100 seventy-year-old handwritten letters written to my father from his large Lewis County family during World War II, a cache that can best be described as a long-forgotten buried treasure.

Letters, to me, are irresistible, the ultimate snoop. They are not an overheard conversation, not an electronic text or e mail, and not a recorded voicemail left on one's answering machine. A letter is authentic, a first-hand peek into another's personal thoughts and experiences made with that person's very own hand. It's a hard copy part of someone, and in my case, some very special someones. Dad's family was always dear to me, and there they were – my four aunts, my three uncles, my grandfather, and best of all, my grandmother – nine different personalities and voices all writing honestly and lovingly to their brother and son, my father.

Fascinated, I took my tin can full of letters to bed with me at night and began to read. Undaunted by some challenging handwriting, I first read the letters in random order, pulling them one by one from the crowded can.

They kept me awake long past bed time, but I couldn't stop reading until I had read them all. I knew that some of the handwriting would pose a problem to my parents' eyes and decided to type them. Seventy thousand words and a year later, the letters needed to be put in order. And that's when the story began to emerge.

My first intention was to simply make my original transcription of the letters available to my parents, my four siblings, my three daughters, and my Markham clan of cousins. But my dad had enjoyed photography and had put together a well-organized photo album of his war years. As I read and re-read the letters, it became clear that I already had the photographs that could give life to the letters. Most of the photographs in the book are from my father's album.

Next, a cousin, Ron Klossner, gave me letters that his mother had saved along with a small collection of letters written to another aunt. Finally, five years after my initial find, my sister, Leigh, discovered a heretofore unopened shoe box in my parents' basement. In it was the rest of the story – the many, many letters that my dad had written to his family. Here was one of the biggest challenges of all. Dad was a prolific writer and including all of his letters would have almost doubled the size of the book. They needed to be sorted through, some eliminated, and the rest dove-tailed by date into the body of the letters, and that's when the story became complete.

———

It's a timeless story, one that has repeated itself over and over as long as there have been families and as long as there have been wars. It's a story that has been capitalized on and sometimes sensationalized. The story has been repeated in novels and on movie screens. But the only ones who can truly tell the story are the ones who made it, the mothers and fathers, the sisters and brothers, who didn't know if their most recent goodbyes were their last. It was made by the wives who hadn't heard from their husbands for months at a time, and who endured the ever-present threat of the arrival of the telegram that would tell them that their worst fears had come true. It was made by the soldiers who learned, one by one, of the deaths of their schoolmates, friends, and fraternity brothers. There were the soldier's good friends, newly made and just as suddenly taken away as the military trained and honed its personnel. There was the soldier yearning to serve but held in limbo by the military bureaucracy. There was the soldier waiting to hear of the birth of his first child. Most of all, there was the soldier who witnessed the horrors of war and there were the families whose lives were shattered by the war's carnage. All of these people are the real authors of the war stories. My father's family wrote the story of their journey through the greatest debacle in human history, World War II.

The setting for this story is Lewis County on the eastern edge of the Tug Hill Plateau region of New York State. Tug Hill is a notoriously rugged place, known for catching the most snow in the United States east of the Rocky Mountains. In the late 19th century, the water power of the Black River and numerous other creeks and waterways combined forces with the vast hardwood forests and the logging industry of the region. First sawmills and then paper mills became the county's largest employers in the early 20th century. According to U.S. Census figures, in 1940 the total population of the county was 22,815.

Like millions of other Depression-era rural families, Ernest and Evelyn Markham, my grandparents, raised their large family on a small farm. Theirs was located half way between Turin and Constableville on West Road. Ernest and Evelyn provided a diverse cast of characters to author this book.

The eldest child was Ernestine. At the start of World War II, Ernestine was a newly married young mother. She had earned her teaching degree at the Plattsburg Normal School and aspired to teach. Her husband, Bob O'Brien, and her young sons, Billy and David, are also characters who play their parts in the story.

Marian was just a year younger than Ernestine. In 1941 Marian was a young, single mother, already married and already divorced. The scant employment opportunities of the Depression necessitated her separation from her son as she worked as a live-in housekeeper for a well-known businessman in Ithaca, Mr. Edwin B. Baxter. Marian's son, Alton, lived in Turin with his grandparents, Ernest and Evelyn.

Robert (Bob) graduated from the College of Agriculture at Cornell University in 1939. He enlisted in the Naval Reserves in early 1942 and began pilot training in May of that year. Bob served two tours of duty as a patrol bomber pilot and wrote his letters home often from an undisclosed location "somewhere in the Pacific."

The next-born son, Burton (Burt), graduated from the College of Agriculture at Cornell in 1941. Shortly after graduation he married Melrose

Marriott, and in 1943 they were living in Ithaca. They were the parents of a one-year-old daughter, Linda. Both Melrose and Linda are important players in the story.

Theodore (Ted) was three years younger than Burt and was a junior at Cornell when he enlisted in the Army Reserve Corps in 1942. In March of 1943, he was activated. Most of the letters in this story are written by the family to him as he was transferred to a total of eleven different military bases for the duration of the war.

Janice was the next daughter and, as our story begins, was newly graduated from the New York State Agriculture and Technical School at Canton. In 1943 she married John Klossner and began life as a farmer's wife on Highmarket Road, not far from home. Happy in her new role as a homemaker and wife, she watched in disbelief as the war stripped the men from her family.

Willis was the youngest son. In 1943, at the age of 18, he was living at home on the farm with the sometimes overwhelming responsibility of keeping it running. He milked the cows, managed the field work, and was the head mechanic – all at the same time. When he could, he enjoyed hunting and fishing in his bountiful Tug Hill neighborhood.

Shirley was the last-born of the family and was a freshman in high school as the story begins. Like any other high school girl, her world was full of social events as well as her successes and her struggles with her high school classes. She wrote very fondly and colorfully of her nieces and nephews: Alton, Billy, Linda, and David.

My grandfather, Ernest Markham, was the writer of very few letters. He was not a man of words. Beginning in 1915, Ernest worked as a rural mail carrier with a horse and buggy and a 23-mile route. By the 40's his route had grown to 38 miles and the war's tire rationing had slowed him down. The strain of the war showed on him, and Evelyn feared that he might not have the strength to see retirement.

Evelyn Wasmuth Markham, my grandmother, is the heroine of this story. She was a tiny woman who possessed extraordinary amounts of wisdom, grace, and compassion. Evelyn had already known loss. On what must have been a bitter and frigid day in January of 1913, Ernest and Evelyn's first-born daughter, Laura, died. She was five months old. Evelyn never wrote about what she didn't have. Instead, she would rejoice in the gift of what she did have – her family. She would write, "Ernestine and her babies – they make me live over my happiest days again when my own little ones were in my arms." And in another letter, "Oh Ted, these grandchildren are the greatest joy and comfort to us now. Without them I don't know how we could bear these days."

To me, it is my father's story that provides the main plot of the book. He was no war hero but simply an enlisted man doing his best to serve his country in the best way that he could. As in any good story, Ted's struggles provide a rising conflict, a climax, and a resolution that only he could do. His family supplies the characters, and the Tug Hill serves as a background, all set within the framework of the drama and the tragedy of World War II.

As I worked at assembling the letters, I became uncomfortably aware of how much of the war I simply didn't know about. My comments about the war and my footnotes are meant to provide a historical reference point for the reader. Rough casualty figures have been given when appropriate but casualty figures are inconsistently documented and sometimes difficult to interpret. Casualties are often reported as "Allied casualties," or "Allied dead," or "American deaths," or "Allied wounded." My historical comments have all been researched and my references are included in a bibliography, but this work should in no way be used as a reference itself.

Finally, these letters have been transcribed as they were written. The Markhams were all fluent writers, but their sometimes colloquial writing – as in their use of "tho" for "though" and their occasional errors in punctuation – were all copied as they were written in order to preserve the unique voice of each writer. I hope you enjoy hearing their voices again as much as I do.

Jill S. Markham

The Markham Family in 1945

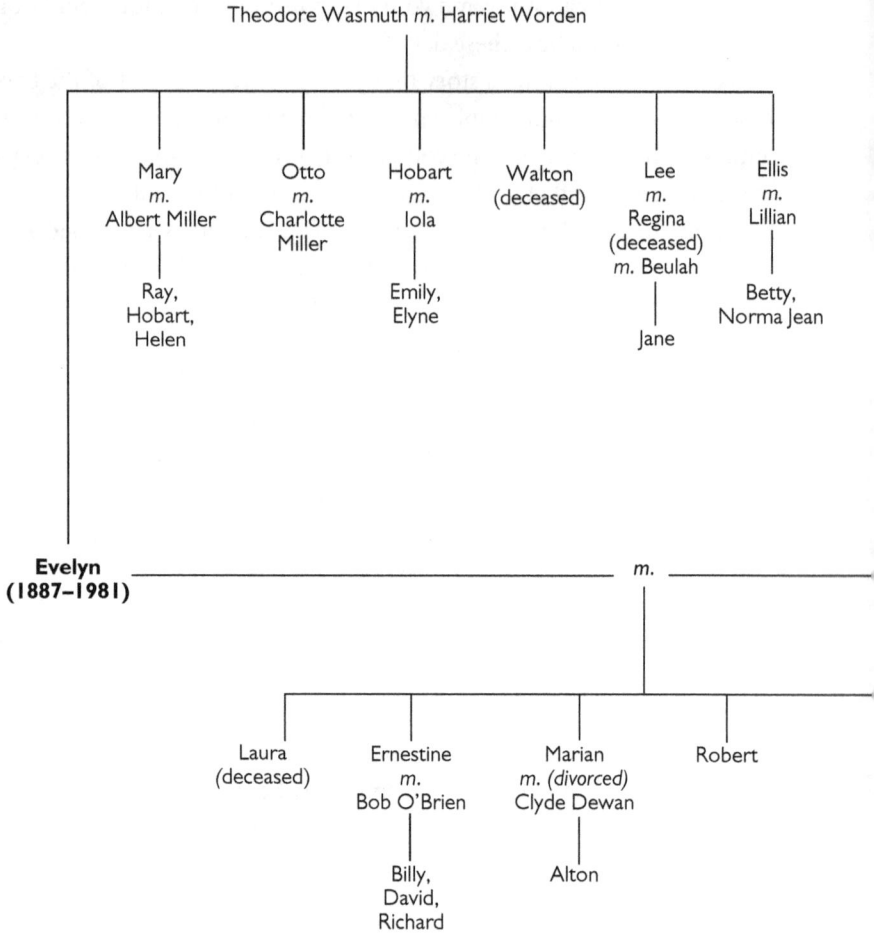

Theodore Wasmuth *m.* Harriet Worden

Mary *m.* Albert Miller	Otto *m.* Charlotte Miller	Hobart *m.* Iola	Walton (deceased)	Lee *m.* Regina (deceased) *m.* Beulah	Ellis *m.* Lillian
Ray, Hobart, Helen		Emily, Elyne		Jane	Betty, Norma Jean

Evelyn
(1887–1981) ———————————————————————— *m.* ——————

Laura (deceased)	Ernestine *m.* Bob O'Brien	Marian *m. (divorced)* Clyde Dewan	Robert
	Billy, David, Richard	Alton	

William Markham *m.* Laura Jones

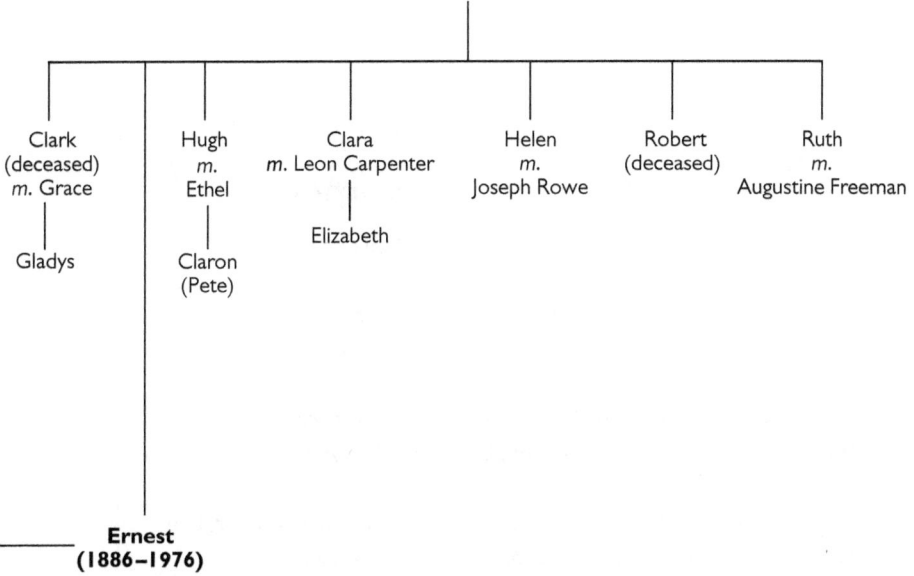

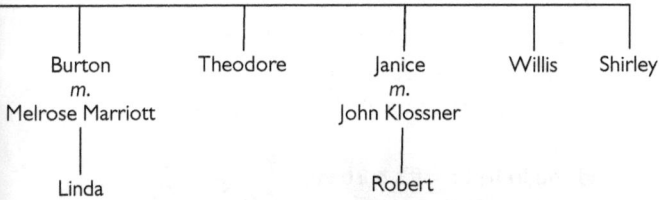

Clark
(deceased)
m. Grace

Gladys

Hugh
m.
Ethel

Claron
(Pete)

Clara
m. Leon Carpenter

Elizabeth

Helen
m.
Joseph Rowe

Robert
(deceased)

Ruth
m.
Augustine Freeman

**Ernest
(1886–1976)**

Burton
m.
Melrose Marriott

Linda

Theodore

Janice
m.
John Klossner

Robert

Willis

Shirley

Glossary of Names
(listed by first name)

Adrial Jones – Ernest's eccentric uncle, said to be a recluse

Albert Miller – Evelyn's brother-in-law, married to her sister Mary, and father of Ray and Hele

Alf Phelps – a fraternity brother of Ted's, killed in France

Alton (Altie) Dewan – Marian's son, Ernest and Evelyn's oldest grandchild

Beulah Wasmuth – Evelyn's sister-in-law, married to her brother, Lee

Bill Barnum – a fraternity brother of Ted's, killed in France

Bill Healt – a Constableville friend, married Marion Long in December, 1944

Billy O'Brien – Ernestine and Bob O'Brien's first-born son

Bob (Robert) Markham – Ernest and Evelyn's oldest son

Bob O'Brien – Ernestine's husband

Burt Goulko – a fraternity brother of Ted's, killed in France

Burt Markham – Ernest and Evelyn's second son and Melrose's husband

Chet Freeman – a family friend and Irene Schoff's husband

Clara Klossner – John Klossner's sister

Clara Markham Carpenter – Ernest's sister, married to M. Leon Carpenter

Clyde Dewan – Marian's ex-husband, Altie's father

David O'Brien – Ernestine and Bob's second son

Don McGovern – graduated with Ted in 1939, John Klossner's best man

E.B. or Mr. B. (Edwin) Baxter – Marian's employer and owner of the Quality Shop in Ithaca

Ellis Wasmuth – Evelyn's brother

Ethel Markham – Ernest's sister-in-law, married to Hugh Markham, Pete's mother

Fay Ackerman – a friend and neighbor, father of Leonard and Lincoln

Glossary of Names

George Waters – Marian's gentleman friend

Gladys Markham – daughter of Ernest's brother Clark and Grace Markham

Grace Markham – Widow of Clark Markham, Ernest's older brother

Grandma – Hattie Worden Wasmuth, Evelyn's mother

Grandpa – W.B. (William) Markham, Ernest's father

Harland Abbey - graduated with Ted in 1939, killed in the war

Harold O'Brien – Bob O'Brien's brother and partner in their family farm

Harold Baxter – E.B. Baxter's son

Harold Baxter Jr. – E.B. Baxter's grandson

Helen Markham Rowe – Ernest's sister, wife of Joseph Rowe

Helen Miller - Ted's cousin, Evelyn's niece, daughter of Mary and Albert Miller,
    married Paul Seitz

Hugh Markham – Ernest's brother, Pete's father, Ethel's husband

Irene Schoff Freeman - Chet Freeman's wife and Rita Schoff's sister

Jan (Janice) Markham Klossner – Ernest and Evelyn's third daughter, married to
    John Klossner

Jane Wasmuth- Evelyn's niece, daughter of Lee and Beulah Wasmuth

Jerry Freeman – Chet and Irene Freeman's son

Jerry (Gerald) Nuffer – a friend from home

Joe (Joseph) Rowe – Ernest's brother-in-law, married to his sister, Helen Markham

Johnnie – John Klossner, Jan's husband

Kate Kraeger – Willie's girlfriend and Robert Kraeger's sister

Lee Wasmuth – Evelyn's brother, Beaulah's husband, and Jane's father

Len (Leonard) Ackerman – family friend, Fay's son and Lincoln's brother

Lillian – Mr. Baxter's daughter

Linc (Lincoln) Ackerman – family friend, Fay and Amelia's son and Leonard's
    brother, died in the Battle of the Bulge

Linda Markham – Burt and Melrose's daughter

Liz –daughter of Ernest's sister, Clara Markham Carpenter

Mary Wasmuth Miller – Evelyn's younger sister, married to Albert Miller and
    mother of Ted's cousins Ray, Helen, and Hobart

Marian Markham Dewan – Evelyn and Ernest's second oldest daughter, Ted's
    sister, and Alton's mother

Glossary of Names

Marion Long – graduated with Ted in 1939
Marion Regetz – graduated with Ted in 1939
Mr. Kaskela (William Kaskela) – Constableville High School Principal

Otto Wasmuth – Evelyn's brother

Peggy Kuhn – Ted's girl from Williamsport
Pete (Claron) Markham – son of Hugh and Ethel Markham, Ernest's nephew, and
    Ted's cousin

Ray Miller – Ted's cousin, son of Mary and Albert Miller, Evelyn's nephew
Rita – Rita Schoff, Irene Freeman's sister
Robert Kraeger – graduated with Ted in 1939, killed in the South Pacific (MIA)
Robert Klossner – newborn son of Jan and Bob Klossner, born on VE Day

Shirley Markham – Ernest and Evelyn's youngest child

Ted (Theodore) Markham – Ernest and Evelyn's third son
Teen (Ernestine) Markham O'Brien, Ernest and Evelyn's oldest daughter, married
    to Bob O'Brien
Teny (Augustine) Freeman – married to Ernest's sister Ruth
Tom Dawley – hired man on the farm

W.B. – the family's nickname for William Markham, Ernest's father
Willis (Willie) Markham – Ernest and Evelyn's youngest son

Dear to Us

U.S. ARMY AIR FORCE

U.S. ARMY AIR FORCES

U. S. ARMY AIR FORCES

Service Club

U. S. ARMY

C.A.A.F.
COLUMBUS, MISS.

CAMP WHEELER, GEORGIA

U. S. ARMY AIR FORCES

San Angelo Army Air Field
BOMBARDIER SCHOOL
SAN ANGELO, TEXAS

TECHNICAL TRAINING COMMAND

U. S. ARMY AIR FORCES
MAXWELL FIELD, ALA.

U. S. NAVAL AIR STATION
ALAMEDA, CALIFORNIA

AVIATION CADETS
AIR CORPS TRAINING DETACHMENT
DECATUR, ALABAMA

ARMY AIR FORCES GUNNERY SCHOOL

U.S. ARMY

U. S. AIR FORCES

ARMY AIR FORCES

UNITED STATES

ARMY AIR FORCES

U.S. NAVAL RESERVE AVIATION BASE
ATLANTA, GEORGIA

AIR CORPS TRAINING DETACHMENT
DECATUR, ALABAMA

1942

Summer 1942

On December 7, 1941, in an attempt to cripple the United States Pacific Fleet, Japan launched an early morning air attack on Pearl Harbor. The following day President Franklin D. Roosevelt asked Congress for a declaration of war against Japan, and the United States of America plunged into the most devastating war in human history. Robert (Bob) W. Markham, eldest son of Ernest and Evelyn Markham and a recent graduate of Cornell University, wasted no time in enlisting in the Naval Reserves. In May of 1942, he began Naval Reserve pilot training in Atlanta, Georgia. The collection begins with a letter from Bob written to his 13-year-old youngest sister, Shirley, affectionately known by all as "Blondie." Writing from Atlanta, Bob is clearly enjoying southern hospitality.

U. S. NAVAL RESERVE AVIATION BASE
ATLANTA, GEORGIA

Atlanta, Georgia
June 1, 1942
Monday AM

Dear Shirley,

This has got to be quick as we have to get going in a few minutes. We just had inspection and I am pretty well caught up for a few minutes, it's 7:00 and our classes don't start for 25 min.

This letter is written strictly for you but if there is any news you wish to tell the others it's OK with me.

We are just starting a new week after our first weekend out. We all had a wonderful time but mine was best of all. A Mrs. Dutton arranges for students to be invited out for Sunday dinner and when the sheet was up last week I was first to sign up. We all met down at one of the churches and the people met us there. Milt Thornquist from Syracuse and I were guests of Mrs. Vaughan Nixon who must be about the grandest hostess in Atlanta. Her daughter, Mrs. Malon Courts and her little son and daughter met us and drove us to the Nixon house where we met the rest. Mr. Nixon

4

is president-treasurer of the Atlanta Woolen Mills and Mr. Courts has some sort of business, I didn't quite make out.

The only people I can think of to compare them to are the Goulds* or the Sissons but they have a much nicer home and grounds than either and want to talk about everything but themselves which is at least different from Mr. Sisson. We had southern fried chicken with two servants serving us and the whole atmosphere just upheld all the best things we have heard about the south.

Mr. Nixon took pictures of us, then we played shuffleboard out in their garden where they have beautiful trees, flowers, a rose garden, badminton court etc. I hope you folks can see one or two of the pictures. Later Mr. Courts took us down to his club where they were having some tennis matches.

Mr. Courts is pretty good, used to be state champion for 3 or 4 years and won a whole string of winnings a yard long, however we didn't know that until I ran into his pictures and pedigree while waiting for him to take a shower.

Little Richard is one of the brightest and most gentlemanly little fellows you could imagine and he and I had a great time. He is going to fly someday and is afraid the war will be over before he is old enough, he is six. I showed him how to salute and do the West Point breather which is one of our exercises to develop the chest. I was crazy about the kid confidentially.

Don't worry about me, Blondie. I am taking advantage of my uniform and have met two nice Georgia "peaches", one at the Bob Hope show and one at a dancing class that I got into the other night. My old heart is going flippity flop, Blondie, had a date with one Sat. night, the other this Sat. You see you don't need to worry.

It's noon now and the papers just came, thanks. Here are some things I wish somebody would get together and send sometime, probably Ted can do it. White shoes, couple of pairs of socks, handkerchiefs (ants ate holes in a couple), colored glasses. That's all I can think of now. I have decided to get a white uniform, that's why the shoes, maybe they are in pretty bad shape but it will save me some money for awhile.

Things are going better all the time and a week from today we start to do some flying.

Love to all

Bob

---

*The Goulds owned the Gould Paper Company (later the Lyons Falls Pulp and Paper Company).

Bob at Cornell, 1939

Bob in his "whites"

Japan's domination of the Pacific was dependent on establishing military bases on strategic islands, controlling critical shipping lanes, and securing abundant oil sources. They wasted no time. Within six months of the attack on Pearl Harbor, the Japanese had invaded the Philippines, Guam, Wake Island, the Solomon Islands, the Dutch East Indies (Indonesia), and even two islands, Attu and Kiska, in Alaska's Aleutian chain. On the Asian mainland, French Indochina (Vietnam), Hong Kong, Malaya, Burma, Thailand, and significant regions in China were taken.

Finally, in May of 1942, the Allies were able to halt the Japanese drive toward Australia at the Battle of the Coral Sea. On June 4, the Americans delivered a blow to the Japanese at the Battle of Midway, and the tide was turned as the Allies began a campaign of "island hopping," fighting their way toward Japan to gain control of strategically important islands.

In August 1942, Bob was sent for advanced flight instruction to Jacksonville, Florida, where he was in training for several months.

1943

Spring 1943

In February 1943, Bob was commissioned an Ensign and was stationed at the naval base in San Diego, California, home of the Pacific Fleet. Writing to his sister, Jan, Bob is enjoying the challenges he faces as a pilot but seems a bit worried about his dating prospects. Nineteen-year-old Jan will soon graduate from the New York State Agricultural and Technical School at Canton.

Tues. night
Mar. 2

Dear Jan,

I guess there is time to scribble a little note before I turn in. My roomie is out tonight anyway and probably will wake me up if I'm asleep when he comes in. He has been griping about how dark things are around here, has been in Honolulu and says our blackout* is more complete than the one there. Boy! I have found that it would be easy to break my precious neck on some of the steps at the ends of the barracks.

I hope your social life hasn't taken such a beating as mine has lately. I guess I was due for a rest after that leave though. My blood pressure was down to 95 when I got here and they wouldn't clear me for flying but last week I passed the Schneider** with a +17 which is only one point below the top so you see I am responding well to good food, rest, and sunshine. Things are really okay here except that sometimes there hasn't been quite enough to do to keep me from getting plenty down in the mouth.

They put me in an operational training unit which will keep me here several weeks, then we don't know what will happen. Part of the gang went out to the Salton Sea in the Imperial Valley yesterday and the rest of us will probably go out there in a couple of days.

I looked up the Evans family and spent two Sundays with them. Murial took me to a dance and has shown me around a bit. I never guessed I would be going around with girls your age but that's about all there is left for us old timers. Sometimes I worry about me.

---

*San Diego was one of several cities on the West Coast with an enforced blackout.
**The Schneider Index was a test of physical fitness given to all pilots, the highest score possible being an 18.

Golly – it's nice and warm out here most of the time and plumb hot sometimes. The grass is nice and green, but like N.Y. in late May. Today we flew down along the coast of Mexico a ways and the mountains were beautiful, in fact they look pretty nice from here. We are on an island with the ocean on one side and the bay, city, and mountains on the other.

The trip out here was very interesting but a bit hard. I came by way of New York, Washington, Atlanta – New Orleans etc. Pete and Doris* met me at the station in Tucson but I couldn't stop over with them. We saw lots of desert and mountains and then went down into Mexico a bit. It was quite an experience, hard to describe though and I couldn't get any pictures.

Well, drop me a line Jan and who knows, maybe I'll write again. Hope this gets to the right place.

Love
Bob

Bob writes from Sandy Beach to Shirley about meeting a celebrity and watching the making of a classic war movie.

Sunday morning
Mar. 7

Dear Shirley,

This is my first morning at Sandy Beach as poor flying weather kept us in San Diego until yesterday. This is a quiet spot, only a small group here and nothing but desert around. I guess it's almost like being on a desert island. I like it a lot so far. You can hardly see the base from the air as the buildings are the same color as the sand and would be anyway for when the wind blows everything gets peppered. Everything is just a little sandy, including the beds and especially our shoes.

We wear anything we want to around here, mostly just cotton pants & shirts and no ties. Mostly I wear my tennis shoes, and a sweat shirt when it's cool, and a baseball cap. It seems good after San Diego where we

---

*2nd Lt. Claron (Pete) Markham was a cousin serving as a bombardier in the Army Air Forces. Claron's Uncle Ernest, Bob's father, gave Claron his nickname, Pete. Pete married Doris C. Cummings on November 22, 1942.

BOONVILLE, N. Y., THURSDAY, FEBRUARY 4, 19

Turin Man Wins Navy "Wings"

From the Boonville Herald, *February 4, 1943*

25-YEAR-OLD FLIER BECOMES ENSIGN

Robert W. Markham Completes Year's Work At Florida Station

U. S. Naval Air Station, Jacksonville, Fla., Jan. 30—After almost a year of aviation instruction involving ground school and actual flight training, Robert Wm. Markham, of Turin, N. Y., completed the final stages of schooling and has been commissioned an Ensign in the Naval Reserve, it was announced here today.

The 25-year-old flier was presented his Navy "wings" and commission by Captain J. D. Price, commandant of the Jacksonville Naval Air Station, at brief graduation ceremonies.

Markham completed elimination training at the Naval Air Station, Atlanta, Ga., last August and was sent to Jacksonville for advanced flight instruction.

Since Navy pilots fly over uncharted water-ways, Markham's Jacksonville studies in celestial navigation and communications were exacting. Combat flying demands professional skill in all branches of training. Proficiency at the gunnery range, in the classrooms, and in actual flight was necessary to give him a thorough background in aeronautics.

The young officer is the son of Mr. and Mrs. Ernest L. Markham of Turin. He is a graduate of Turin High School and received his B. S. degree at Cornell University.

had to be in full uniform all the time except when flying and we couldn't go to town except in blues.

Columbia Pictures Corporation is making a movie just a few miles from here and some of us went over there yesterday afternoon. It is a desert war picture starring Humphrey Bogart as a sergeant. Bogie, as they call him, told us the name was to be "Somewhere in Sahara" but they will probably change it.* He is a very friendly and ordinary sort of guy, in fact the whole group was very nice to us. I had quite a nice little visit with a few of the sound and camera men. The only complaint I have is that there are no pretty girls and no horses in the picture, just a modern desert war. We watched them film a scene from the bottom of a well. It's all above ground – built up against a bank. In a few days we may be able to see some of the fighting scenes.

Most of the pictures I took at home and in Atlanta were good but they didn't enlarge them for me, just made small prints. When I get them enlarged I may send some home. Also I may be able to get some around here.

Thanks for the letter, Blondie. I hope I'll rate another soon.

Love
Bob

---

*Sahara, a 1943 war film.

11

Spring 1943

Ted at the Alpha Zeta fraternity house, Cornell, 1943

At the beginning of his junior year at Cornell, third-born-son Ted enlisted in the Army Reserve Corps. He was activated in February 1943, but in mid-March was still attending classes in Ithaca.

Bob writes to Ted of flying long-range patrol bombers on the West Coast. His love of farming is evident as he writes about California's climate and agriculture.

Sat. nite
Mar. 13

Dear Ted,

The last report from home tells me that you are still in school & know it must be hard to keep interested in school but you might as well stay as long as you can. Was glad to hear that you can use some of my old clothes. I should have thought of it when I was there.

Things out here aren't too exciting. I haven't done much flying yet as the unit is short of planes and instructors and there are several fellows who have been here longer and they are trying to get them through. We are getting quite a bit of navigation and a good Link Trainer schedule. We

12

have a small base on Salton here out in Imperial Valley that makes a good place to fly. We were out there a few days but a couple of cases of measles broke out and they brought us back. The fellows who have checked out to solo are not there now and the rest of us will probably go back as soon as we are checked out or maybe sooner.

We are still flying PBYs but newer ones of course and fully equipped. They plan to qualify us as first pilots here and then we will be turned over to another outfit maybe to fly B24s, PB 2ys, or Venturas.* Things aren't moving too fast tho so we might be quite awhile yet.

This is pretty nice country out here, at least the grass will grow when it rains and things are nice and clean and the scenery is good. It's a relief after Georgia and Florida. Clover and alfalfa grow pretty well around here and I've seen quite a bit of topsoil so the soil is apparently quite sweet. I was out to Foster Evans and helped him plant a little garden, take care of the chickens and had a good time. Poultry is quite important here and I've seen quite a bit of celery, lettuce, carrots and other vegetables.

In an hour or less we can go up over 8,000 ft. mountains and down below sea level to Salton and it's real desert over there. The few bushes around in the sand don't even look alive. There is an irrigated section where they grow alfalfa and some vegetables but nothing grows without water.

Tonight I'm on duty as 2nd pilot for the ready plane. If there is a job to do out in our area we will have to go out. There is a possibility at the moment but we don't have definite word yet. Ordinarily a fellow gets more sleep down here than otherwise for we just stand by unless something turns up. The plane crew sleeps in the plane.

Pete is still in Turin and not doing very much I guess. He is training as a navigator now but doesn't fly much. I saw him a few minutes on the way out and had a letter from him but didn't find out too much about his work but am still glad I'm in the navy.

Drop me a line to let me know what's going on and don't work too hard in the meantime. Have a good time while you can and if you need a bit of money let me know.

Bob

---

*The PBY Catalina, PBY-2, B-24 Liberator, and Ventura were long-range, land-based bombers used against enemy shipping and submarines. The PB 2y was a flying boat/patrol bomber.

Ted was sent to Fort Niagara, New York, for processing in early April. He's glad to get rid of his civilian clothes, and he's proud to be a Cornellian.

Fort Niagara, April '43

Dear Folks,

Well here I am, and where I'll go I don't know. I have asked for Flying Cadet, but I don't know whether or not I'll get it. We arrived yesterday afternoon after looking around the Falls. We immediately started processing and we will probably finish tomorrow noon.

I have no idea how long I will be here but most of the fellows stay for about 30 days before they're shipped. We won't know when until the morning before and we don't know where until we get there.

I have my uniform now so I shipped a mess of stuff home tonight. I shipped my camera and film, but I may call for it later, so keep it handy. I was glad to get rid of those clothes because they were getting badly mussed and linted up around here.

I rather like the place so far. The fellows who have been processing us have been swell. Jerry sleeps over me and Les on the lower bunk on my left side while Alex Dugan has the lower bunk on my right. We have about 8 A.Z. men here and many other Cornellians whom I know very well.

We Cornellians made quite a showing in the "I.Q." test this morning. The lowest in the whole bunch got 117 while 110 is required for O.C.S.* I got 130, Jerry 129, Les 129, Baker 125, Seldon 140, Tiny 125, and etc. We're proud of it, and they tell us we can be because the average from other schools has been considerably lower. We are amongst Harvard, Syracuse, Rochester, Princeton, Penn, Bucknell, and etc. We take quite a ribbing as well as dish it out.

I wish sometime when you're in Lowville you would pick up a kit which the county is giving each service-man and send it to me. You probably shouldn't write for 3-4 days but I guess it doesn't make too much difference. Well I guess I'll quit now, so write when you can.

As ever,

Ted

---

*O.C.S. = Officer Candidate School.

In her first letter to Ted, his mother, Evelyn Markham, shares one of Bob's flying adventures.

MRS. ERNEST L. MARKHAM
BOX 143
TURIN, NEW YORK

Apr.13

Dear Ted,

Your letter came yesterday and the bag full of clothes today. Everything in fine shape.

We are proud to know that your I.Q. was so good. And Hooray for Cornell! There are so many Cornellians in your bunch, it would seem that some of them would be going on with you.

We have had a letter from Bob since you went away. It was written a week ago today, up in the air, off the coast of Mexico. Three of them, Dick, Smithy and himself, were up from seven to twelve taking turns as pilot and second pilot and one resting. He had taken her off, climbed to 11,000 to get above the clouds, which were about a mile deep, and then under the hood for instrument flying. Said no one could imagine how beautiful clouds could be till they see them like this with the early morning sun on them. They are like snow so they have to wear dark glasses up there. He said it was quite cold up there but they had a good heater and had just made coffee. "All the comforts of home – even some music happened to come in on the radio."

We were up at Uncle Hugh's Sunday.* Doris and Pete are at Alamagordo, Ariz. Pete expects a short leave to come home – Doris to stay here.

Harry Mathis has gone to Salt Lake City.

You said, "better not write for 3 or 4 days," but I guess it is that long now.

Your pictures came, so I'll send them. If you want the negatives and the other stuff they sent, let me know and I'll send them. Everyone is OK and sends love.

"Mom"

*Hugh Markham was Ernest's younger brother and Pete's father.

It didn't take Ted long to do some grousing about his new situation (Ted's letter to Bob is not available). In this next letter, Bob gives Ted some brotherly advice about how to cope with the frustrations and bureaucracy of the military. Next, he writes about a tragedy at sea. Bob finishes his letter to Ted with his ideas of how he would manage the family's herd of Jersey cows if he were at home and in charge.

Their father, Ernest Markham, worked for thirty years as a rural mail carrier. His first love, though, was his small herd of Jersey cows. Ted and Bob both shared their father's lifelong interest in the dairy industry and farming.

Ready Room
Easter Sunday Morning

Dear Ted,

I was sure glad to get your letter yesterday. It was about what I had sort of expected from you. Ray and I were both plenty disgusted with military life at first too you know.* We would still rather be back on the farm and at times are sure we could do more good there, but that's not for us to decide. The only thing you can do is accept the inefficiency and chicken shit procedure and try to get adjusted so that it doesn't bother too much but for god's sake don't let it spoil you.

After you get acquainted and get a little responsibility it isn't nearly as bad. You'll be shoved around and be ready to tell some officer to go roll his hoop but it won't do any good. You might as well learn how to play and make good use of your leisure time for there will be lots of it. I never knew how to play or be a social whirler until I joined the navy. Out here it's really terrific and I'm getting to like it.

In another few days our class will be qualified first pilots and assigned to a squadron. We may be flying PBY's, PB2Y's, B24s, or Venturas and might be sent to almost any field of action or inaction. All we have left here is one five hundred mile daytime navigation hop and one all night nav. hop. The night hop will be by celestial navigation entirely and will be about fourteen hundred miles.

I took Bill Zimmer out with me one day and now he wants to go again so he must have enjoyed it. Yesterday we took a couple of doctors along on a bombing run to Salton Sea.

---

*Ray Miller was a first cousin, Evelyn's nephew.

Spring 1943

Last week we had some excitement around here. A TBY was found down about a hundred miles out and the three men were in a rubber boat.* They were first seen on Saturday afternoon by another of their planes but they couldn't get to them with boats or seaplanes that night. On Sunday there were several seaplanes and small boats out there but the weather was bad and no one spotted them. Monday one of our pilots sighted them but there was a thirty knot wind and he couldn't land and they soon lost sight of them. Tuesday they were again sighted by a carrier plane but Wednesday we didn't even see them. On Thursday we were out again and I happened to be the lucky one and spotted the boat about one o'clock and we got a destroyer that was only about five miles away to pick him up. There was only one man left and he was suffering from exposure. The others had died. It was a tough grind for I was out there sixteen hours in two days and was on duty the night between but it was a great thrill and relief to find him. Of course it was a splendid experience too.

I know how you feel about things at home. I felt the same way a year ago. We have a damned good bunch of cows there and they would make some money with the proper care. We can't expect too much though and after all it really shouldn't worry us too much. We can't do much to keep things going right and will be just as happy if we forget about it.

As for the bull situation, I would be in favor of seeing Prim's son that they tell me is now back from Riebenahet's. There are few cows around the county better than that old girl and since Ellen, Phoebe, and Nell are looking fairly good there shouldn't be too much risk from the sire's side. The bull that Sampsons have should be worth using too so personally I see no point in buying anything for a couple of years as long as we have Pedro** for the best cows anyway.

Well, I better quit and get this mailed. I'll try to keep up with you though my correspondence has slipped badly lately. Let me know how things go. Just take it as it comes though and don't let it bother you. Have as much fun as you can and see the sights.

As Always

Bob

---

*A TBY was a torpedo bomber with a three-man crew.
**Pedro was the bull kept on the farm.

Ted has been shipped and is writing from a hot, dirty train on his way to an unknown destination. It's been a long, two-day trip and already he misses his buddies.

U. S. ARMY

April 26
Monday night

Dear Folks,

I have at last got my chance to ship. We were shipped Saturday afternoon and we have been riding since that time. (It has been 48 hrs.) At present I am writing while riding the train through Tampa, Florida. I don't know where I am going, but we're told we will reach our destination tomorrow morning. The postmark on this letter will probably tell, because we cannot mail until we reach the end of the line.

We are told that we're in the Medical Detachment of the Air Corp,* so chances are that we wind up at Miami. It is going to be lonesome for me because I left all of the boys I knew back at Ft. Niagara. Perhaps some will follow; I only hope they do. I have no idea what this will mean for me, whether Vet, Flying Cadet, or Buck Private, but I am going to try my best to make something out of it.

It has been a long trip so far because most of the trains we've ridden have been locals. Fortunately we have had a Pullman since we left Niagara Falls, but it is old and terribly dirty. It is warm and the soot grinds right into our sweat. I'll sure be glad to reach Base Camp where I can take a shower and put on clean clothes.

I don't seem to be having much luck in writing while the train is moving, so I guess I'll have to quit. I'll write as quickly as I have an address. The post mark on this letter should tell you where I am. My return address on the letter will be that of Ft. Niagara, but I'll be many miles from there.

Love,
Ted

*The United States Air Force wasn't established until 1947.

The Tug Hill region is famous for its formidable winters. In this next letter, Evelyn welcomes spring but typically, it is a very late spring. It is the end of April, and a lingering pile of ice by the front steps has just vanished. Evelyn never fails to write about the beauty she observes around her.

MRS. ERNEST L. MARKHAM
BOX 143
TURIN, NEW YORK

Friday, Apr. 30th

Dear Ted,

Your letter [postmarked April 24; not included in this collection] came Monday. I meant to write sooner, but hope it will be forwarded if you have moved.

We hope you have recovered from that sore throat. It sounds bad. The "strep" is a bad bug.

You should have received that service kit the first of this week. At first we thought we should go to Lowville and get it, but finally got the idea of asking Mr. Hart. He brought it right out the same day and we got it off in that day's mail. Sorry we did not think about that so you could have had it sooner.

Spring, which seemed to start early, is coming along very slowly. The pile of ice by the front steps has just vanished and there is still plenty on the north side of all buildings. Sugar season is over about a week. The grass is slowly greening, robins beginning to nest, daffodils show buds; pussywillows are just beginning to come out, woods up on old Forest Hill still full of snow and streams very high.

We have had a "tearing up" time this week. Moved everything we could out of the dining room, pulled down paper and loose plaster and such a mess as it was! Dad has put on sixteen patches, some large and some small. We have to do a lot of scraping and sanding and scrubbing and then paint woodwork and paper. Harvey Sage will help me some, I expect.

Don Kentner will give Dad ten dollars to go and get Clark's* garden

---

*Clark was Ernest's older brother and had recently passed away.

tractor, so tomorrow afternoon, Dad, Shirley and I expect to start out, going by way of Utica to get Shirley something to wear. We will come back Sunday. Howard Cuter will help Willis.

The Baxter-Dewan crowd* expect to arrive here Sunday afternoon or evening, stay overnight and then proceed to Old Forge – excepting Alton who will stay and resume school.

Did we tell you that Janice was home last week from Thursday evening to Sunday afternoon? Her graduation will be a week from today, Shirley's birthday. Bob's next day, you know. Jan's yesterday.

We haven't heard from Teen** lately. Grandma*** went over to her home Fri. a week ago. She came here yesterday afternoon and stayed overnight. She seems to be getting along well.

Grandpa**** seems to be as usual. He is anxious to hear all about you boys. If you have a chance, send him a post card once in a while. He'd like it. I must write to Bob now. We had a letter from him the same day yours came. Bill Zimmer had been up on an operational hop with him, and took a good <u>nap</u>.

Hope to hear good news from you soon. We are pulling for you, son, every way we know.

Love,
Mother

---

*Edward B. Baxter was Marian's employer; Marian Dewan was Ted's sister; and Alton was Marian's son.
**The family's nickname for Ernestine, the oldest daughter.
***Evelyn's mother, Harriet Wasmuth.
****Ernest's father, William Markham.

Ernestine O'Brien, Evelyn and Ernest's eldest daughter, was married to Robert O'Brien. She writes from their home in Lowville and describes some of the antics of their two-year-old son, Billy. Ted is in Miami Beach, Florida, where he has qualified for the Air Corps with hopes of becoming an Aviation Cadet.

Spring 1943

Lowville, N.Y.
May 3, 1943

Dear Ted,

We got your card today. It was very welcome. We haven't been home so know very little about you.

(Ernestine wrote the following in a childish script. Scribble marks from Billy are on the page.)

I GO TO THE BARN TO HELP DADDY. WE MILK THE COWS. GRANDPA AND I FEED THE COWS.

TO MARKET, TO MARKET TO BUY A FAT PIG.

LOVE,
BILLY

Billy always wants to write to everyone I do. He gets to be more of a great little chap every day. He talks a streak.

He's a great help in the barn. One night he was scolding at the cows. I listened and this is what he was saying, "Over there, damn cow. Over there, damn old cow."

Ernestine and Billy in 1941

Bob was certainly coming down with the grippe the night you were here. He had quite a session of it, too. It hung on for a week or more. We all had it. I couldn't make it to school one morning.

We're all busy as bees. Harold and Bob made about 100 gals. of syrup but have been done a week. They could have made a little more – most of the neighbors are still boiling some but there was so much else to do they quit.

It's still winter here. Today is cold and rainy but Friday it was cold and snowy. The temperature was only 12 degrees above zero on the first of May. There are lots of snow banks left.

I'm still teaching! Mrs. Alexander has her baby but no one to take care of it. This is my 11th week.

Marian called last night. She and E.B.* arrived in Turin yesterday and were going to Old Forge today. I'll bet it snowed there today.

Spring's work is pretty far behind here. I don't know anyone who has been able to do a thing. Bob has spread one of the winter's piles and got out some fence stakes but that's all. The snow broke the fences terribly.

Bob sees Joe Pendergast every Sunday in church. He's busy as can be, I guess but likes it. People like him too.

You know old Judge Merrill died last winter. Mother O's brother works there. Recently Merrill's farm foreman left and they got a new one.

Nat told Hanno – the new man – that the farm had cost them about $2000 a year for years so Hanno has persuaded him to sell all the Jerseys and buy Holsteins.

I'm feeling pretty rich and secure and comfortable. We have two new recaps! I guess we could get a new tire but I don't figure we need it much.**

Black River flats look like a huge lake. Several of the crossings have been closed. We've had a lot of rain and a lot of snow to melt.

It seems winter has been interminable. Next winter, Bob says, we're going to be in Florida. He loves it, you know. Wouldn't it be good luck if you were there if we are there?

---

*E.B. was one of the family's nicknames for Mr. Baxter. They also often referred to him as Mr. B.
**Tires were strictly rationed by the OPA (Office of Price Administration), which imposed restrictions on some foods as well as gasoline and tires. Ninety per cent of the U.S. natural rubber supply was cut off with the Japanese invasion of the Malay Peninsula and Dutch East Indies in 1942.

Mother probably tells you the family news and I don't know much.

Grandma is home now. Aunt Mary & A.J. have moved to the Heily house and Beatrice & Habe to the farm.

Janice was home a week ago from Thursday until Sunday.

Mother, Dad, & Shirley went to Richfield Springs to get Aunt Grace's garden tractor for Don Kentner.

Alton came back with Marian and began school today, I suppose.

There is certainly fierce fighting on all fronts – Africa, Alaska, Russia, & the Pacific. Lowell Thomas** is just saying that Hitler still plans to invade England this summer.

There's small comfort except that our men are giving the Axis Hell. I hope every last Axis man personally meets our brand of Hell.

In the spring of 1943, the Allies faced off once more against Field Marshal Erwin Rommel's German forces in Tunisia. Finally, on May 7, the Allies prevailed, taking 200,000 prisoners, and the war in North Africa was over.

In June of 1942, the Alaskan islands of Attu and Kiska were taken by the Japanese in an attempt to lure American forces away from Midway Island. On May 11, 1943, the U.S. 7th Infantry Division landed on Attu, where 600 Americans and more than 2,000 Japanese soldiers lost their lives.

On the Russian front, after the surrender of the German Sixth Army at Stalingrad in February 1943, the Russian counter-offensive moved to retake Rostov, Kharkov, Kursk, and more, and the Russians began their march toward Berlin. The combined Russian/German losses at Stalingrad alone were estimated to be more than two million dead.

In March of 1943, the Allies delivered a disastrous defeat to the Japanese in the Battle of the Bismarck Sea by destroying a convoy of Japanese ships carrying critical weapons and supplies.

We're happy and proud to know you can get in the Air Corps. I hope you can make cadet. I'd be very proud to wear two wings. Bob sent us each one and we are all delighted, of course.

----

*Lowell Thomas was a well-known journalist with a popular weekly radio broadcast.

Susanna's brother, James McCarthy, is in Miami Beach. Did you ever meet him? He was Cornell Vet. in about '40, I think. He was very recently married to a girl from Harrisville. James is a Lowville chap, about my age. A nice fellow. I'll get his address and enclose it. It might be good to see someone from Lewis Co.

I've been wondering what you'd like or need – besides money. I've had some ideas. Are any appealing to you?

Duffle bag
Apron for shaving etc.
Sewing kit
Wallet
Writing folio
Picture album
Writing paper
Toilet articles (specify)
Our copies of *Reader's Digest* (we certainly enjoy that so much)
Fountain pen
Camera (Have you one?)
Clothes (specify)
Luggage
Lowville Journal
Herald

Please let us know what you need. We'll be expecting to send you a present soon. Don't forget sizes, color preferences, etc.

I've certainly written all our news!

Write when you can.

Love from all,
Ernestine

P.S. I didn't get McCarthy's address last night but will send this along and send the address in a couple of days.

Ted writes from his new base at Miami Beach. Except for having to do his own laundry, life at a beach-side hotel isn't so bad.

U. S. ARMY

Sunday afternoon
May 3, 1943

Dear Folks,

I am writing this letter on my bed so perhaps it will be hard to read. I have just come in from having my first swim in salt water, and I find it quite nice. The sun is quite hot so I started a pretty good burn from the few moments I was out there. It is very warm out there, but it is nice and cool up here in my room.

I just finished my washing and you should see it. It is far from being as white as that I am accustomed to. We have to wash a lot of our clothes because it isn't always easy or cheap to send it to the G.I. Laundry. Things are beginning to shape up to the point where I know more about my status. I am in the Med Corp. of the Air Force, but it is in name only. It looks as if I have a good chance to apply for Aviation Cadet so I will be trying for that as quickly as possible. If I fail there I will probably end up in some school learning meat and dairy inspection. We were classified yesterday and my interviews gave me quite a little encouragement. We will finish processing sometime this week and then go into the Basic Training for which we came. This period will last about seven more weeks, and from that point on depends upon the way I play my cards now.

It is a great deal nicer here than it was at Ft. Niagara. The meals are better; we have better facilities for taking care of our clothes; and I have nearly recovered from the bad throat which everyone at Ft. Niagara had. My only kick is that I miss good friendship, and it gets sort of lonely.

We have found that we can keep cameras here under certain

conditions. I wish you could send me mine. I'd appreciate it a lot if you could put it in a good strong box so that I could pack it thereafter.

There are many things which I could tell you about this place, but it is for our own safety that we don't. I haven't seen too much of the town yet, but I hope eventually that I can. It is nice here and we have a very nice hotel on the beach. I'd rather be here than at many inland posts because of the breezes from the sea and the shorter days later in the summer.

Well, I guess it's about time for me to quit for this time, so write when you can.

Love,
Ted

P.S. – I got a funny feeling yesterday when I saw an Ensign turn a corner in a car. The head and shoulders looked for the world like Bob's. I felt like hollering but of course it couldn't have been.

Evelyn writes the news from home including more proof of a very late spring. It is the first week in May and the pond was frozen over just last night. Lewis County has just finished a very successful bond drive.

MRS. ERNEST L. MARKHAM
BOX 143
TURIN, NEW YORK

May 5

Dear Ted,

Your two letters reached us last Friday and Saturday – the later one first. We are glad you reached there safely and hope you have gotten all over that bad throat.

Dad got your letter just in time so he could re-direct one we were sending to you. Did you ever get that service kit we sent to Ft. Niagara? Don K. says it should follow you all right. It's too bad we did not get it sent sooner.

A nice letter from Bob came the same time as yours. We haven't heard from him very often of late. Guess he's pretty busy. He said Bill Zimmer went up on an operational hop one day.

Dad, Shirley and I went to get Grace's tractor last weekend, going by

This advertisement from the Black River Democrat *announces the start of the 2nd War Loan. Image courtesy of New York State Historic Newspapers.*

way of Utica, Sat. afternoon to get some clothes for Shirley – back Sunday afternoon. Howard and Willis "batched it" here.

Howard will stay with Willis again tomorrow night and we three will go to Canton to see Janice graduate and bring her and her belongings home.

Sunday evening, the Baxter-Dewan bunch came. Monday Mr. B. and Marian went on to camp and Alton started school. He seems very peppy and happy.

Marian brought a letter from Mel and some new pictures of Linda. They are all fine.

The bond drive* was a big success hereabouts. Lewis Co. went $50,000 over the top.

---

*The War Finance Committee, in a series of eight bond drives, raised a total of $185.7 billion in securities by December 1945. By the end of the war, over 85 million Americans had invested in bonds.

We made about 15 quarts of maple syrup in pans out doors burning brush. Of course we finished it off in the house. We will send you some sugar soon if we are sure you will be staying there.

Today is the first nice day in quite awhile tho there was a white frost this morning and quite thick ice on the pond. The ground is like a sponge full of water, streams very high and the grass just beginning to show in sheltered places.

Nell had a bull calf yesterday. We have come through clean on the T.B. test and cows seem to be doing well. The last check was $211.00. Willis will have to tell you the test, etc.

Be good to yourself.

Love,
Mom & All
Dad is plowing.

Ernest's news in his next letter is all about his Jerseys and recent events on the farm.

Turin NY May 9 '43

Dear Ted

Your special letter came last nite while I was milking. Willie went to Kentners & got it. After supper I went to Lodge & got Harry Ayers to go down & get the paper.

This morning when we went into the barn was some surprised to find a calf being Phoebe's of course a heifer from Pedro apparently doing fine one night the past week "Nell" freshened with a bull something went haywire and we lost it not much loss altho probably could have got more than the price of a hide but have not seen a picker for quite a number of days.* The old cow from "Bulls" is making around 35 to 40# daily and tested 4.3 she has had some trouble sometime with the near [left] front quarter some flakes at times.** Am going to have her dry when we have inspection in Dec.

---

*A "picker" would take dead livestock off the farm to be further processed.
**A flake found in milk would indicate that the cow has mastitis, an infection in her udder.

Went up in the woods today snow is about gone could not see as the ice did much damage one or two sparrow's nest to Woodcock lot were bent over but I straightened them o.k. found one adder tongue* out & brought down to Mom.

The seeding in the south meadow looks good but the Alfalfa does not show up much in the north meadow but will show up more later Pastures look green. Have not been able to plough only one afternoon but I guess the rains have quit for a few days.

Willis says to tell you that the cows are all bred now but four – Old Prim, Phoebe, Nell and I don't know what other. He says he'll write soon about the test, etc. The bull we got home from Wes's is looking much better – filling out. You know the one Fay had died, don't you?

(Dad)

Bob writes the next letter from Washington State where he is looking forward to trying out a new plane. He has just spent a whirlwind weekend in Los Angeles where he and a buddy were royally entertained.

May 12
Wed. nite

Dear Ted,

I'm glad to hear that you got into the air corps and now hope you can get to fly if that's what you want. Flying isn't the only thing though.

As you see I have moved again. The address may be confusing but I'm really on Whidbey Island in Puget Sound about eighty miles north of Seattle. Those of us from San Diego are to be here though the others haven't checked in yet. One of them is Dick Durham, my closest friend for the past couple of months. We will be in a squadron which is forming here and will be commissioned June 1. We will now fly Venturas (PV.1) so our training goes on from here again and it might be a couple of months before we get out.

---

*An adder's tongue is an early spring flower.

Bob poses with a PT-17, or Stearman, used as a primary trainer for both the navy and the army.

These planes are apparently quite the thing though I haven't been up in one yet. They are practically a two engine fighter and will chink and maneuver on one engine. They sound plenty hot for me.

This country is a lot like home and seems good after Georgia, Florida, and California. I like all of them but it seems good to see lots of green grass, trees, clean water and hills again. There are some good looking dairy farms around Mt. Vernon, which is the nearest town and the cows are knee deep in good grass now. We even have some cows inside the base here – a herd of Guernseys just over across the road and the soil looks good. It's a heavy black loam. They call this place Clover Valley. We can see snow covered mountains off to the east and we came through some beautiful ones in Oregon – nice big trees too.

Spring 1943

Last weekend in Los Angeles was one of the nicest I have ever had. Dick has a girlfriend in LA (really OK too) and my latest heartthrob from Coronada was up there staying in Beverly Hills. We were met at the station and chauffered around (rather we drove it and loved it) in a '42 Buick Super, stayed at the Ambassador in a suite that would have cost a civilian about fifteen dollars a night, danced to Freddie Martin at the Coconut Grove and really did the town. Sat. (my birthday you know) we had lunch out at the ranch where Jean's folks live, a swim in their pool and an all around good day. We boarded the train at eight Sun. AM after about three hours sleep in two nights.

It will be pretty quiet here especially after being spoiled by Coronada social life. I hope to get over to see Uncle Ellis* sometime and am going to try to see Carnation Farms but don't know how soon I can arrange it.

I'd like to see Miami but then I guess it isn't quite like it used to be. I understand that southern Florida is much nicer than northern. Better see all you can while you're there.

Let me know how things go.

As always,
Bob

Evelyn writes that now that she knows where Ted is stationed, she can finally mail him a long-awaited package. In this letter, we hear for the first time that someone has had a "big event." A "big event" is the term all family members used to mean the birth of a child.

MRS. ERNEST L. MARKHAM
BOX 143
TURIN, NEW YORK

May 26

Dear Ted,

Your letters of Friday night and Saturday night reached us on Monday and Tuesday and we are glad to know where you are.

Now I am venturing to send the little package I have been holding

---

*Uncle Ellis was one of Evelyn's younger brothers.

31

for reasons of security – your camera, films, some maple sugar, etc.

It is a relief to know that at last you have received the service kit. Too bad we did not get it off to you when you first went to Niagara.

Bob evidently has written to you so you know more about him than we do. He wrote to us as soon as he reached this new base and we probably will get another letter soon.

Chet Freeman* has passed his first stage of training and gone on to Alabama. Ray has washed out** and may be home to get his uniforms, etc. to go back to his former job. Howard Ross has recently gone into pilot training. I do not know whether it is in army or navy.

Did we tell you that Doris and Pete came home a week ago Sunday? Aunt Ethel had a party for them on Tuesday evening – a sort of wedding reception – and had all the nearest relatives who live nearby. Doris' family were all there except Marion who is in the hospital with a little son. Willard came though, and he is at least a foot taller since the big event. Pete went back Wednesday, but not so far – only to Nebraska or Kansas, I think. Lucy Wiedrick was at the party, just back from spending the winter near Lyle who has moved. Howard Chapman is in Denver training for an aerial photographer. Francis C is in the army somewhere.

Did Teen tell you that James McCarthy is at Miami Beach? We hear that Ken Trainor is too.

The O'Brien's were here a little while Sunday. They are all just fine. She is through teaching. Feels like her old peppy self lately – looks so nice. And I can't begin to tell you how Bill grows and talks right along in sentences.

Must get this mailed. Uncle A.J. is coming.

Love,
Mom

---

*Chet Freeman, a friend and future Cornell professor in the College of Agriculture and Life Sciences.
**"Washed out" means eliminated from pilot training.

Ernest enclosed the next letter, one of the few from him, in the same envelope as the preceding letter from Evelyn.

Dear Ted,

Last Friday we had a distinguished guest in the form of John & Katherine Luchsinger.* Well John had to see the cows, then the heifers and by gosh he wanted to buy a heifer and the calves well he did not say anything about buying them but it would not be a very hard job. He got four yearlings in a corner then said that they would be hard to beat them in Aug Show. I said that I just as soon beat John L – as anybody Mrs said that it was no disgrace to be beaten by such heifers as those. (B.S.)

Sunday I was walking around the pasture and up on the old potato piece near where we found Weatha's twins I saw some clover I turned a leaf out by darn it was Ladino.** I went along a ways turned another leaf & Ladino again there seems quite a bit & I don't know how it got there unless carried by the cows. The Ladino across from Fays is a mess about 2 ft high & as thick as blazes all over the 2 acres the piece which was grazed quite close last fall does not show any effects now in fact just in the meadow by the gate is as good if not better than the South Meadow.

Corn is just peeping thro potatoes are up Oats look good. The Seeding is as good as we ever had. We had a whale of a rain just as we got part of the piece sowed & I guess the seed was covered too deep.

Cows are avg about 200# – 5.2 test per day 11 cows etc.***

Dad

Get me a GI watch if you can

---

*John and Katherine Luchsinger were well known in the American Jersey Cattle Association for their excellent Jersey cows. Sixty-three years after this letter was written, Ernest and Evelyn's great granddaughter, Amy Markham, would marry the Luchsinger's great grandson, Charlie Luchsinger.

**Ladino = white clover.

***Most dairy herds are still tested monthly for the amount of milk produced and for the milk's butterfat percentage. 200# meant the average weight of milk produced per day, and 5.2 meant the percentage of butter fat in the milk. Jersey cows were, and still are, favorites for a small farm because of their higher than average butterfat content.

Mr. Baxter and Altie at Gray Lake

In 1943 Marian was the single mother of Alton, age 9, and working as a live-in housekeeper for Mr. Edward Baxter in Ithaca. Alton lived with Evelyn and Ernest on the farm in Turin. Marian wrote this letter from Old Forge, where Mr. Baxter owned property on Gray Lake. In this letter, she proves why Mr. B appreciated her so much as a housekeeper.

May 31

8:30

(Old Forge)

Dear Ted,

This is a beautiful morning and the lake is still as glass. It's a bit muggy and may rain later but will be nice for the Memorial Day parades. The temp is 55 degrees. A little different down there isn't it?

I enjoyed your letter and a couple days after it came, we went to the show and saw a short of the A.A.F.T.T.C.* at Miami Beach. So you see I have some idea of where you are and what you do. We saw drilling and marching. Seems as tho they said the fellows average about 12 miles a day.

---

*A.A.F.T.T.C. = Army Air Forces Technical Training Command.

I hope you haven't had "Freshman's cramp." We saw drilling & training on the polo grounds and golf courses and beaches and marching thru the streets. It showed a lot of the hotels and restaurants etc. We also saw soldiers scrubbing and washing windows. More fun, huh?

I saw a letter you wrote home that said you had just finished some of your laundry but it wasn't as white as you were used to. Now will you learn to change your clothes oftener? Maybe you'd like a few tips on the "how to do it." I think the easiest (and best) way to have a really white wash is to use two suds and always two rinses (or until water is clear.) White clothes respond best to hot water but get stains out first. Blood stains soak in cold water & then soap. Never put clothes with elastic in hot water as it ruins the rubber. Never wash colored clothes in hot water, (just warm) and don't hang in bright sunshine to dry. Never wash silks, rayons or woolens in hot or cold water – lukewarm and use same temperature for all suds & rinses. If you soak your handkerchiefs first in cold water with plenty of salt, it cuts the mucus. A cake of lava soap to rub on dirty places works slick and I don't have to tell you it cuts grease do I? There now, you ought to put the other guys to shame! Don't neglect shaking the clothes good before you hang them up so they'll dry smooth. Hang them as straight as you can and they'll fit better – hangers help on some things.

Have you any more of an idea what division you'll get in? It sounds to me as tho you're in a good outfit and the training would be excellent and also practical.

I'm enclosing some clippings I thot you'd be interested in – especially about the war certificates.

The garden is coming up, the leaves are almost half size and the black flies are here so we think spring has come. And the trout are beginning to bite. Mr. B. got his limit (10) Sat. I've only got 2 so far but have only been out 3 times.

We have got the linoleum laid on the living & dining room and are very pleased with it. It adds light and gives the appearance of more room.

I'm about out of news. Will try to write sooner next time. Alton is at home and full of pep and having no trouble making up school work. Write.

Love, Marian

Mr. B. just proposed pulling out & going down home to Lowville on business. I'm saying yes.

Summer 1943

U. S. ARMY AIR FORCES

Thursday night
June 4

Dear Folks,

I have just finished my examinations for Aviation Cadet, and I have some news which sounds better. I passed my mental yesterday and I passed my physical today so far as could be determined today. However, they have no returns on my chest Xray nor serology yet, so I can't quite say that I have passed my physical yet. My only worry, though, is the interview which I will have next week before I am finally accepted.

I might tell you a little about the present set up for training Aviation Cadets. After we finish basic we wait until we are sent to some college for Pre-Aviation Training. Here we receive the present pay and get essential training in Math, Physics, English, and etc. After this we're classified as to Pilot, Navigator, Bombardier, or Meteorologist and start on the $75 rate of pay. From here we go to our respective training schools and proceed with Advanced Training. All in all it takes about 15 months for training after we leave here which means that if I am successful it will take about 18 months before I am commissioned.

However you folks will have to remember that I haven't made A.C. yet, and that there are many chances of "washing out" after one does make A.C.

I have taken a few pictures lately and I hope to be able to send you some before long. I would like to have some pictures taken at the photographer's but I'll have to wait until I get a little more money. It

36

seems to have been all that I could afford to get my uniforms altered and cleaned. These stores etc. really ream the devil out of the soldiers here.

Our work has been a cinch lately. The only things which require any effort is K.P. and Guard Duty which we draw about once a week. It looks as if we have completed our training in the field because about all we do out there is to listen to unimportant lectures and participate in P.T. once in a while.

It isn't quite as convenient to write letters and read here at our new hotel because we have no Service Club in the basement as we did before. I hope to send you a card before long which has a picture of my former hotel on it. It will be the second hotel from the right and its name is the Whitman. I shouldn't tell you this, but I guess there'll be no harm.

News seems to be running low, so write when you can.

Love,
Ted

Willis, or Willie, is just 18 years old and ready to graduate from high school when he writes this letter. He has no plans to go to college because he is needed to work on the farm during the war years. He is pleased with recent events at the farm but wants to boast a bit about baseball and fishing, too.

Turin, NY
June 4, 1943

Dear Ted;

Sorry I haven't written before, but here goes. We got the oats in last night. It sure has been a tough year to try to get any crops in. It rains about every two days and the ground no more than gets dry enough to work and it rains again. The corn ground isn't plowed as yet but Dad has gotten Denis Koster to plow it with a tractor and he will be over Tuesday.*

The pastures are in excellent condition. I never saw them better. Boy you can see the difference where we spread manure last year. We have quite a little pasture manured this spring.

---

*Horses were still commonly used for farm work.

Will's high school graduation, 1943

The new seeding is like we have never had before. It sure is thick.

The cows went up when we turned them out.* We have to put the milk in 6 cans now. Cymbie had a heifer and she is coming along fine. We sure got a darned good bunch of calves this year. Beauty's heifer is as pretty a calf as I ever saw. Old Prim's is pretty too. Dad sold Phoebe's heifer to George for $20.

Our baseball team is pretty good considering the number of new players. Boonville beat us by 7 points when they came up to C-ville but we sure wupped them today at B-ville 21-7, not bad huh! We were all batting good today. There were 11 men up in the first inning and we got 8 runs.

The film that was in your camera I finished and I will send you the pictures as soon as I get it back.

_____

*A cow's milk weight would increase when it was turned out to pasture.

The fishing is pretty good, so far I have gotten 11 trout from White River. 2 – 7", 2 – 10", 2 – 11" and the others 8 & 9".

I sort of envy you, getting all that target practice with some darned good rifles.

Can't think of any more.

So long

Willie

Ted's youngest sibling, Shirley, was a sophomore in high school in 1943. She writes that the war is putting a damper on her social life. Not everyone had enough gasoline to make it to a high school dance, and attendance wasn't good.

Turin, New York
June 4, 1943

Dear Ted,

Well it's about time I sat down and wrote you a letter. I'm really ashamed I haven't gotten around to this before, but there's seemed to be something most of the time lately.

Willie took samples last nite and I guess all the cows did very well. He's going to write to you about it later, I guess. He is very much taken up with his dyeing feathers for flies. Nights, lately he has been tying flies. He's made quite a few, I guess. Mr. Kaskela had a fly once he liked and wanted another like it.* He asked an expert to do it and it wasn't what he wanted. He told Willie about it and seemed pleased to have Will make one like he wanted. Willie, of course, didn't want him to pay for the three he made, but Mr. Kaskela said he'd go bankrupt some day at that rate.

Dad told Mom tonite he doesn't believe he has ever seen as nice pastures as we have this year. Dad got the oats in yesterday and will probably get the potatoes in tomorrow. It's been rather impossible to do much this year on the land because it seems as tho it has rained a continuous stream all the time. The grass on our lawn even has jumped up so we ought to mow it every day. Dad says the seeds that didn't germinate last year did this year.

---

*William Kaskela was the Constableville High School principal.

Mr. Baxter

It has been rather hot and muggy this week. Today, when I got home from school, the temperature was 87 or 88, and so muggy that everything just stuck to you. The gym was so wet we couldn't have dance club tonite.

Jan is up to Mr. Baxter's camp this week & probably next. She really ought to be home helping Mother, but I guess she wouldn't do anything anyway. She went to see Doc Vadney and he said there was nothing wrong with her physically but her nerves are all shot.

Burt and Mel want me to come down this summer as long as I can, and when I told Mr. B he said I couldn't go down there until I came up there and he would disown me if I didn't.* Teen expects to have a house in Lowville from now on and she asked me to come down there this summer. I really ought to stay home this summer. There will be plenty to do.

---

*Burt and Mel were living in Ithaca. Mr. Baxter had a residence in Ithaca but was at his summer home in Old Forge. Mr. Baxter was a widower, Marian's boss, and a loyal friend to the whole Markham family as well. He welcomed any and all of them to his home for frequent visits.

We had a dance a week ago tonite. It was quite nice, but there weren't an awful lot there because of the ban on gasoline. There were a few boys from Boonville and a few from Turin, but other than them, only the C-ville kids came. The orchestra was good – Bernie's from Rome. Everyone seems to like them best from around. Willie and I didn't get there until late because he and Dad went up to Hughs' for a doodlebug. It's quite a jitney! What a noise it makes!! The men were fixing it Sunday and Mom said you would be right in your glory if you could be puttering around with it. Billy & Teen were down with Susannah & her two youngest boys over the weekend. Billy didn't quite like the sound of the doodlebug at first but finally said "A doodlebug won't hurt me." Gosh, he's cute now. He went to church one day and he lost his nickel just as a man was going by. Just as soon as the man got by he picked it up and said, "I got it, man." He talks right along in sentences. Mom says he either makes up his mind one way or the other, there aren't any shades in between. He kind of stuck to me this time, too. He likes me, I guess, because he knows I'll stick up for him.

Well, everyone else has gone to bed, and my hand is so tired from writing I can hardly stand it. I wrote to Mel, Bob, besides what I wrote in school. I guess I ought to have a secretary.

I'll get Will & Jan & Altie to write next.

Love,
Blondie

Once again, Evelyn paints a picture with words. Jan has graduated from Canton and is living at home.

MRS. ERNEST L. MARKHAM
BOX 143
TURIN, NEW YORK

June 14, '43

Dear Ted,

Someway, the letters I mean to write just do not get written, though I believe I think of you every hour I am awake.

We all realized you must be pretty bored and homesick when you wrote that long letter [letter not included] and we all resolved to write more often. We received one since, telling of your examinations and then Shirley had your card.

Last week, off and on, we had Harvey Sage here papering and painting. We started on the dining room the day after Easter, tearing off loose paper and plaster. Dad put on sixteen patches of plaster. The woodwork, as you remember, was a mess. The paint was badly chipped so we have worked a lot getting it scraped, sanded, and even removed some of it with a blowtorch. Mr. Sage, like all other workmen, is much in demand so he has had to come here at odd times. The dining room looks different now with the new wall paper and woodwork done. He will come again when he can to do the windows, floor and radiator. He has the kitchen ceiling papered and maybe will paper the rest and paint.

About the spring's work, the very rainy weather has held us up as it has everyone but we are getting nearly through. We got Howard Koster to plow the corn ground last week and we have it partly fitted. Oats are up, so are most of the small garden stuff. Potatoes, sweets and popcorn are in, some of the beans, tomatoes, etc. still to be put in. We got our oats in just after George and before Fay. His ground is still very wet and he, like some others has decided to plant no corn. Many meadows still are very wet and streams are high for this season. Grass is simply wonderful though. The orchard here looks nearly ready to mow, the cows are knee deep in grass and you should see how the white clover has come in in new places as well as all the old ones. Last year's seeding is wonderful. Dad says he thinks seed which did not germinate last year has come up this spring. Everywhere is the beautiful lush greenness of June with patches of yellow buttercups and mustard – a beautiful picture. This morning I looked from the back porch and saw the cows down near the pond, some lying down, some drinking in the pond and they and the hill and woods reflected in it as in a mirror. I said, "How I wish I could get that, colors and all, in a picture to send to the boys!"

Dad has been plenty worried about the planting, but he has worked very hard at it and things seem to be coming as well as can be expected. Willis is about done with school now.

All the stock is looking well. You wouldn't know the bull we brought home from Wes'. He is pretty sleek now. We send six cans of milk a day. Willis will have to report more fully on that.

Janice is still at home but talks about finding a job. Guess she doesn't know what she wants to do. She <u>could</u> join the WAAC's,* couldn't she? I would, if I were young and unencumbered. Hope you are getting on well. We think of you and pray for you. We need your prayers too. Keep your <u>faith</u> all will come out right.

Love,

Mother

Ted writes home with some good news.

H. S. Army Air Forces

Monday noon [postmarked June 15, 1943]

Dear Folks,

I just got word this morning that I passed my interview, so I am now a "Qualified Aviation Cadet." This means that I'll probably be moved to another flight within a short time. Maybe I'll be sent up the Beach a ways or next door, but send my mail and etc. to the same address until I send word that I have moved. I'll probably start taking basic for A.C.** which will take about another month.

I am including a picture of myself which one of my roommates took. The light was poor so consequently it isn't too clear. The uniform which I have on is the "Fatigue Uniform" which we wear in the field and for work purposes. It is green to blend with the grass and trees. The picture was taken looking up the boardwalk in front of our hotel, taking in another hotel, mess hall, beach, and ocean in the upper right hand corner. There is a guard at my left shoulder who is walking his beat. This is the beat I

---

*WAAC = Women's Army Auxillary Corps.
**A.C. = Aviation Cadet.

Ted's camera needed some tape to cover a light leak!

A better photo of Ted, in his "Class A Uniform"

walked last time I had Guard Duty. Within a few days I hope to have more pictures to send you which show me in my "Class A Uniform."

We have a parade this afternoon which I don't look forward to. We have these twice a week and I'd rather do anything else than this. You have to stand in your squadron for about 2 ½ hrs. on the hot sand and under the glaring sun. This has to be at "attention" or "parade rest" which is as bad as "attention." Each day there are about 10 fellows who pass out of each squadron (250 men). You literally suffocate from the dust and lack of air and water.

We had K.P. yesterday and I can frankly say that I would have enjoyed it were it not Sunday. This mess hall is some different from the last one. They don't treat you like slaves and when you get your work caught up you can sit down.

Well write when you can.

As ever,
Ted

Second-born son, Burt, is 24 years old when he writes his first letter to Ted in Miami Beach. He is a Cornell graduate, married to Melrose Marriott, and the father of a one-year-old daughter, Linda. He writes from their very hot apartment in Ithaca.

varna apartments
ithaca, n. y.

melrose , burt , and linda say :

June 20, 1943

Dear Ted,

I've meant to write long before but there always seems to be some reason why I haven't. It's been nearly 2 months since you landed there and I hope you will excuse me for this time.

It's hot as all get out here tonight but I imagine it's hotter down there. I was working out in the garden for a couple of hours without my shirt this morning and I have a sweet sunburn. It's 86 in our living room and not a breath of air is stirring. It makes it a bit tough on Linda.

We had a nice letter from Bob last week & I hope to answer it yet tonight. He's out on an island off the west coast but I imagine you've heard from him.

Mother wrote that things are fine at home except the cold, wet weather this spring makes everything backward.

There are a lot around here that don't have their corn planted yet and a lot more that didn't get any grain in at all. The feed situation was bad enough before this spring but it looks now as if a lot of poultry and dairy cows will be eaten next winter. The hay crop appears good but very few have started cutting yet. We've had miserable weather.

Our garden is fairly good though. I think we have as good a one as I've seen yet. We've had spinach, beet greens, onions, lettuce & radishes and will have peas before the week is over. Our string beans & early potatoes are blossoming.

Work has kept me quite busy up until lately but it has slacked off a bit now. The opening of the office at Cortland took a lot of work but the fellow over there is getting things going well.*

---

*Burt was working for the Produce Credit Association.

The office forces for the three offices had their annual picnic yesterday out at Monkey Run. It was the first time this year that any of us had been in swimming. Linda had a pretty good time eating pretzels and drinking ginger ale out of a bottle.

It looks as if we might move. Not very far, though. The Janses downstairs are buying a place & we are thinking of moving down where they are. It will be much cooler and of course we won't have to be trotting Linda upstairs all of the time.

Linda is wild to get outdoors so we bought the playpen of the Janses that is in the yard. It will be very convenient & Linda likes it.

Linda is growing like a little pig and advancing fast. She gets all over and chatters all the time. When I come home at night, the first thing I hear when I get out of the car is "Hi Daddee, Hi, Daddee" no matter where she is. We don't have any recent pictures of her & I believe you have seen the last we took.

I'm running out of news but I'll try to keep it more current from now on. Write when you have a minute.

Burt, Mel, and Linda

Evelyn writes from Mr. Baxter's summer home on Gray Lake. Marian, Shirley, and Mr. Baxter have insisted that she take a little vacation.

MRS. ERNEST L. MARKHAM
BOX 143
TURIN, NEW YORK

(late June)
Thurs. eve

Dear Ted,

Here I sit by the window in the dining room at Gray Lake watching the sunshine filter through the leaves and dance on the rippling water as the shadows lengthen. At supper last night we saw a doe and fawn just across the little bay on the north side. They were feeding and capering about among the trees, quite unconscious of watchers. It is beautiful here.

Yesterday, Marian came down home as Mr. Baxter went to Lowville to see Dr. Germann. She packed Alton all up to move up here and it was understood that Shirley was to come too. Then, at the last minute, they decided that I'd better come. It seemed to me that they were adopting a pretty big family, but they were quite insistent, and I came. Ernestine and Janice are both at home and they seemed glad to get rid of me.

When I wrote to you last, I told you, did I not, that I had been having a bothersome time with a peculiar skin disease, and that Ernestine was coming to help out? I have not been sick, and it is not a serious thing, but I've been quite uncomfortable with it some of the time. It is not communicable, the doctors say, does not come from any internal condition and will run for about six weeks in all. I went to a skin specialist in Utica. He called it the same as Dr. Vadney did, gave me a prescription for a soothing lotion and said not to put any soap, oil or anything else on except I might bathe with boric solution and use the lotion. The treatment is helping and I am quite comfortable now. It gets to itching sometimes yet when I get warm or something rubs the sore spots, but they are healing fast.

Up here it is so lovely I can't help getting better fast. I've made molasses cookies and fussed around at small house keeping jobs, walked around the garden and all around, read some, went over town in the car for mail and groceries, taken a nap and had just a quiet day.

Mr. Baxter has two old men, a brother in law and a cousin, who are visiting him and we all get a great kick out of them. They are really nice old boys, good sports, and as tickled as a couple of kids to have such a rare chance to go fishing. They are out in the boat nearly all the time they aren't eating or sleeping. I just wish I were Norman Rockwell so I could paint them for you. You'd surely appreciate them.

Mr. Baxter fished a while this morning and he and Alton went again this afternoon about four. I might have gone but the flies are pretty hot. The punkies even come through the screens some. Mosquitoes are thick, too. They are having fair luck fishing.

Ernestine and Billy have been down home a little over a week and we've had Grandpa there nearly a week. He seems to be having a good time. The change will do him good.

Shirley adds the following to her mother's letter:

Dear Ted,

I don't know really what to write to you, but will make an attempt. It's swell up here all except for the bugs. I bet I've got bites from one end to the other. I was trying to take a sun bath yesterday on the dock and read too. Between trying to focus my eyes and swatting the _____ bugs I didn't get much time for the sun to get at me.

Mr. Baxter's brother-in-law, Harry Fudge, is up here. Funny! Oh my gosh! He's deaf as a post, but he's always coming out with a funny crack – always has an answer for everything. It's funnier because of his squeaky voice.

Marian says she was awfully glad to get your letter and that by the looks of the picture you haven't lost much weight. She says she'll write soon.

Billy is quite a boy now. My gosh what he doesn't say. We told him not to pick up the cat, that he stunk. He said he was all cow manure.

Well Mr. B is going now so I'll have to go. I'll write more later.

Love,
Blondie

Burt writes with news of their garden and the perils of living with a one-year-old daughter.

---

varna apartments
ithaca, n. y.

m e l r o s e   ,   b u r t   ,   a n d   l i n d a   s a y   :

Sunday nite
(Ithaca, late June '43)

Dear Ted,

Don't die of shock but I did get to answer your last letter better than I did your first.

We've been pretty busy around here lately with the garden. Everything has been growing great, including the weeds & it's all I can do to get caught up with them. We've been canning string beans today! Pretty good don't you think. Most people around here are just getting the first few to eat. I dug a hill or two of potatoes yesterday and found one the size of a baseball. If you can judge by the tops we should have a good crop. The vines come nearly to my arm pits.

I've been pretty busy at the office for the last few days. We are in the process of having an examination of some of the loans and believe me those boys can find things wrong. Of course, that's their job and we learn plenty by the exam. Linda has been a real terror lately. She can get into any kind of trouble you can imagine. She climbs into everything and we can't keep her put. We have the play pen down back for her and she has a lot of fun down there. She jabbers a blue streak all of the time and gets now so she puts two or three words together. I had hoped that we could send you some pictures of her but I haven't been able to buy any film for about 2 months. I keep trying all the time, though.

We had a letter from Mother & Shirley a few days ago. They were up at Old Forge for a few days because Mother had some kind of skin trouble but you have probably heard from them.

The campus down here seems rather strange this summer. There are a lot of sailors and soldiers everywhere. And then, the regular term has started and there aren't as many people vacationing in the state. I drove past the house a few days ago.* There didn't seem to be any activity around.

There doesn't seem to be much out of the ordinary happening around abouts. We keep pretty busy with our garden & baby and of course there's gas rationing. Oh yes! I nearly forgot. Mel is going to do some part time work for the college, 35 days a year plus a week's training school. She'll be teaching "foods" to 4-H leaders in counties near Ithaca. They sure are short of qualified people for such work & Mel will welcome an occasional change from housework.

I guess I'll sign off and hit the sack. Write when you have a chance.

Burt, Mel, & Linda

---

*Burt is referring to the Alpha Zeta fraternity house at Cornell. Both he and Ted were members.

Bob writes next from Whidbey Island, Washington. He shares his observations of the cattle, the horses, and the crops.

U. S. NAVAL AIR STATION
WHIDBEY ISLAND, WASHINGTON

Wed. nite
June 30

Dear Ted,

Glad to hear you made A/C and hope you like it as much as you expect to. I think you might get quite interested in aviation. It's a big field and you'll find the men have a rather different way of looking at things.

Probably you know that Chet made the grade for pilot training and has been at Maxwell Field and about due to go to primary somewhere. Irene* has been down there or expected to be for awhile. Ray wrote that he was waiting to be sent back to S.C. but I haven't heard from him since and didn't write because I thought he would be moving.

Vin Davis, the ag. teacher at Richburg, wrote me a letter the other day and mentioned some of the Allegany news.** Do you remember Kay Kniffen the home-ec teacher from there that I met at the drill hall dance at the '42 F.&H. Week? He said she would like to hear from me so maybe I'd better write. She certainly was good company.

Have I written to you only once? I was thinking I wrote a couple of weeks ago but my records don't show it. If I didn't you haven't heard about my trips to Uncle Ellis or Carnation Farms. I had a little vacation for myself after the tonsillectomy (four days AWOL) and had a nice trip over to Coulee Dam. Saw some of the apple country, wheat and livestock

---

*Chet's wife.
**Bob worked as a farm bureau agent in Allegany County following his graduation from Cornell.

country and of course in spots quite a bit of dairying. There aren't any trees to speak of over east of the mountains – just sagebrush and the canyons are big, especially the coulee where the Columbia used to run.

The dam is quite a thing, over 4,000 ft. long and 330 ft. high, backs water up 150 miles, has about three times the flow of Niagara now but of course it isn't quite as steady throughout the year. The light metals industries are really making use of the electricity now and they are wishing they had all the generators installed.

Uncle E. & Aunt V. have a new daughter Norma Jean since then which wasn't a complete surprise to me. Too bad Wasie* didn't get a son tho. He sure would be a good dad for one.

One day in Seattle I went to the Carnation office to find out where the farm is located and if it would be possible to get there. I met Mr. Moore who is advertising man for the company and found out that he was born in Potsdam and used to work for Mr. Sisson. The farm is nearly forty miles out but he called them and they sent a car to meet me at the ferry. I spent the afternoon there with Mr. Lowry the herd superintendent. He used to be field man for the Holstein assoc. up this way and hasn't been there long enough to know the herd real well but was very nice and did a good job of showing me around.

It certainly is the best herd of Holsteins I have seen but of course they do have a few that aren't too beautiful. He must have showed me at least fifteen mature bulls and their milking herd is around 250. They have over 600 head in all and have some wonderful pasture but don't grow any hay. They can buy good quality stuff from the other side of the mountains and it's really hard to cure it in this section. Their calf raising system is similar to Cornell's but they feed a little more milk or at least keep it up longer. They don't let them get fat though and feed lots of good hay.

I saw the Madcap cow that holds the milk record but she is pretty badly broken down now after the two big records. They have a young son by Imperial that looks good. They have two sons of the Buthoking cow but they don't look like much and apparently aren't doing much for the herd. Old Governor is still in heavy service and his daughters make up the best of the herd. Imperial has lots of good daughters around four years old and the first daughters of Renown look very good. The three are father,

---

*"Wasie" was Ellis Wasmuth's nickname.

son, and grandson respectively you know. Old Sir Luka May is still alive at twenty.*

They also have some Percherons out there but I didn't get to see all of them. Charlie Hardy is their horseman and knows Bob Watt quite well I guess. The stallion they are using is a son of Dan Again the full brother of Dan Action that you probably have heard about. He has been grand champion at Chicago three times I believe and his gets have won consistently.**

Did I tell you about my visit with the local county agent? Guess I just wrote home about it. Anyway we had a good visit and he took me out to a farm where we saw some good Jerseys. Also I found that their testing program is very good here and they have a high percentage of cows on test – at least 25% or maybe it's more – I have forgotten. This small county of 3,000 farms has more than thirty herds over 400 lbs. and some up around 550 consistently. Other important enterprises here are growing spinach, cabbage and turnip seed. Canning peas and other seed are fairly important too. This little county grows nearly all the cabbage seed for the country and a high percentage of the spinach and turnip seed. There are some really wonderful pastures here too tho they are limited to the valleys and most of them are on good level land that would grow almost anything.

Burt finally got around to write after I asked him for a new picture of Linda. They may move downstairs but otherwise there wasn't too much news. I haven't done very well myself lately so can't complain about anyone.

Our squadron is slowly getting underway but I don't seem to do much yet. I may not get to solo the PV for awhile because we are short of planes and I'll be a second pilot anyway as far as operations are concerned.*** These planes have got a lot of stuff but are plenty hard to keep in commission. I'm not too enthusiastic about them at the moment. I'll be in charge of the machine guns and gunners as ass't gunnery officer in the squadron, may work some with bombing and torpedo equipment some too. Dick has radio and radar equipment.

Well this is getting long for me. I'll have to save some for another time. Write when you can.

As always,

Bob

_____

*Bob is writing about Holstein cows and bulls.
**The "get" of sire is the progeny of a male animal.
***A PV was a long-range bomber that also carried four guns.

Nine-year-old Alton writes the next letter from Gray Lake in Old Forge. Alton lived with Evelyn and Ernest during the school year but spent summers at Gray Lake with his mother as she kept house for Mr. Baxter.

Altie, age 9, 1943

July 1, 1943
Old Forge, N.Y.

Dear Ted

How are you? I am fine. I caught 13 trout this year. What planes are you flying? Or aren't you flying any yet? Mister Baxter lost a forteen or fifteen inch rainbow trout. Blondie is writing to Mel. I wrote to Bob yesterday by air mail. Do you want the pictures back? I am building an airplane and am planning to build another soon. This morning Gram saw a fox track Sometime in May a buck had a broken back up here. Last night we went for a ride and saw 4 deer. We can't get chickens, boy am I glad because I don't have to feed'em. I have to put up the flag now days. I captured a dragon fly yesterday. Gram and Blondie came up to camp to for awhile. I'm getting the weekly reader and it tells about differnt planes. How do you like the card I wrote? Guess what we had for breakfast? Eggs, toast, corn flakes, and milk. I can't Think of much more news.

Love
Alton

P.S. Bobs address is Ens. R.W. Markham
VB 142   C/O Pacific Fleet P.O. San Francisco, Calif.

Evelyn writes again from Gray Lake, where she is beginning to feel better.

Old Forge, N.Y.
July 2, 1943

Dear Ted,

Alton has written a nice long letter to Bob and one to you, so I will scribble a bit to add to it.

Your letter, and one from Bob, which came down home since I have been here, the home folks sent on to us.

Your pictures look very like "Our Ted" even though the streak of light nearly spoiled them. Guess you'll have to put on some more adhesive tape, eh?* Well, thank you, we like them all the same. And we are glad you qualified to A.C. if that is what you wanted. We'd be just as proud of you even if it had been some other branch of the service.

Did we tell you that Doris had a cable about two weeks ago from Pete, that he had arrived safe, Somewhere? She has been to see us a couple of times with Ethel and Hugh. So nice for them! Has Bob written you about his visit to Ellis and Kathleen and of the birth on June thirteenth of Norma Jean? Ray Miller has been home. Ernestine wrote that he and Ted Kangas had been over to our house. Grandpa is making a little visit down home – if still there. Billy keeps things lively down there. Will caught five nice trout Sunday so Billy said he was "going to have them for bre'fus a woner day an' a woner day an' a woner day." Alton was spreading some bread for him and Bill said, "Half it in two an' shut it up." (Sandwich) While Teen was washing dishes she gave him some tin can tops to play with. He said, "I making pies – strawberry pies. I helpa my gramma. She got so much to do, her's tired." He comes rushing into the house looking for his dad and says, "Whersa my Pop?" Another time he says, "Here come my "Fodder." Though usually Bob is just Daddy.

---

*See photo from Ted on page 44. Ted's camera had a small crack on the body that would allow light to spoil whatever film it touched. A simple piece of tape placed over the crack worked to block the light.

I am getting over my skin trouble as fast as can be expected. I've been having a swell time and a good rest though I find lots of useful and interesting things to do. I see I must close.

Love, as ever. Mother

We've seen lots of deer and tracks galore, once a baby fox and once a doe and fawn. Think we'll be going home Sunday.

Marian writes the next letter from Gray Lake. In it, she expresses appreciation for a neighbor's gift of broiler chickens, but it sounds like she isn't looking forward to spending a hot summer afternoon plucking and dressing them.

July 2

Dear Ted,

Mom has been writing so many letters since she came up she makes me ashamed. I don't know as I've any news that she and Alton didn't write.

I was awfully glad to hear from you and get the picture. It doesn't look to me as tho' Army chow had made you thin.

That movie short wasn't advertising Miami as you thot. I think it was O.W.I.* or Army or something like that. It showed very little of the city except as a back ground. It merely showed what you guys do and where you do it – what we all want to know about. That's what made it so interesting.

While you are "beefing" about Miami remember that it is a tourist city and probably treats you the same as the tourists get. And don't forget the people up this way did the same thing. Before Pine Camp was enlarged, rent and everything else had jumped high as the moon.**

The papers sound as tho Watertown was getting a good cleaning up. I guess the Army threatened to call it out of bounds if it didn't.

---

*Office of War Information.
**Pine Camp, in Watertown, became Fort Drum in 1951.

The Alpha Zeta house at Cornell University.

I'll send you a clipping that is in today's paper. I saw one awhile ago but forgot to cut it out. It told the frats that were being taken over by navy or army, (I don't remember which) and A.Z. was one of them.* The army has moved in a lot lately. The navy mess hall is being enlarged. I doubt there'll be much but uniforms from now on.

We had hot weather last week 80 degrees and better but the last few days have been cool – about 40 degrees in the morning.

It's 9:20 p.m. and a man from town just brought us two broilers as a present so Mom and I'll pick them and dress them. Since I wrote that he brought another one. Some friend! Water is boiling so I'll stop.**

Will try to write again.

Love,
Marian

---

*Ted and Burt's fraternity, Alpha Zeta.
**A chicken is plunged into boiling water, then hung for plucking and cleaning.

Ted is frustrated with his lack of opportunity on the firing range but clearly enjoys sharing what he has learned about firearms.

U. S. ARMY AIR FORCES   TECHNICAL TRAINING COMMAND

Tuesday noon
July 13

Dear Folks,

I have a few moments to spare, so I'd better get off a note to you.
I imagine that you all survived the holiday and are pecking away at the
hay. We didn't get any time off, but it wouldn't have made any difference
anyway.

As yet my status remains unchanged, and it probably will until I get
a chance to qualify on the range. We were at Tent City last week for three
days for the purpose of qualifying, but they didn't give us the chance.
We were firing and completed the slow fire when they ordered us to
cease firing. It burnt me a bit because we waited for three days for the
opportunity and then only twenty minutes would have given us enough
time to finish. On top of this I had run up a good score and thought I
could be one of the few to get medal. However, I expect we will be going
back tomorrow for another three day stay when we can try again.

I might tell you a bit about the guns we have shot up there. First we
shot the Caliber 30 Carbine. This is a slick little rifle developed to replace
the side arm. It weighs only 5½# and can be slung so that it is drawn faster
than a 45 caliber revolver. In addition to this it is semi-automatic, very
accurate, and for carrying. Secondly we fired the "Tommy" (Thompson
Automatic Sub-machine). We fired 20 rounds and I'll swear that it
seemed like 5. It has a semi-automatic position whereby you can fire
single, and then it has a full automatic position where few can fire in less
than three rounds per burst. This will throw lead pretty fast but, it takes
a lot of practice in order to make that lead amount to anything. It rises
to the right so fast that without a lot of practice, anyone trying to fire
on the automatic would hit his target only once, with the first round. In

57

the movies you often see where the hero merely waves it back and forth and fires in a plane parallel to the ground, but that just doesn't happen. Paratroopers have developed a means of holding it down, whereby they drop the sling and step on it with their foot. Thirdly, we fired the Enfields Cal. 30. This was developed in 1917 for use by the English and French. Because we mfg. so many, they are found very commonly throughout the country where they're used for practice. It is a fairly good gun with a high velocity shell, but it is inferior to most other army rifles. The last gun we shot was the Springfield. This resembles the Enfield in many respects but it has many advantages over the Enfield. It was developed in 1903 and is still used on some of our battlefronts. It carries the same cartridge as the Enfield, but its velocity and accuracy is greater. This is the gun which we'll use if we get a chance to shoot for qualification.

I got a letter from Bob this morning and he says that Chet Freeman is about due to go to primary training soon. Boy, I don't know how he would so fast. The way things are working down here it looks as if it'll be quite awhile before I even get shipped for classification. It's pretty tedious to have to wait around here and to have to take things so many times. Someplace up the line someone seems to be in an awful tangled mess. They don't seem to know what to do with us. It wouldn't surprise me a bit if they started giving me basic again.

I got a nice letter from Mom, Marian, and Altie yesterday. It thrills the devil out of me to see the nice letter that Altie writes. The good grammar and punctuation he uses is quite an achievement, I think. It's nice that Mom had an opportunity to have such a good vacation. I hope that after this war is over that both Mom and Dad will have the opportunity to take a real vacation.

Bob said he went AWOL a while back to see the state. I'd sure have liked to visit the farm lands that he saw, as well as the more scenic areas. I guess he had quite a visit with Uncle Ellis's folks. He seems to think a lot of his Uncle "Wasie."

I'm glad you liked the poor pictures I sent. I hope I can get some more before long. I seem to put the task off. I'd like to have a picture taken of myself before long, but it's hard to get a good cadet picture taken here. I perhaps should wait until I get my cadet's uniform before I have it taken.

Seems as if I have written long enough, so I'll sign off. Everybody write and tell me a little about the activities around home.

Love,

Ted

P.S. I just got a nice letter from Ray saying that he was home for awhile.

Following the end of German resistance in North Africa in May, Allied forces moved on to successfully liberate Sicily. The next step was the invasion of Italy, and on July 25 Mussolini was arrested.

One of Ted's high school friends, Marion Regetz, writes this next letter. In it she describes a difficult commute to work and expresses some optimism about how long she thinks this war will go on.

Saturday P.M.

July 17

Dear Ted,

I received your letter this A.M. and was surprised to get one because I have not written, but as always before I never answer letters very promptly. I could think up plenty of excuses but it's the same old thing, I've got so much else going on that I don't get time.

I'm working at the Rome Air Depot this summer as an accounting & property clerk. And I am working the night shift, 4:15 to 1:45 in the a.m. We drive back and forth with some kids from Lyons Falls. By "we" I mean Marion Long and I. At the present time there are seven of us gals riding in one car, which makes it very cozy, don't you know.

The work isn't too bad but we all manage to keep busy and the pay is fair, about $30 a week after all the taxes have been taken out.

I'm so glad that at last you have been accepted as aviation cadet. I believe your mother was talking something about it and how you hoped you would be accepted.

The Constableville High School Band. Shirley with her trombone, second row, far right.

Marion* has heard from Bill** three times in the past two weeks. The last letter she got was dated July 2. He's having a nice time, playing baseball, swimming & dancing. At least he was when he wrote the letters. He sent a picture of himself and he has a mustache, no less. He really looks tough, rough & ready with it.

Mrs. Wendt has taken over the band. I guess it is going to improve somewhat. They are going to have band concerts every 2 weeks in the village park this summer.

The gas situation is still pretty bad. We had an awful time trying to get some to drive back & forth to work, but this won't last too long now.

Well, I've got to start for work so I'll have to make this short. Excuse me for not writing sooner. And you keep up the good work.

As ever,
Marion

*Marion Long, another high school friend.
**Bill Healt.

Alton decides to show off his cursive writing skills in the middle of this next letter. It looks like he will have to take care of chickens after all.

Summer 1943

Old Forge New York

July, 22 1943

Dear Ted

We are sending you some more clipps. Mom just got your letter. It rained all day. I am going to buy a fly tying outfit like Willies when I finish my Stuka divebomber. We picked a quart of raspberries in the garden tonight. [Alton now changes to cursive writing.] *If you don't mind I'll write. I just got around to write you, I've been so busy. You don't need to boast. Are you to old for fighters? Or can't you take it? Or don't you study for, fighters? We got 14 hens, 13 White Legorns and, Rodeisland Red. They cost $2 apieace. We've picked 83 roses this year. We had _____ _____ muffins yesterday and today. pleasefill in*

Love

Alton

Marian deplores a temperature of forty-eight degrees in July and the high price of produce.

Fri. Morning

9:00

Dear Ted,

I'll just scribble a bit on Alton's letter. Mr. B. is going to the p.o. and Alton says his letter has to go.

I'm sending some more clippings – some are pretty stale. I cut them out when I see something I think might interest you. The one about snow is authentic. The man at Woodgate who sold Mr. B the berries said his beans froze. The temp here this morning was 48 degrees. It rained yesterday and we hoped for more. It's very dry and the garden shows it. We are getting a few raspberries but they need rain. Hope to have some to eat and can. The red raspberries have sold for $1 a qt. in Utica. Saw where first corn on the cob in Rochester was $1 a dz. Tried to get some fruit for Alton last wk. All there was on the market was oranges (like marbles) @39 cents dz., plums 45 cents dz., orchard cherries @49 cents a lb., peas 10 cents per and white grapes I didn't dare price. I don't know how the working man feeds his family.

There's not much news. Mom & Shirley were here 2½ weeks. We may have more guests later if the O.P.A.* decides whether it's coming or going. It's a mess now. No pleasure driving but can take a trip for vacation (with a car full). There doesn't seem to be any checking up here so we get around a bit. Shirley wrote yesterday Dad is going to get Bill a pup if he stops sucking his thumb. Said she didn't know which one would have the most fun. Will try to write again soon.

Marian

Mrs. Weigard wrote Susan is back in Ithaca

Will writes the next letter using his mother's stationery. He is keeping a meticulous tally of the number of trout he has caught this year.

MRS. ERNEST L. MARKHAM

BOX 143

TURIN, NEW YORK

Dear Ted,

I guess it has been quite a while since I have written to you.

We finished haying Saturday the 24th. I lost count of the loads but the barn is full. There is more hay than we had last year with second cutting and the hay Uncle Albert gave us. Clarence Higby offered to give up his new seeding that was just as good as ours but we haven't room for it. George's hired man had boils under his arm so I'm helping George finish up. For the last few days it's been darn poor hay weather.

Two weeks ago Sunday I went fishing down in White River and got 14. Two were 13" one 11½" one 10" and the rest 7 & 8". The week after that I got 14 more but none were over 10". In all I have caught 70 trout so far this year.

I would like to take some cows to the fair this year but I don't know much about showing and we hate to take the time. Joe P. says I ought to

---

*Office of Price Administration.

take Beatrice anyway. He said Mr. Markham would come home with a blue ribbon.

The cows are milking pretty good and the calves are looking good. Cymbie's calf is sure a pretty little thing.

Must hurry this, will write some more later.

Willie

Ted has been transferred from the Basic Training Center in Miami Beach to the Collective Training Directorate in Williamsport, Pennsylvania, where he officially becomes an aviation student. Shirley writes this next letter. Her summer is going by fast.

Turin, NY
July 27, 1943

Dear Ted,

Your letters today reminded me I better get busy and write to you. I'm awfully sorry I neglected to write before. I'd been thinking about it all the time but seemed to be occupied some other way.

I bet you're glad you were shipped to Pennsylvania and we certainly are. We were even hoping you might be shipped to Cornell.

I'm going to take care of Linda next week while Mel goes to the college for training for some part-time job. I'm planning to go Friday on the bus. They'd wanted me to come sometime this summer and this is about as good a time as any.

I got a permanent today. It's kind of frizzy now.

We had quite a rain storm this afternoon – two, in fact. The wind blew quite a bit. We've had quite a few electric storms lately. Sunday it struck a tree this side of Murphy's and Walt and Dad each think it struck down a big branch in the elm tree. One night Willie and Kate* were going to the movies and it was thundering and lightening and he was telling her how to tell how far away it is and just as he got "and when it lightnings and thunders about the same time it's pretty close" out of his mouth

---

*Kate Kraeger, Will's girlfriend.

Fourteen-year-old Shirley and
her new perm

– crash! And splinters began coming down from a telephone pole right in front of them.

Burt just interrupted me to ask me when I'm coming down. Gee, I was rather surprised, but glad.

Johnny and Janice have just gone to a hot dog roast altho it is rather wet.

Jan has been trying to get a job at the Rome Air Depot, but they aren't taking anymore summer workers. She's been making me a couple of dresses and made herself one. Aunt Lottie wanted her to sew for her this fall too.

Dad said to tell you we're all through haying and both bays are filled to the peak. Clarence Higby gave us three acres besides. It certainly was a wonderful year for hay after the farmers could start.

Most were so late with their spring's work they couldn't start very soon and aren't only about half through tho. Some of the vegetables and fruit aren't so hot this year either because there was such a late frost and so much rain. Raspberries are 45 cents a Qt., cherries, 30 cents. Strawberries are bad too.

Willie went to see Mr. Kaskela tonite to take him his rod he's just rewound. You should see all the flies Willie's tied. Every time he gets a few minutes – up he goes. He and Mr. Kaskela have been quite thick this spring and summer. They're going camping for about three days or so. Nearly every Sunday they go fishing somewhere. It's nice Willie can be with Mr. Kaskela. Well it looks as if I was running out of paper and blab so I'll call it quits.

P.S. Altie was awfully pleased with your letter and wasn't his nice?

Love,
Blondie

Evelyn is relieved to have Ted in Pennsylvania. Compared to Miami Beach, he is close to home.

Turin, N.Y.
July 28, 1943

Dear Ted,

We are all so happy about your being in this new place! It seems that it is the answer to our prayers. It must make you feel quite at home to see farmlands, woods and hills which I imagine are not very different from the ones we know. And you are only about a hundred miles from Ithaca! Burt called on the phone last night and we told him about you.

We have received your three letters in a few days, one saying that you would be leaving Miami came about Friday or Saturday; the other two yesterday.

I think I have not told you I received the letter with the money order and have had the deposit made. Also, the receipt for your life insurance premium came. I took the liberty of opening it and put it away with policy.

Two very good and useful men have passed on within a few days – Dean Ladd of Cornell and Fred Grubel of West Leyden.

Otto's family is moving to Naumburg which will be only a mile, I believe, from his office.* They sold the house in Lowville. We have had two or three big rains in a few days. A lot of hay got wet, but not ours. We finished a week ago. Dad and Will have been working on the potatoes and cutting down a big limb which the wind brought down from the big elm

---

*Otto Wasmuth, another of Evelyn's brothers.

65

on the south side of the little garden. If there is any hay weather Geo. H. wants Willie. His man has been sick.

Well, I must put breakfast on.

Lots of love,
Mom

Shall I keep your bank book?

Now that he's closer to home, Ted is hoping for a visit from the family.

U. S. ARMY AIR FORCES

August 2, 1943

Dear Folks,

I have been a bit busy lately and haven't found time to write much of a letter. I got Mom's, Blondie's, and Willie's letters Friday.

I hadn't heard of Dean Ladd's death before. Of course it is a great shock to everyone who knew him. The loss of his usefulness will not only be felt statewide but perhaps world wide. Jerry Wanderstock wrote me today telling of his death as well as the very poorly condition of Prof. Savage and Prof. Hinman. Prof. Hinman has had to retire as you probably already know. Charlie Norton, one of the good students and a good friend of mine gave him a blood transfusion, though I doubt if that will give him strength for long. Men like these men aren't born everyday, though to us they tried to act like everyday people. Their efforts and guidance will long profit we to whom they gave their life's work. Though I am apart from Cornell now, I very often run into the indirect work of some of these great men like Dean Bailey, Andrew D. White, and many others from Cornell who built the pattern which has been so worldly accepted. Today, though it ceases to be the great peacetime institution, its military research, military teachings, and wartime programs* make it part of the nerve system of this country.

*As a land grant university, Cornell was obligated to teach military tactics as well as agriculture and engineering.

66

Looks as if Willie has been having a bit of luck at fishing. If those aren't "fish stories", they are sure as good stories of fishing in White River as I have ever known. Is the water in the stream quite high?

I'm glad to hear that Willie has been helping George out. When he goes out like that, he can help the neighbors a lot, improve his position with the Draft Board and certainly do himself a lot of good in working for other men which he hasn't had much of an opportunity to do.

Yes, I want you to keep my bankbook, and of course to open and take care of things like receipts which come. I would like to send money to have you bank when I do want to bank some because it would be a bit hard to keep changing addresses and still keep contact with the bank by mail. It is hard to be able to save any, but I expect I'll be able to send a little every once in a while. Has my G.I. Insurance Policy ever arrived? I think I mailed you my receipt to keep, but I believe the government should have sent you a policy.

I wish you folks could get down here some weekend while I'm here without making it too inconvenient for yourselves. I hope I can get home for a weekend, but because of the poor train connections I'll only be able to stay a few hours. If you decide to come I wish you could let me know and plan about a week ahead of time so that I could try to get a pass to get away more that weekend. It will be difficult to get away without early planning.

It would be nice if I could get to see some of the farmland around here, while I'm here. There is a county agent who I believe lives here in town, and I think I'll try to get acquainted with him. Maybe I could weadle a ride with him some Saturday afternoon, who knows.

Well, I seem to be nearly run down, and I want to send this letter in tonight's mail.

Write when you can.

Love,
Ted

Ted's next letter to Shirley is full of appreciation for his new location.

August 6, 1943

Dear Blondie,

I hope I can scribble you a few lines before "Taps."

We just got back from having a picnic out at a nearby park. Can you imagine the army giving its men a picnic? I couldn't until tonight, and it was really swell. Of course with small numbers of men such as we have here it can be done whereas with more men it would be impossible. I guess we were pretty much on the ball during the past week and that was our pay for it. This is a fine place to be and the officers and instructors are swell to us. It is so much different than we were accustomed to in Miami.

I had a few hours to look the town over last Sunday and it is quite a nice town. It is spread out over quite a little area as are most towns of its sort in Penn. It is also a bit dark from the soft coal dust which floats through the air in this section and that everyone heats their homes with. This week end we get a longer chance to leave the post so maybe I can climb a few of the hills around here.

Life here makes me feel swell. It is so cool and refreshing around here mornings and never gets terribly warm. Each morning we have an hour of drill and then PT (Physical Training) another hour before classes. Our exercises are quite rigid and we do a lot of double timing. Next week we'll be in good enough shape so that we'll be running six miles every other day. Our muscles were in good condition when we left Miami but our wind was poor. I weighed 172 lbs. the other day, stripped, and I think it is pretty solid weight too. We have a nice swimming pool here, and they usually let us swim about five minutes every day. It loosens you up a lot after doing good rigid exercises and running.

We heard a rumor tonight that our CO (Commanding Officer) is leaving us. We hate to see him go because he gets a lot out of us and we still have fun doing it. Our only hope is that our new CO is that sort of a fellow.

You know, Blondie, I got to thinking that Willie's fishing might be more than an accident. I take it that he gets around the good fishing of White River more than one would ordinarily imagine.

Looks as if I'll have to go to bed now, so take it easy, huh?

Love,
Ted

Marian has some news for Ted about their younger sister, Jan. She is a bit skeptical about her little sister's readiness for this event.

Aug. 9

Dear Ted,

I'm ashamed I haven't written but we had guests and have been gadding, etc.

I was pleased that you got out of the heat and somewhere near home. If you get a short leave you might get to Troy, Pa. and visit the Tates. They would be tickled to have you and I'll write and tell them you may drop in. He's deputy postmaster so everybody knows him. (Charles Tate). She is Mr. B's youngest sister. Richard (their son) has just been discharged from the Army because of allergy trouble. He was in the hospital (army) for weeks. He's allergic to 50 different items – including all sorts of food. They finally told him to get out before he got a bad case of asthma. After his discharge he took a flying trip all over the country. I think he flew over 5000 mi. and hitch-hiked several hundred besides.

I'm sending another bunch of clippings – mostly about Dean Ladd's death and also Prof. Hinman's.* I hadn't heard of Prof. Savage's illness until you mentioned it in Alton's letter. The loss of these men is a loss to the whole country.

About your birthday – I'm awfully sorry I haven't anything for you.** I've been trying to find a watch but it's impossible. I know that old thing of mine is next to no good. It takes months now even to get one repaired.

Could you tell me something you'd like or would you prefer to buy it yourself? <u>Let me know</u>. Maybe you could use money.

About the news about Janice. It's straight and not gossip. Mom probably left it to her to tell you and she hasn't. She has a diamond. None of us are terribly excited about it and she doesn't seem to be either. Don't repeat it but I think it's a case of her being afraid of being an old maid. I

---

*Carl Edwin Ladd was Dean of the New York State College of Agriculture and the New York State College of Home Economics at Cornell, and also Director of the Geneva Experiment Station. Robert B. Hinman was Professor of Animal Husbandry at Cornell.
**Ted's birthday was August 12.

guess she's going to get rich first and at the present it looks as tho it wouldn't be right away.

We went down home Thurs. nite and stayed and the next day went to Lowville and came back that night. Saw Teen, Bob & Bill a few minutes. Bob has lost 25 lbs. since last Sept. – says he works for a living. Teen said that morning Bill sneezed and she asked him if he had a "fuzzy" up his nose. He said, "No, he had 'hay feber'."

Mom has gotten over her skin trouble but Janice and Alton both have it. Don't think Mom feels too good and Janice doesn't look good – doesn't weigh much more than I do.

Going to take Alton to Dr. Lindsay for the skin trouble today. Took him about 3 wks. ago and then it was cleared up. Broke out again last week. The skin specialist and Dr. Vadney both said it wasn't contagious. Nice going.

I've got to go to town and have to run. Got lots to do and shouldn't have stopped to write this morning but wanted to send you birthday greetings. Have a good celebration but don't get too drunk.

Love,
Marian

Evelyn writes that Bob will soon be sent overseas. It feels like a "big wave of cold water" to her.

MRS. ERNEST L. MARKHAM
BOX 143
TURIN, NEW YORK

August 11, '43

Dear Ted,

Your nice long letter came about a week ago. It seems so nice to have you nearer so the letters are not long on the way.

It has taken quite awhile to get Bob's letters and some of ours to him took a very long time. Some he never did get I guess. One to him from Ray, sent by airmail June 4, reached him July 24. He just got some maple sugar we sent for his birthday and some Otto's folks sent, Aug. 1. He did

Bob and Evelyn,
circa 1939

think his sea chest was lost, but Rosemary finally located it in San Diego.*

Have you heard from him lately? We have a letter, dated Aug. 4, saying that he would soon be going out – probably fly to California, then ship to Hawaii, then fly again south. Though we have been expecting it, the full realization sort of comes like a big wave of cold water.

You mentioned Dean Ladd's death. We had intended to send you some clippings, but Marian said she had sent some. We sent ours to Bob. Do you know that Prof. Hinman died a few days later?

Yes, Ted, the certificate showing that you have insurance** came some little time ago, also a second one of Bob's. We only hope we will never have occasion to use them.

Bob says he probably will have more time to write after a little but very little he can write about. His address will be the same as now. Mail connections will be poor, he says, but we must try to write often just the same.

Marian has planned for a birthday present for you from all of us, and we were to pay her later. I don't know what luck she has had. Sorry this is a bit late but we are wishing you loads of good luck and happiness.

Love from us all,
Mother

P.S. Did you borrow some money from Bob that time last spring when you went to the bank and made a deposit for him? I am a bit uncertain about how much I borrowed for Janice. Harry Mathis is home on furlough. Clyde Sage is home – discharged.

---

*Rosemary was Bob's California girlfriend.
**Life insurance for soldiers.

Ted writes home with some reflections on his birthday and on growing another year older.

August 13, 1943

Dear Folks,

It was nice to get the birthday cards today with everyone's signatures upon them. Somehow I don't seem to feel any older than I did Wednesday. I used to think that a fellow twenty-two years old was an old man, but when I stop to think about it, I realize that I'm still the young kid who makes mistakes and continually looks to those older than he. I also once thought that a fellow of that age had passed the big stages of learning and that his life from then on was that of a mature nature, but I still find myself studying and anticipating the same for quite a while henceforth. It would be great though to get on top of the heap once so that life could be enjoyed as most people live it.

There wasn't a great deal exciting about the big day yesterday, except that the boys saw my cards on Wednesday. Thursday morning during chow the mess hall suddenly broke out with a "Happy Birthday dear Markham," and then during drill when we are allowed to sing as we march, the popular song seemed to be the same. It made me blush a bit, but it was one more thing that gives a fellow self-satisfaction with good fellowship.

I spoke of trying to get a pass to come north before long. Since that time we have had a new CO and he may change the picture; I have no idea as yet. Different CO's have their own opinions as to how their particular organizations should be run.

Last weekend was our first real week end to see the town and I found the people to be swell. The parents of one of my roommates back at Miami had me over for dinner and then a girl I met on Saturday had me out to her folk's farm for the afternoon and evening. They have a vegetable farm, and it sure seemed great to get out on the soil again.

I guess I never told you a great deal about my roommates at Miami Beach. They came from Buffalo, Syracuse, Rochester, Watertown, and Pulaski. There is no special one for me to speak of for most of them were about the same sort of good fellows. Of the twelve I had at different times all except three were married men. Four of these had one child and one of the four had two, one two and the other four years old. This fellow was a swell fellow, but he had received an awful deal from his draft board. His health wasn't good and he was employed at the Syracuse Ordinance. How many of these fellows bit their lip and dug in was a surprise to me. It seemed that most of my associates back there were all men of thirty except for one lad who was my closest friend and an E.R.C.* man. He was Bill Kane, an Irishman who went to school in Olean.

My roommates here are Dick Baier from Newark, N.J. who finished two years of engineering at N.C.E.** He can get about the most music from a piano that I've ever heard though he is only nineteen years old. The second is a married man, Vern Westcott, from Lewistown, N.Y. though his wife lives in Pittsburgh. They're good fellows and make the best kind of roommates.

Looks as if I have written a great deal more than I'm accustomed to. I'm waiting to go on guard Duty at 9 o'clock. This will be my first Guard Duty here. I won't be carrying a rifle for a change and I won't have to bother to stop anyone for another change. It won't be nearly so lonesome as the twenty four hour, four shift duty which we pulled so often at Miami. Well, I guess I'd better leave now. Write when you can.

Love,

Ted

Ernestine updates Ted on what birthday gifts he can expect to receive in the mail. She hopes to be able to find enough gasoline to be able to visit him in Williamsport.

Turin, NY

Aug. 14, 1943

Dear Ted,

As usual, this letter will be hurried. I'm waiting to go to Turin but will write as much as I can.

We're sending a package, too. Willis selected a duffle bag for you a couple of days ago. I never go shopping any more or would have got it for you long ago. I hope you still can use it and it is a kind you will like.

---

*E.R.C. = Enlisted Reserve Corps.
**N.C.E. = Newark College of Engineering.

If you have another bag or would prefer a different kind, will you send it back and tell me what is wrong? We can exchange it. Maybe, by now, you can use the money, rather than the bag. If it isn't worth five bucks, say so, too.

Mom is sending some cookies and a hand brush, too. I guess they are birthday presents, too.

Marian organized all of us to get you a good watch. I haven't heard what she got. Have you received it yet?

I'm looking forward to seeing you, now that you're so near. Of course, tires and gasoline are scarce, but we'll find a way.

There's little news, I guess. Have you heard that Lieut. Howard Ross, U.S. Army Air Corps, was sent to Miami Beach about the time you left? Chet Freeman is in Florida, too, Sarasota, I think.

Our Bill is getting to be some youngster. He has an amazing vocabulary and surely uses it. He tells great tales, some true and some imagined.

A few days ago, when I was bathing him, he held up his hand and said, "I caught a little fish in my hand, mommy. Tell Grandma put on the fry pan – cook it for supper." Then, very thoughtfully he put his hand back in the water, and said, "I let the fish go away. He doesn't like to be cooked. It's too hot."

You should see him swim. We take him out where it is about waist deep on us, put a hand under his chest and he propels himself along through the water. Bob brags about his powerful stroke!

Mother got her last uncensored letter from Bob from San Francisco.* He mailed it Monday. They were to sail the next day, probably any time after midnight. They were to go by carrier to Hawaii and fly south from there.

Rosemary found his chest at the last moment and met him in San F. with it. She will send it on here. Evidently quite a lot of our mail never has caught up with him.

Doris had a letter from Pete. He says he's well, it's hot where he is, and he's very busy.

Janice goes to work in Rome at the Depot Monday. She will be a civil service clerk at $1440 a year, plus overtime.

---

*A soldier's outgoing mail was censored.

Bill O'Brien, age two, climbs his backyard fence in Lowville.

I'd love to work there myself. It's a busy place. I was pretty thrilled one day to see all the planes coming and going.

Shirley is in Ithaca helping Melrose, who is doing some sort of part time work. Blondie is enjoying Linda, of course.

Jan is here today for a short visit. She & Bill are having fun. I don't know any farm news and everyone is ready to go to Turin.

Love from all,
Ernestine

P.S. Billy & I are here only on a very short visit. We leave on the bus tonight.

Ernest and Shirley have visited Ted in Williamsport. Ted writes that his squadron is in need of some disciplinary action.

September 2, 1943

Dear Folks,

I am sorry that I've been so tardy in writing. I didn't mean to, for I wanted all of you to know how nice it was for me that I had an opportunity to spend a little time with Dad and Blondie. Though I couldn't give Dad much of my time after we returned to Williamsport, it seemed swell to me to have him return with me. I only regretted that Mom couldn't have also made it.

I seems that lately they have kept us so busy that I haven't even had a chance to catch up on my housework. It is a good thing for me that studies are easy for I would have little time out of formation to study. It seems that lately we have had out of routine formations to make whenever we ordinarily get a chance to study, write letters, launder, polish shoes, and etc. Then too it seems that we got badly out of line during the past two weeks and our superiors have had to issue severe disciplinary actions to us. It kept building up with minor things until the parade which Dad saw was the first major fault and then more followed. From now out the discipline is going to be rigid and require more time devoted to military bearing. I'll have less time to write, but it may be a good thing because the extra time is going to be used in building us to what we are supposed to be.

Time slips by pretty fast here and I hate to think of the small time we will have to spend here. Only two and one half more months and I'll be leaving the north for some time. I like this place and the thought of being closer to home. As Dad has probably told you I hope I can make it home if and when I get my next pass. I won't have long to spend there, but I think it is possible to make it. In that connection I hope you will surely telegraph me immediately if there should be family sickness, financial crisis, or any other thing for which I might be able to get a furlough. It must require my presence at home in order that I get one.

I happened to think of the pictures of mine the other day which Willie had developed from the film which was in the camera at the time I sent my camera home. Would you be so good as to send them to me Willie?

I would like to thank the family for the swell package they sent me for my birthday. The bag is swell, the cookies vanished like mad, the brush comes in handy, and the Boonville Herald helps me to keep up on local gossip. I know Dad was responsible for sending the Herald, but I take it he meant to include the rest of the family.

Would you please send me Bob's new address and latest developments from him. I haven't heard from him since he shipped, and I figure I should write.

I guess this is all tonight. Everyone write.

Love,
Ted

P.S. I see that the Boonville Herald has me for a cadet. I thought I had made it clear that I was an Aviation Student and not a cadet until as classified at Nashville. I didn't mean to deceive you folks in that way because I may never make the grade.

Bob writes from an undisclosed location in the South Pacific. U.S. forces have continued their strategy of island hopping to isolate Japanese air bases.

Monday 6 Sept.

Dear Ted,

It took your last letter about three weeks to get to me this time and then I might have been a bit more prompt in answering. Some of the time here hasn't been a lot else to do but write letters but somehow we seem to do a lot of fooling around.

No doubt the family has told you that I shoved off about a month ago. It was a bit sooner than we expected but it's good to get started on our little tour and get it over with. There are some things about this experience that I'd hate to miss but that doesn't mean that it's anything to look forward to. The first part of the trip was aboard ship and of course a new experience for me. Luckily I wasn't seasick and really enjoyed the trip but was glad to get my feet on the ground again. The first stop was interesting and in some respects almost glamorous. The food and quarters were swell. Here things aren't quite so luxurious.

Glad you got back up north, for at this time of year you'll get a kick out of it. Hope you have a chance to go to Ithaca and up home. I'd sure like to see that country right now. Get a little tired of so much water.

Washington is nice country and we had some good times up there. Hope you get a chance to go there sometime except that it usually means you are on your way to Alaska. I never did get to visit the cousins in Bremerton. Was going over on a Sunday that they suggested and we left the day before. Anyway I don't really know them. It was good to see Uncle Ellis again though.

We have a good gang in the squadron and that means a lot up here. There are a few guys that I seem to hit it off with as well as anyone since Tracy, Harold Wallace or other old pals. The fellow I fly with is a great guy too. A screwball in some ways – always seems to enjoy himself and provides amusement for the whole gang. He was in Alaska for about eight months then instructed in these planes for awhile and can handle them pretty well.

Do you still hear from Ray? The last letter I had was addressed wrong and took a month to get to me so I figured he had moved. I hear from Chet now and then and guess he is coming along pretty well.

Wish I could tell you more about what we are doing as I know you would be interested. Will have to stick to incidentals.

Let me know how they do things in the army. Also be sure to have some fun while you can. It's a fine chance to get around and meet lots of nice people.

Drop me a line.

As always
Bob

Evelyn writes to Ted that the family is doing all that it can to keep the farm and home safe for her boys to return to. There is a bee buzzing in Jan's bonnet, and Ernest's visit to Williamsport has done him a lot of good.

Turin, N.Y.
Sept. 13, '43

Dear Ted,

This is Marian's birthday, isn't it? I had not thought about it until I wrote the date.

Yes, we have been very remiss about our letter writing of late. For me, at least, it has seemed that every minute is crowded with things that demand immediate attention or else my hands and brain are too numb to write. But we are happiest when busy. We can still think a lot about you boys and try to do the things you'd like most to have us do. We are sorry we can't always write and tell you what is in our hands and in our hearts but it's mostly of or for you two who we know are carrying the huge load of responsibility of fighting for us. We are trying to back you up the best

Engaged

Miss Janice Elizabeth Markham, daughter of Mr. and Mrs. Ernest L. Markham of Turin, is engaged to John Francis Klossner of Constableville, according to a recent announcement made by her parents.

we know how by trying to make and save and to keep home just as you'd hope to find it when you come back.

Dad has just bought a $100 bond for Willis and hopes to get some more before long. He is sending, in a few days, the interest and $500 to Mrs. Hinckley. We do not owe anything on any stock, tools or farm equipment or cars. We pay the co-op for feed, etc. each month. So, you see, things have got caught up a bit financially. Between Dad, Willis and me, we have $550 in bonds, and we will get more. I guess Jan will have to buy some. She is working for Uncle Sam, you know.

Has she or anyone told you what kind of a bee she has in her bonnet tho? It has been buzzing so loudly all summer she has not had room for a thought of anything else. If it has to be, I'm glad Johnny is her choice, but it seems to me she needn't have been so afraid of old age, just yet. The two Marians gave her a shower of personal things, undies, etc. last Thursday evening as they were about to go back to school. The big date is to be Oct. 30, we expect. You'll be able to come, won't you?

Dad had a wonderful time, visiting you. I think it did him lots of good. He has seemed sort of old and tired and more muddled than ever sometimes. We must get him out to lodge or church or something oftener or he'll be like Adriel before long.*

Melrose, Burt, Shirley and Linda came Friday night, a week ago, and Mel and Burt stayed until Monday night, then started for Fillmore. My, but it was all too short a time. None of us except Shirley ever got Linda in our arms but she did begin to play with Billy and pick up the kitten. She liked Lad too. Marian and Alton were here over Saturday night and the O'Brien's were here a little while Sat. evening and then again Sunday.

Silo filling has begun and Willis is working on the job. They began at Walt's and have finished Sampson's today. I guess they'll go to Millard's and Herb's next. Willie came home from Sampson's and took Dan** up in the woods skidding for awhile. Guess the corn harvesters have to catch up. Our corn is still growing fine – nice dark green, good & high, ears not quite milky. A light frost nipped squash vines here last night but tomatoes and such are all right. We hope it holds off. Many late-planted things are still growing. Potatoes are a good crop hereabouts but mostly blighted. Oats have turned out better than expected. There has been so much rain lately we have only one load drawn in. We have some nice second cutting on the upper south meadow, some in barn, some drawn up in pasture and some more to cut. All pastures are good for the time of year. We have had lots of early and Dutchess apples to use and give away. We seem to be fortunate. I am canning and drying a good lot as other fruit is scarce and high. We got eighteen quarts of huckleberries and then a few more for Mel.

Grandma was over last week and Grandpa was here with Clara and "Liz" yesterday. They are all as usual. Helen and Joe are going to buy the old house and come "after the war."*** She is starting school today, I think. Did I ever tell you her address? It is 401 Crossett St.

I seem to have run out of paper, so I'll write to Bob. He wrote to us from Hawaii and from farther out – we think maybe Wake – pretty wild and barren. His address remains the same – Fleet P.O. San Fran.

Love,

Mom

Yes, we had read of Flansburg's death. One more of the civilian casualties of the war. A great loss to his field of work and influence.

---

*Adrial was an eccentric uncle.
**Dan was a work horse. Horses were still used to skid logs out of the woods.
***Clara and Helen were Ernest's sisters. Joe was Helen's husband. Liz was Clara's daughter.

Will has been working hard on the fall harvest and is proud of it.

Sep't. '43

Dear Ted

I sent that film away to be developed but it has not returned as yet. When it comes I will see that you get your pictures.

We got a pretty darn nice hay wagon now, even if I did build it myself. Everybody on the corn job thinks it is a pretty nice little hay wagon.

A week ago I cut a couple of loads of second cutting. It would have been ready to draw next day but it rained on it that night and it was wet all week. It got so black I put it in the pasture and the cows ate some.

This week the weather has been grand – no rain, and I got in a load that was in darn good shape, nice and green but plenty dry.

We finished our two wheeled manure wagon and that works good too. It will hold as much as the sleigh and it draws real easy. Neither wagons with the rubber tires will cut in wet ground as much as an iron wheeled wagon.

Our oats look a lot better than most of them around here but we won't know for sure until we have thrashed. The stalks are good and long,

Silo filling. Fay Ackerman's gray horse and Ben's "rear view" [Evelyn's writing]

Fay Ackerman on the "corn job" [Evelyn's writing]

almost as tall as last year. The corn job is coming along good. We have finished Walts and Bens and will probably finish Millards today. Ben had corn about 15' tall and was it mean to handle. The bundles were tied too close to the butts and were tied very loose. It's a good thing there weren't two ears to the stalk as we wouldn't have been able to handle them. They weren't eared at all. Ours is earing up good. Dad and I finished that strip of floor in the new part of the barn and now we can drive right in with the wagon. We have built a scaffold on the second bent in the new part and are putting the oats up there.

It has been pretty cold for about a week and it froze Sunday night, but I don't think it hurt our corn much.

Charlie Eavens said to me the first day of silo filling that he would come over and get our wagon when they got on their end of the job and I said like hell he would and he shut up.

Willie

Ted is clearly miffed at Janice about hearing the news of her engagement from someone else. He's doubtful that he will be granted leave so that he can attend her wedding but proposes a scheme that may enable him to get there. Ted ends this letter by echoing his mother's concern over the state of his father's mental health. The war seems to be taking a toll on Ernest.

September 17, 1943

Dear Janice,

I would like to give you my best wishes upon the announcement of your engagement. I have been waiting eagerly to hear the news from you, but I was disappointed in your neglect. I was a bit put out because I had to learn of the event in a round about means of local gossip.

Mother, in her last letter, told me that you expected to hold the grand event on Oct. 30. If it meets with your approval, I would like to be at the occasion if it is in any way possible. However, I may have difficulties. Firstly I will have to reject the pass which will be coming in about three weeks, and hope that I can have it deferred until the weekend of the 30th. Secondly, and most important, is the fact that weekend passes begin at 1 PM on Saturday. This type of an organization is particularly exacting and I will have to do some tall thinking in order to get away from here Friday night I will have to make it look like an emergency, and this is a part which you might be able to help me with.

Do you suppose that you could get Johnny or yourself to fake up a letter whereby you asked me to be best man? Now don't get me wrong, I don't ask to be best man; I merely want that put in writing so that I can show the letter to the Captain. Far be it for me to meddle with your personal business and arrangements for your wedding. I really wouldn't accept such a job anyway for it will be all I can do to get home and enjoy home as I'm entitled to for those short hours.

I guess I had better tell you now that if I can make it, it will be hard to get there before late Saturday afternoon. Perhaps if Burt and Mel attend I can make connections with them someway.

I wish you a lot of success with your future with Johnny. Johnny is a swell fellow and should make the best kind of a husband. I hope you can make him the best kind of wife and home that he is entitled to. I hope you realize that the role of a farmer's wife is a difficult one, and that you will have to dig in as never before.

As you have by now realized this letter is intended especially for you and so I'm going to say a few things that I would not say to the whole family. When Dad spent the weekend with me a month ago, it shook me to realize how he has aged during the last six months. Mother also complains of the fact when she often writes me. You have got to hand it to him for the way he takes his work for his age, but it looks as if something is wearing him faster than physical labor. He would be the last one to admit it, but I think I can read his reactions as easily as my own. He seems to be thinking too much of Bob and me if my guess is correct. He was touched pretty deeply when he left me that morning, more so than I've ever seen him before. I know what must have built up with him before that. This isn't the way I like you folks to feel, and I'm sure that Bob feels the same. We have a lot of faith in ourselves, and God knows we want the same of our homefolks so that their life will be more cheerful and carefree. I speak of this to you because I realize you look at it differently than Mom or Dad. Wouldn't you try to think of something that would divert their attention so that they can enjoy life easier and longer?

I guess I can say little more tonight. I wish you would write me and discuss my scheme.

As ever,
Ted

P.S. Perhaps if Johnny should write that note* it would look good to the captain if he touched it a bit with personal feelings between himself and me.

—————————

*Johnny Klossner did "fake up" a letter for Ted in an attempt to get Ted home for the wedding. Unfortunately, Johnny's contrived letter was not included in Ted's collection.

—————————

On September 3, Italy surrendered to the Allies. Ted writes that he is enthusiastic about the war effort, not knowing that German forces would battle back and the liberation of Italy would not be finished until May of 1945. Ted is enjoying himself in Williamsport and writes with some news: he has found himself a girlfriend.

—————————

SERVICE MEN'S CENTER
ACACIA CLUB
WILLIAMSPORT 6, PA.

September 18, 1943
Sunday afternoon

Dear folks,

I am spending this afternoon in the new Servicemen's Center which the Masons have provided us. They are really going all out to make this an enjoyable place for us. It opened a week ago last Saturday night by giving us a big dance. They are giving us a dance every second Saturday night with an orchestra and then every Saturday night in between they give us a rec-dance. At each occasion like this we may bring our lady-friends by means of a special pass they provide for us. They provide soft drinks, rec-music, books and magazines, facilities for letter writing, and anything else which we might want. This place is always open and they lean over backward to make our life here more pleasant. This is an example of the sort of people we have to live with here. A bit different than Miami.

Tomorrow we move into Squadron D on our third class of Pre-Aviation. It means that we have completed eight weeks here and we have eight more weeks before shipment to Nashville. I finished this last class with about a 92 average. Studying is far from what we at Cornell were used to. I only hope they don't shove me ahead for I am going to feel badly when I have to leave here.

In one of my previous letters I spoke of the general tightening of military training here. Along with this they began scoring the squadrons according to their perfection in drill, physical training, academics, and general military bearing. After two weeks of this scoring our squadron finished last week in first place. We really cleaned up in academics, won three of four parades last week, won for the third consecutive week the inter-squadron physical competition on Saturday, and had the fewest demerits for the week. The spirit of our squadron is in top condition right now.

I am going to devote this paragraph to Blondie who seems to keep the family record of the family's love life. Yes, Blondie, I have found myself a girl-friend here. Her name is Peggy Kuhn, and she is a very nice girl with a fine father and mother. We get along pretty well, Blondie.

85

To Willie and Altie, I want to say that I will start flying in four weeks. I will have ten hours of dual-control work aboard a cub. This flying is just to give us the feeling of the air. These planes are powered by a 50 or 75 H.P. Franklin or Continental motor. Contrast this motor with the two 2,000 H.P. Double Wasp, Pratt and Whitney's that Bob has in his control. You can imagine what he has a hold of when he takes hold of the throttle of his Ventura (B-34 or PV-1).

I enjoyed the letters which I got last week from Mom and Willie. Willie must be revolutionizing our farm wagons.

I am going to try my best to get home for Janice's wedding. I'll have to play my card pretty shrewdly if I do. Perhaps I can make arrangements with Burt and Mel if they attend.

I had a letter from Jerry yesterday and find that he is in Sheppard Fields, Texas. He has made PFC and now he is trying for AC. His rank will help his financial status a bit if he makes cadet. By the way you should read an article in the last Post about the Naval Pre-flight at Colgate. It describes our set-up to quite an extent.

I am pretty enthusiastic about our war news lately. It indicates that we still have a long and tough fight but at least we have the initiative. Neither Germany nor Japan seems to be producing air power that can compete with ours. There seems to be a tremendous margin between the abilities of our airmen and theirs at present.

I had my first letter from Bob the other day. As nearly as I could read between his lines, I would <u>guess</u> that he is in the area of Midway or south of there. He wouldn't be at Wake because that is still enemy territory.

I guess I can't say a great deal more.

Everybody write.

Love,
Ted

P.S. Altie do I owe you a letter or do you owe me one?

In a letter to Jan, Bob expresses his appreciation for the work Willie is doing on the home front. He also tells Jan that she is fortunate to be one of the lucky individuals who can be married in this time of war. He approves of her decision.

Sat. afternoon
Sept.18

Dear Jan,

It certainly was good to get your letter yesterday. Had meant to write you for some time but you know how I am at corresponding. Wish I could talk with you. Say – that letter was postmarked Sept. 10 out of C-ville and that isn't bad service, huh? So you think you know where I am – yes? You might as well go ahead and guess for it's an interesting game and no one reads your letters anyway.*

No one had told me you were working in Rome and I was wondering if you had a job. Seems like other people are as bad as I am at dishing out the news tho I have an excuse because there are things I shouldn't tell – even things I shouldn't have told, no doubt. Haven't heard much from Willie either. No doubt he feels funny not to be going back to school this fall. Perhaps his role will get a little monotonous and there will be times when he will wish that he could do something more exciting.

I wish he could too for it's good experience to get out on your own whether it's to go to college or join the army. I hope that can come later for him and I'm sure he is doing as much good where he is. I do know that he is doing a lot for the rest of the family – especially Ted & me because he is helping hold together the thing we think of as our home. When we get back we hope to find things the way they were when we left except for the few improvements that are bound to come along. Perhaps we are selfish in that respect.

Jan, – it's sort of hard to think of you being married only because I hate to lose my "little sisters." Don't think I don't approve. It sounds like a sensible decision for both of you. I am especially glad that it is John for we know him so well. I would do a lot of wondering if it was someone I don't know but then "we Markhams" make up our own minds. Right?

It was thoughtful of you to wish I could be there. You can bet I would like to make it too. Chances are if and when this old rooster makes the decision, tho he won't worry too much about the rest of the family and might not give much notice.

You and John are very fortunate to be able to plan a normal married life. There are thousands of young people who would like to and should

---

*Only the outgoing letters of soldiers were censored.

be doing the same. And then what is even worse (I think) is the thousands of cases of young married couples being separated especially when they have been married only a short time. We get to see too many marriages that just don't have a chance.

Perhaps you folks are wondering about me, especially since Rosemary wrote to Mother. Maybe I have let her assume too much. She is a swell friend tho such as you seldom find. Very definitely tho – I am sure of nothing, especially my own feelings and therefore there are no plans. There is lots of time for thinking out here tho too much.

Wish you could see our nifty tans. It isn't necessary to wear much of anything so a lot of the time we don't. Yesterday I pitched horseshoes and hung around the beach all forenoon and got a bit of a burn especially on my nose tho I was already quite brown. We get up at 4 a m two out of three days and at about 7 on the others and go to bed around nine or ten so we have quite a long day and there isn't a lot of flying to do. It would be a pretty soft life if the entertainment situation was better. Anyway we are a healthy lot and we have a lot of foolishness to keep things lively.

At the moment, as I'm finishing this thot I started in an odd moment this afternoon, there is quite a congregation here. I am seated on Dave Walbinshaw's bed and tending his record player while he and three others play Bridge. The records are nice to have and also we have two radios that will pick up California stations pretty well. We heard the "Hit Parade" this morning. You see there is eight hours difference between our time and yours.

Tell everybody to write, Jan. Also be sure to let me know how all your plans turn out. Don't spare the details.

Bet you are getting some cool evening by now and maybe some colored leaves. I have nearly forgotten what both are like. Wish I could go hunting up there this fall.

Love
Bob

Evelyn writes that Marian has found Ted a birthday gift, a watch, but she had to go as far as Utica to find it. Alton has returned to his grandparents' home on West Road, Turin, for the school year.

Turin, N.Y.
Sept. 20, '43

Dear Ted,

By this same mail we are sending you a watch. I guess it is the long delayed gift we intended for your twenty-first birthday.

Marian found it in Utica and left it here with us. Several of us are contributing toward it. We hope it will prove useful and satisfactory. Marian says the buckle is not very substantial. If you need a sturdier one, let us know and maybe we can get one for you. We'll try.

Marian and Mr. B. were here for overnight and left Alton here, as usual to go to school. They had just taken Aunt Em. to Utica to take the train.

Teen and Billy were here a couple of days, went back yesterday afternoon but will come again soon. She and I are doing some co-operative canning. Bill is getting to be a great boy. He told his mother the other day he wasn't her little boy and when she asked whose he was, he said, "Markhams." He has a big time when he is here. (And so do we).

Merrill Dewan and his little family have been home and Clyde* was there too. Marian and Alton stopped in and saw them all.

Guess there is no big news. We are having nice weather except that nights are very cool – several light frosts. Everybody is digging in at the harvesting of crops. Silo filling is progressing well. We are canning a lot of apples, vegetables and tomatoes.

We hope you are feeling fine and liking your work.

Everybody sends love,

Mother

---

*Clyde Dewan, Marian's ex-husband.

Autumn 1943

Ted writes that he likes his new watch a lot. He knows that he has a special family.

September 23, 1943

Dear Folks,

The nice watch arrived today and it pleases me like the devil. I was a bit put out by the fact that you spent too much for it. Nevertheless it is swell. I want to thank everyone for it even though I don't know just who contributed toward it. To me it stands for the thoughtfulness of the best darn family a fellow could have.

Nothing very exciting has taken place since I wrote you on Sunday. We have started our studies in our new squadron and find them about the same except that we are taking History this month instead of Geography. Our PT (physical training) is getting stiffer because we are now in a class by ourselves and have no green squadron with us to slow us up.

Today a new squadron pulled in. This will be squadron A. Since we arrived we have now had three squadrons arrive after us. They are namely Squadrons A,B,C, while we are Squadron D with Squadron E above us.

I learned of my marks this week and even though I am pleased with them, I am a bit worried. I have an average of 92 which is the highest of the squadron at present. It worries me because the possibility of shipping with Squadron E is very good. That would mean I would leave here four weeks too soon. I don't mean to shirk, but I would like to fly here. I want those four weeks of academics, and I hate to leave Williamsport and the north.

It seems that I should write some more letters tonight, so I will close. Everyone write.

Love,
Ted

Marian is planning to stay at Gray Lake until after Jan's wedding on October 30. Then she will close up Mr. Baxter's camp and open his house on Mitchell Street in Ithaca.

Thurs. Sept. 23

Dear Ted,

I've been promising myself every day that I'd write you but then put it off so I'm doing it right after breakfast.

There's not too much news here except we are a bit lonesome since Alton and Aunt Em left. That was a week ago yesterday. Alton's skin trouble was spreading so Dr. Lindsay thot he should see a specialist. (Teen says – Alton & his specialists!) So we went to Utica and put Aunt Em on the train. The Dr. gave Alton an x-ray treatment – an ointment for night, a lotion for day and some medicine to take. It didn't bother him but it was spreading and I wanted it taken care of before he went home.

We stopped in Boonville on the way back for a pair of shoes for Alton and a haircut. While he was in the barber shop, he found out that his father and Merrill were both home so we went down. Dub was there and Merrell's wife and baby. Clyde looks fine and Merrill and Dub are big as barrels. The baby is cute – looks like Merrill's baby pictures. His wife seems awfully nice.

Then we went on home and stayed all night. Mr. B. had an appointment the next morning in Boonville to have his wheels lined up. Then we went to Millers* for dinner and stayed for supper at Markham's and on home (camp) to sleep. Quite a trip these days.

It seems Janice is getting married Oct. 30. I hope you can make it. It won't seem quite right if you can't. Willis is laughing up his sleeve because he thinks she won't be able to quit her job at the Rome Air Depot. (Not pronounced dee pot but de pot). Mom said Mr. Klossner was lovely to Janice when they told him they were going to be married. I said it was nice he was because none of us had been. Bob wrote it was hard to believe

*Mary Miller was Evelyn's younger sister.

but he was glad it was John. Even admitted he might consider the step someday when things were more settled. Of course he didn't commit himself any further.

I've been wracking my brain (or rather the substitute the Lord blessed me with) for stuff to send Bob for Christmas. The packages have to be sent by Oct. 15. It's so hard to guess what he might be able to use. I've finally gotten a cloth kit with pockets in it which I've filled with shaving cream, toothpaste, razor blades, handkerchiefs, sewing kit, washcloths, lava soap. He wrote in his last letter that it was pretty rough where he is and rather hard to clean up.

By the way, when I was in Utica I found a watch for you. Perhaps you have it by now as I left it down home. I'm sorry it's not nicer but watches are as scarce as hen's teeth. There are a few expensive watches and hardly anything else. That watch is a service watch and guaranteed for a year. I got it at one of the nicest jewelry stores in Utica – can't remember the name. I bet I'd be safe betting there aren't two dozen watches (of all descriptions) for sale in all of Utica and it's he__ to try and get one fixed.

I'm doing a little canning. Don't know how we'll get what we've got down to Ithaca. By next week I'll probably get to the chickens. We had ten and got 8 more from Millers for canning. They are moulting to beat all so I'll have pinfeathers till I can't see.

There has been a frost over town and there had been frost down home a week ago but we haven't been touched yet. The nearness to the lake and fog save us here. The foliage is turning but probably won't be at their peak for at least a week. The garden is getting pretty well whipped (and canned). We had a few green peas on Monday. We still have cucumbers, tomatoes, beets & carrots, parsnips, Swiss chard, string beans. In the flower garden we have lovely glads and dahlias, roses (we counted around 50 buds yesterday), morning glories, zinnias, asters, canna, phlox, pansies, hydrangea(?), and of course the petunias. The petunias on the wall have been lovely this year but are getting pretty large and blossomed out. Of course the chrysanthemums are just beginning to be nice and they last a long time.

All in all it's beginning to look as though winter weren't far off.

With hunting season starting Oct. 20 this year, I was going to get to Ithaca somewhere around Nov. 1 this year. But Janice's getting married has upset my applecart. I won't mix moving and a wedding for anybody.

I hope maybe to get my work arranged so I can get down home to help Mom a few days. This business of two houses – closing one and opening another is worse than moving. I wouldn't know myself if I stayed in one place a year. I've jumped around for ten years and can't say I like it. Guess I'm getting old anyway.

Probably I'd better get to work. It's a gorgeous day – makes me want to be outdoors but it wouldn't be very practical with all the work I've got inside.

Write when you can. I'll try to do better next time.

Love,
Marian

Shirley told me long ago, she wished I'd get a typewriter so she could read my letters. If you can't decipher some of it, figure it isn't important.

Jan writes about her engagement to Johnnie Klossner. There could be no more doubts in anyone's mind about her sincerity. She is looking forward to a wonderful future.

Monday night
September 27, 1943

Dear Ted –

I guess I've started at least half a dozen letters to you lately but never got any of them finished. Things have been pretty busy around here lately!

Ted – I'm awfully sorry if you were hurt because I neglected to write you of my engagement. It certainly wasn't because I didn't want everyone to share my happiness but each time I'd try to put it into words later I'd wonder if it didn't sound foolish to others. But – I guess everyone naturally expects that when things of this nature suddenly happen. It's needless to say I've never been so thrilled or happy in my life and still people say one's happiness and fulfillment of life grows after being married. It truly seems impossible at the moment. Johnnie and I certainly get along fine together. If we continue to get along as we have our future certainly will be a bright one and as yet I see no reason why it won't. The whole Klossner family is wonderful to me and were afraid I wouldn't like them instead of wondering whether they would accept me or not. It sometimes makes me feel humble they are offering so much to us but they are the type that would do the same to most any friend of the family's.

Clara* is quitting her job in Lyons Falls and coming home to live with us about a month to help me get settled, etc. She is then getting a job in the city somewhere I guess. She wondered if I'd mind her helping me out. Naturally it will be grand having someone to show me the way in which I can make both Johnnie & his father the happiest.**

I expect Johnnie is writing you tonight about acting as best man. Of course he understands you wouldn't be able to accept it but was only too pleased to think he could make it easier for you to get a short furlough at that time. He has asked Don McGovern to stand up for him and I expect Blondie will do the honors for me. If Johnnie's letter doesn't have the proper amount of sentiment ,etc, don't hesitate to ask him to write another because we definitely want you to be here for the big event.

Ted – when Burt & Mel were here Labor Day, Burt seemed to think he couldn't make it for my wedding so I wish when You wrote to them that you would asume (I know my spelling is awful) that they were coming and perhaps say something to the effect that they certainly wouldn't miss it. Maybe that's "laying it on pretty thick" but I want so much to have all the family that's possible to come. I'll write myself & ask them again hoping it will help.

I got an awfully nice letter from Bob to-day. We are quite sure he is at Wake Island.*** Tho of course, he can't tell us, he said we could do all the guessing we wanted. It appears he hasn't seen too much action as yet (thank god) and is enjoying himself as much as possible. He appears to like it except there is not enough entertainment for them. He spoke about Rosemary & his indefinite plans for the future. I can't begin to tell all he said but it will be here for you to read when you come.

I don't know whether you heard or not that Teen is pregnant again and it threatens to be a trying time for her. She was planning to stand up for me but she isn't feeling well and the excitement & all would be too much for her.

---

*Clara was Johnnie's aunt.
**Johnnie's father, Albert, was a widower.
***Bob was not at Wake Island, as it was occupied by the Japanese for the duration of the war.

Everything here at home is buzzing lately. Fay* got our corn down to-day & the men will be here tomorrow to fill the silos. The oats are ready to be threshed & potatoes & vegetables are in the progress of being stored for the winter. We had a hard frost Sat. night & most of the plants are black now.

Harvey Sage is coming to do more painting & papering in the kitchen & dining room & it looks as if we'll be pretty well fixed for the winter before it catches us.

It seems strange to think I'll be packing up once more to move from home to another permanent home but I'm so glad that I'll be near enough so that I can keep watch of things here at home.

Shirley and Altie are a real help. It's comical to see Altie planning with Dad about what he'll do to help. The other night he wanted to know just how Dad wanted him to take the old silage out of the silo.

Dad is busy nights now selling more bonds in this third war loan & seems to take a greater interest in the Masons. Last Sat. nite he went to a Past Master's Club meeting at Black River where they visited the Service club at Pine Camp that the Masons are setting up.

I'm so tired & sleepy my writing & spelling is worse than ever so I'd better get some sleep. I'm thinking, write & tell me what you hear from Burt.

Love,
Jan

---

*Fay Ackerman was a neighbor and friend. His sons, Leonard and Lincoln, were on active duty.

In this next letter to Shirley, Melrose makes a very generous offer to Jan.

---

varna apartments
ithaca, n. y.

melrose , burt , and linda say :

Oct. 3, 1943

Dear Shirley,

It was quite a treat to have such a nice long entertaining letter from you. We do miss your "eternal chattering." In fact I was quite lonesome at first I wished you could have come back with us. Maybe you can come again next summer. Linda said "bye-bye Shirley" & "Shirley all gone" for a long time. Sometimes she would call to you when she woke up. Now she says "Shirley" once in awhile. I'm sure she'd be delighted to see you.

We have lots of butter now. We just finished the butter you gave us. I have been buying my ¼# allowance right along & we got 1# in Fillmore Friday. I went over to see Old Man Mose & he had lots of butter so I said "I see you have butter" and he said "Sure. Do you want 5# ?" I laughed & he said I'd better get it because the points go up Mon, as if there was lots of butter.* So I bought it & I guess we have 8# plus in the house – enough to last all winter.

We miss our garden terribly. We took inventory to-nite & we have 201 pts. & 227 qts. of food down cellar. We have done more tomatoes, grape juice, chili sauce, pickles, peach & peach & apple jam. Ruth gave me some drop peaches – not many. We took care of 40 qts. of tomatoes the day after we got back. I'll never see such beautiful tomatoes again. They were lovely. We didn't get many more after that & they weren't as nice. Please tell Mother we have 30 qts. of tomatoes for her & we will contribute our blue points if she'd like to buy tomatoes.** Linda would like them 2 or 3 times a day & so would we.

Linda has changed so much since we got back. She started feeding herself entirely & does very well. The first week the kitchen was literally bathed in milk but she is quite careful now. She eats with us & is good about minding her business. It sure saves me a lot of time. She says, "Pease, Mommy, moi (more)". She says everything she hears us say. She tells me about the potty too, only too late quite often. Boy, does she get into things too. She gets her stool & gets things off the stove, sink & cabinet so the refrigerator is my only refuge. She takes the dishes out of the drainer & puts them on the floor.

Ruth would like to know if Tine would like to sell her teeter-babe. Renee & Linda had Ruth's sister's teeter-babe but she has another baby to put in it now.

Would Janice like to wear my wedding dress? It would fit her to a T.

---

*Foods were allotted a certain number of points based on their availability.
**Individuals were allowed 48 blue points for canned, bottled, or dried foods and 64 red points to buy meat, fish, and dairy products.

Burt and Melrose on their wedding day

I have no veil. They are easy to make but expensive to buy. If she'd like to change her mind, I'd be flattered to have her wear it. I thot about it when we were up there but didn't want to insult her. I got myself a good husband in it. I'm glad you're going to be her attendant.

It will be nice to have my coat soon because it is getting cold but tell Mother not to worry.

I finished my houndstooth dress. It was miserable stuff to work on. I have cloth for another now. It is a light gray-green corduroy. Won't it be luxurious to have 2 dresses?

We probably won't get to Jan's wedding much as we'd like to. I don't know where we'd get the gas especially now they've cut the B & C rations.

I earned myself some dough judging at the Trumansburg Fair last week. It was fun. I go to Chenango Co. to work for a couple of days next week.*

Now I must close. I've tried to write to everybody in your letter. I'll write to somebody else next time.

---

*Melrose worked as an Associate 4-H Club Agent for the Cooperative Extension Service of Tompkins County.

Evelyn with Burt and Melrose

It was really wonderful to have you here this summer. I feel much better than I have for a long time.

Write again.
Love
Mel

Ted writes that his squadron has shaped up and of an unexpected reunion with a frat brother.

October 4, 1943

Dear Folks,

Please excuse the pencil for I haven't my pen with me at present. I am enclosing a money order of $20.00 which I wish you would bank for me when you have a chance to get to the bank.

There seems to be a very good rumor that we will be shipped from here Oct. 30. They have new planes in at the airport and it looks as if they are going to give us our flying quite rapidly. This will cut our time here short of two weeks. I have no idea how this will affect my chances of getting a pass to get home on, and it looks as if it will be impossible to get to Jan's wedding. This is only a rumor though and I won't know for a few days whether or not there is truth in it. I am sure that there will be some sort of a change soon though.

Our squadron won the weekly competition last week for the third consecutive week. In addition to getting an extra night off post during the following week, we were awarded a blue and gold streamer to tie onto our squadron flag. We fellows are pretty proud to think that we beat the pants from the other four squadrons three weeks in a row. Our PT instructor told the Commandant the other day that he can sock it to us a great deal harder than any squadron which he has yet had here. We're pretty proud of these facts and it does a fellow a lot of good to be with a sharp outfit like ours.

I had an odd coincidence Sat. night. We were dancing at the Service Center, sponsored by the Masons, when a damn sailor came up and started working me on the back. I looked around and it was Frank Curtis who was A.Z. and in the same class in school as I was. He is still at Cornell in V-7. It happened that he was with the soccer team which had been at Penn State playing. Coming back something happened to their bus and they had to stop here and await repairs. He was told of the Serviceman's Center and happened to go up there to enjoy himself while he waited. It was a surprise for both of us because I never dreamed of seeing him here, nor did he know I was here in training.

I am anxious to learn whether Willie had good luck in getting the DHIA* records back in shape. I hear about most other farm functions, but I seldom hear of the cows.

I guess this is all for now. Everyone write.

Love, Ted

---

*NYDHIA = New York Dairy Herd Improvement Association, now Dairy 1.

Melrose   *Burt*

Burt writes news of a very successful garden harvest. Ted has recently been able to make a short visit from Williamsport.

Sunday

Oct. 4

Dear Ted,

We've really neglected writing for long enough. We've been meaning to write ever since you were here.

We did appreciate your getting up here but wished that we might have given you a little better welcome. We had just a little more company than we had room for but glad everyone could come.

We took Shirley up home just before Labor Day and stayed for a few days then went along out to Fillmore [Melrose's home]. It was quite a long time for us to be away and there was plenty for us to do when we got back. We had to can 40 qts. of tomatoes the next day. We were gone a little over a week. Linda had a grand time seeing all the animals but she did get pretty tired. She was car sick on the way from Turin to Fillmore and kind of heaved her biscuits.

We got moved downstairs finally. I painted the kitchen beforehand and it took 2 coats. I'm still painting, putting up fixtures, etc. but I guess we'll get settled after a bit. We bought a new old table for $25 & it will cost us $6 to get it refinished. We could easily sell it for $50 anytime we wanted. With our antique corner cupboard & our table we have our living room fairly well filled. We have a writing desk to fix up but don't know yet where we will put it. We like it much better downstairs.

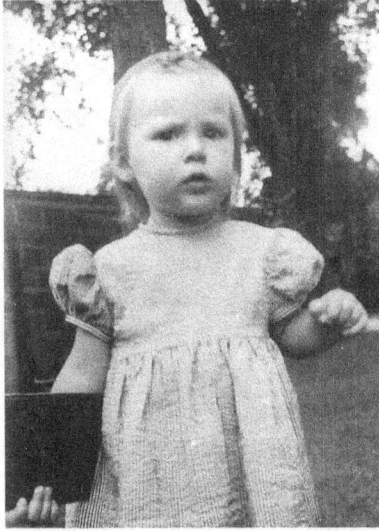

Linda, age 1

We're just getting the last of our garden in. We have carrots & beets, etc. yet to dig but everything else is done. We've canned plenty. We just took inventory and we have over 400 cans of different things, eight bu. of potatoes besides carrots, onions, beets, soy beans, etc. They sure will save on the feed bill next winter.

Talk about potatoes. I was down at Richford watching a man dig a few days ago. He has over 200 acres & they were yielding about 400 bu. 80,000 bu. are a lot to handle. It's costing him plenty to get them dug though. He should do all right because most of them will be sold for seed.

I talked with Earl Beckwith one day since you were here and he has some good prospects with bull calves. He's been selling them pretty fast and getting about $300–400 for them. I might be able to do a little better a little later since the price of cows is falling off a little.

Well, I guess I'll have to sign off because I've got to write to Marian yet tonight.

As ever,
Burt

P.S. Here's a picture of Linda. It isn't exceptionally good but we hope to get some better ones soon. It was taken the day you were here.

Ted writes to his future brother-in-law, Johnnie, thanking him for his efforts to bring Ted home for the wedding.

October 4, 1943

Dear Johnny,

I got your letter Saturday and I would like to say that I appreciate the help which you tried to give me. From Jan's letter I understand that you understand that this is only a pretense and that I couldn't accept such a job even if you wanted me to. Nevertheless I hope that your letter may help me a lot. It is pretty hard to get away for any extra time here.

The Army is supposed to give a man a two-week furlough every six months or thirty days a year. I was thinking the other day that I've nearly six months of service and have no hopes of any time off until at least a year from now. So far I've had one weekend pass when I met Dad in Ithaca. Oh well, this is the sort of a thing we must put up with if there is a hope in the world of getting those "silver wings."

I had more cold water thrown on my hopes to get to your wedding, the other day. It seems that a rumor has it that we will be leaving here Oct. 30 for Nashville. This is only a rumor, but I have reason to believe that there may be something to it. Nevertheless, I shall keep my eyes and ears open so that I can "play my cards" if I can. I will let you know as quickly as I learn more.

I was pleased to hear of your engagement, Johnny. I want to wish the two of you all of the success possible. I am sure you made a good choice, and I have enough confidence in Jan to hope that you did.

We've been having some pretty rugged training here John. Academics have been easy for me, but the military side of the picture is a little difficult. They hammer our asses for all we're worth, and sure figure to keep us on the ball. Every phase of our training is formal and military to the smallest detail. We've had a lot of physical training which sure has made a difference with the boys in my squadron. You'd never know how flabby and skinny around some of these fellows used to be. At last I think I am with an outfit that even a bunch of tough farmers would find difficulty in whipping. The army seems to be pretty determined that the men they pin wings onto, will not be "ninety day wonders."

Well Johnny I wish to thank you again for the letter, and I only hope I can swing a pass from it.

I'm pretty tired tonight so I won't bore you with more of my idle thoughts. I just finished one of my good weekends and need a bit of rest.

As ever,

Ted

P.S. They just got in some new cubs for us to start flying when we get to that phase of training sometime next week. These are some cute little ships.

Ted writes with the news that he will not be able to get home for Jan's wedding. It looks like he won't be home for another year.

October 12, 1943

Dear Folks,

I have been hesitating to write you this week because I felt I would have some important news for you soon. Tonight we learned, officially, just what to expect during the next two weeks.

It seems that our squadron is being hurried out of here by Oct. 30 we believe anyway. We start flying tomorrow morning and hope to finish it in two weeks. We have our graduation dance tomorrow night and will be the E squadron from now on, although the present E squadron won't leave here until the end of this week.

This of course dampens my plans for the next five weeks. It puts a kink in my hopes to get to Jan's wedding as well as getting home at all. The passes for our flight are due for this weekend, but we cannot leave post until after the bus leaves for Elmira. I had hopes of getting home and bringing Peggy with me, but now I see that it is impossible.

I'll try to write more later, Jan, but I haven't time right now. I appreciate the attempt which you and John made to help me, but now it looks as if I can't make it.

I had high hopes of getting home, but now it looks as if we'll have to forget the disappointment. I'll have to hope that home will be even more what I look forward to a year from now.

Tonight, I just got word that I may be a supernumerary* for the squadron which is leaving this week. There are four of us who have high grades and low numbers of demerits that are under consideration. I only hope that I am not chosen for I have a dislike for many of the members of that squadron and as far as I care I would just as soon stay here a bit longer.

Later in the week I hope I'll have some photographs in the mail for you folks. I just got them from the photographer and am waiting an opportunity to mail them. I have two different sittings. I have one large one for you folks at home and one smaller one for each member of the family who are not at home. I can't decide whether I should send the one for Bob or not. I shall send it home and if you folks think it safe to send, you may do so.

Sunday I was entertained by the parents of Dr. Hertel who is college secretary back at school. They live at Trout Run which is about 15 miles north of here. I was quite flattered to think that Johnny (that is what everyone calls him) would remember me and tell his folks of me. Their youngest son is in the same sort of training as I, and it made me feel a bit as if it was my home. They are simple country folk like the rest of us but the swellest kind which the world knows. Johnny is an AZ man and liked well throughout the Cornell campus.

I guess I'll have to quit now and do a few small jobs. I have my laundry soaking in chlorox and must hang it up.

Love,

Ted

---

*Supernumerary: one who exceeds the required number of a group.

Marian writes Ted about the difficulties of finding a new watch or even getting an old watch repaired. The Markham household is being turned upside down in preparation for Jan's wedding.

Oct 14

Dear Ted,

I've written Mel, Burt, Mrs. Wiegard, and Bob so I'll finish up on you. I guess our last letters crossed – we wrote the same day. I'm glad you like the watch. I knew you needed one and after you're used to one it's awful to get along without. Mine is on the blink now and I never know the time. I wore it night and day and almost feel naked without it. In fact I wore that old one in the bathtub twice. No wonder it's goofy, eh? Burt took mine to Patten for me after he was up but Patten wouldn't take it till Nov. 1. All jewelers are swamped with no new watches to be had and everyone needing watches.

I sent out Bob's Christmas present today. He wrote that things were pretty rough where he is and it was hard to keep clean so I sent toilet articles. I got a bag with a lot of pockets and filled it. I put in 2 cakes of lava soap and 2 wash cloths, 2 handkerchiefs, pr. shoe strings, 4 pkgs. Gillette blue blades, big tube shave cream, tube tooth paste, plastic eye cup, pocket game of Chinese Checkers and Reader's Digest (five or six).

Mom and I feel it in our bones (woman's intuition) that Bob was in on the raid on Wake this week.* The Ithaca Journal said one of the accomplishments was breaking in new ships and air squadrons. You mentioned the possibility of his being in the Aleutians. That is out. He said his ships didn't do so well there and besides he didn't take his winter flying gear. They flew from Hawaii so isn't Midway a better guess than the Gilberts?

We went down home yesterday. Things are all abuzz about the wedding. Mom is turning the house wrong side out. She had Emma Hoffman yesterday and expected Harvey Sage. She about wore Blondie out Mon. & Tue. when there wasn't school. Dad got Mr. B. to go to Sasenburg's to help pick out a new suit. They tried regulars and stout on him and Mr. B. told them he wasn't trying to buy an overcoat.** Finally they came to and took his measurements and ordered a suit. He brought the swatch (sample) home. It's an oxford with a pin stripe of grey.

Everybody's getting new clothes but me. Blondie is to be bridesmaid. She has a pink wool and brown accessories. Jan has blue wool and blue hat – and a green going away dress. Mom has a new hat. I'm going to wear the dress I got for Teen's wedding. I tried to get Alton a suit but couldn't

---

*Wake Island was taken by the Japanese shortly after Pearl Harbor was attacked. Until the end of the war, it was subject to U.S. naval air raids.

**Edwin B. Baxter was the owner of The Quality Shop, a well-known men's clothing store in Ithaca.

Marian at Teen's wedding

find a satisfactory one. I got a soldier suit. It's an army officer's suit and beautiful khaki serge. Long pants of course and overseas cap. I got a size 8 but it was too small so when Mr. B & Dad went down changed it for a size 10. I guess he's grown more than I realized.

Jan gave me the job of decorating the church. I wasn't pleased with the job. Told her I guessed it would be jack-lanterns. Don't you think that would be appropriate and good enough?

We shopped in B.-ville on the way down yesterday; were at home for lunch; went to Lowville had treatments and shopped; back home – Dad & Mr. B. & Alton went to B-ville, supper at home, stopped at Miller's for eggs (Ray is taking a girl home this week). Aunt Mary got a new bed for the occasion. Then we stopped in Boonville to the show, "This is the Army" (Alton said we should see it) and something to eat afterward and got home at 1 o'clock. Too much for an old lady like me. I never woke up until nearly eleven. It's been years since I slept as late. I guess my treatments relaxed me.

It's eleven now and I must get to bed and be on deck in the morning. I've got so much to do. Am trying to get my work done for closing so I can go down home for a week and help Mom. I canned 12 chickens last week and had company twice to help eat the bones.

Write when you can. Hope you can get home for the wedding. Burt and Mel think now there's a possibility they can make it. We are trying to find a little gas for them.

Love,
Marian

Keep your average down and maybe they won't ship you so quick and you'll be able to get home after all.

From all reports, Pete is in the thick of it. Sometimes he writes from England and sometimes from Africa. Said awhile ago they had their 4th plane.

106

Alton is more interested in going Halloweening than in the upcoming wedding.

Oct. 14, 1943
Turin, N.Y.

Dear Ted,

I just got done breakfast. Can you come home for Jan's wedding the 31st? Daddy Clyde has been transfered to Boston for anti aircraft guns instead of balloons.* I'm going to get a 22 when I'm sixteen. Anty Marian is going to give me hers. We are studying Denmark in Socal Studies. We got 28 bags of oats, and a silo and a half of silage. We have a lot of wood to get yet. Willy started a letter but I daught if he will finish it. I have history and arithmetic to do for Monday. Jonny the cat is playing with gram's slip. Lad wants me to go out with him. I have an officers suit at the post office. Come up and I'll compare it with yours. Ha, Ha. We have to clean the stables today. Mr. Baxter got me a cat and a punkin made of paper for Halloween. I am going to give one to Bill. Bill and I are going Halloweening together. I can't think any more, so, long

Your Nephew,
Alton Dewan

---

*The Allies used blimps, or barrage balloons, to suspend aerial cables in the sky and foul enemy bombers.

A disappointed Ted writes Jan that he won't be able to attend her wedding.

October 14, 1943

Dear Jan,

I expect that both you and the folks have received the pictures by now. I am in hopes that this will serve as a wedding present for you and John.

You probably know by now how futile it will be for us to think that I can get to your wedding. Things looked quite prospective for me until we were told that we would leave here two weeks early. This means that I will be leaving Williamsport about the same time that you will be taking the great step. Anyway I can think of you and John when I board that troop train.

Tonight I have some visions of leaving here this weekend. I am one of five supernumeraries from the squadron which leaves Saturday. This means that I must pack and accompany them to the train, whether or not I leave with them is purely a guess. I will let you folks know immediately whether or not I leave.

We were supposed to have started flying yesterday, but weather conditions have prevented us as yet. My plane will be a J-3 Piper Cub with a 65 HP Lycoming motor. I am quite anxious to get hold of that stick.

Well I guess this is as well as I can do tonight. Probably soon after this letter arrives you will know whether I am headed for Nashville or whether I'll be here for a couple more weeks.

As ever,
Ted

P.S. Everyone write for a change.

Evelyn is disappointed that Ted is unable to attend Jan's wedding especially since he is so close to home. She has just received Ted's first official portrait in the mail.

MRS. ERNEST L. MARKHAM
BOX 143
TURIN, NEW YORK

Oct. 16, 1943

My dear, dear Ted,

It is hard to know how to write this. I just can't believe that you won't be coming soon. I am just hoping all the time that something will happen to give you the chance. Couldn't you somehow take it up with your commanding officer and let him know how near you are to home and how much it would mean to all of us to have you come?

Of course we are immensely proud that you are doing so well getting advanced into a higher squadron, but it will be a great disappointment if you get moved out so soon.

Private Ted Markham

Your bond came a few days ago and I put it away in the safe with the rest. I have a new one Grandma just gave me. She is buying one for each of her children. Lewis County and even little Turin went over the quota in the last drive. Dad is one of the "Minutemen."

Marian and Mr. B were down Wednesday. She got Alton a little "officer's suit" and he is pretty proud.

Teen has not been very well lately but feels better than she did. She and Billy are coming home tomorrow to stay for awhile. Bill gets to be more of a great guy every day.

We are having some nice real October weather which sort of compensates for the cold rainy time awhile ago. We are hustling to get lots of things done – wood cutting, housecleaning, painting – you can picture it.

Dad has just come home with the mail and your pictures! They are swell! Now I'll go and get a frame just like Bob's if I can. None of them is nicer than yours. You couldn't give us anything nicer.

We don't hear much from Bob. Dad and I haven't sent his Xmas package yet. Suppose we put your picture in it, eh?

I must tell you, Dad has ordered a new suit for himself. He is going to give the bride away, you know. His old suit was looking pretty threadbare, and I am glad he had the excuse to get a new one.

Well, I will just keep hoping and praying that you will be able to come home.

Love,
Mother

Ted writes with some good news and a story about the post's mascot.

October 17, 1943

Dear Folks,

This is Sunday morning here and I am at the airport waiting to fly. It seems that the weather has been so poor lately that we haven't been able to get into the air. However the ceiling is good this morning and we hope that the wind will not be too much for good flying conditions. Waiting here at the airport makes time pass rather slowly.

As you must realize by now, I didn't get shipped with the upper class yesterday. I am tickled to think that I can wait for our squadron for I'd hate like the devil to share the reputation which that class has when they get to Nashville. Our boys have a whole lot better reputation and it will probably be an asset when it comes to classification.

It has been a beautiful fall here. The leaves were colored more than any I can remember. Now they are falling fast and the trees will soon be bare. These hills of Penn. are certainly a beautiful sight.

Willie and Altie might be interested in hearing what I have learned about the new B-29 heavy bomber.* It sounds like quite a ship and expectation hopes that it will soon be in combat. The ship has a wingspan of over 200 feet or about twice that of the Fortress. It is powered by four 2200 H.P. Wright Duplex motors or a total of 4000 H.P. more than the Fortress or 4800 H.P. more than Bob's Ventura. Total capacity for gasoline amounts to 8500 gallons or enough to give it range which again is twice that of the Fortress. Other statistics about the technical devices of the ship are amazing but perhaps best not to tell of. Probably it would be best not to speak of these facts I have given you for the war department has not released this data.

I guess I have never told you that I have been playing in the Drum and Bugle Corp here. I have been beating a drum for nearly a month. My ability has been definitely lacking, but I am slowly gaining confidence in my drumming.

---

*A B-29, the Enola Gay, was used to drop an atomic bomb over the city of Hiroshima, Japan, on the morning of August 6, 1945.

We seem to have a self-appointed mascot here at the post. He is a black and white bull dog who seems to figure that he belongs to us. Someone in town evidently owns him, but I doubt whether they see much of him. He is not at all affectionate but rather very independent. However he loves the boys and is always found on the drill field or whenever there is activity. He likes to go to the airport and usually makes sure he gets on the bus regardless of invitation. At night he makes a few rounds through the barracks and then goes to the guard room to spend the night. He is certainly a peculiar dog for he always acts so independent and unaffectionate.

Since I started this letter I have completed my first hour of flight. It was quite a thrill for me and I believe I liked it a lot. I feel just a bit uncertain because of the many things to think of at first. Later when I feel a bit more confident I think I'll really like it. My instructor seems swell and the plane seems to also be swell.

I guess this is about all for now. I have been asking Willie about the herd records and etc, but I don't get much reply.

Everyone write.

Love,
Ted

Burt writes that they are now planning to attend the wedding. They have some extra gas coupons and want to meet Ted's new girlfriend, Peggy Kuhn.

---

varna apartments
ithaca, n. y.

m e l r o s e , b u r t , a n d l i n d a s a y :

October 22, 1943

Dear Ted,

We were glad to get both your letters and your picture. Your picture came the same day as your letter.

We are planning now to get up for the wedding. At first we didn't think we could manage but we have a few extra gas coupons that won't be missed. It looks as though we would have to go Friday nite because of Linda. If we waited until Saturday she would be too tired and wouldn't have a chance to rest before the doings. We are planning to come back Sunday.

We hope you can make connections so that we can all go up from here together and of course you can ride back to Ithaca with us. We hope Peggy can come too. We would like to meet her. I'm sure she must be "O.K".

Ray Miller stopped in Monday. He is home for 10 days and he brought a young lady from Conn. or rather she brought him. It looked kind of serious. Ted Kangas came out for the evening with them.

Ted called a few minutes ago & says John Hentel is trying to get a bunch to go to a square dance a week from Monday nite. We may go – it sounds like fun.

I've got to drop Mother a line yet tonite so I guess I'll have to make this brief but we're planning on seeing you next Friday nite.

Thanks a lot for the picture,

As ever
Burt

Evelyn writes some encouraging words to Ted on a postcard. She has just learned that he will be in Williamsport a while longer and may be able to come to the wedding.

Oct. 23

Dear Ted,

So glad to get those two last letters telling of your flying and staying where you are. We are so in hope you can come home. It must be a great thrill to fly. Hold 'er straight and keep going true to her course, boy! And be sure we're always thinking of you and pulling for you. Everybody here terribly busy.

Love,
Mom

Bob writes from "somewhere in the Pacific" that he had to dig out his calendar to figure out what day it is. He hasn't had a letter from home in nearly a month.

Oct. 24

Dear Ted,

They tell me that today is Sunday. I guess none of us would have known except that Mac was wondering what day it was and I dug out my calendar. All days are much the same here except that some days you fly and others you don't. Today I don't so I can write a couple of letters, swim & lay around in the sun, and generally relax.

We don't lead a tough life at all, tho the fellows who have been out here for some time get fed up with it. Some of them have had more than just the bad food, hard beds, insects, etc. to bother them. So far I haven't and even the things I mentioned aren't tough – just a little annoying.

You will notice by the new address that I have been changed to a different squadron. It is the same type of outfit tho it is older, more experienced, and probably better organized. I still fly with Fred McFarland of Seattle and we have the same crew. I think it is a pretty nice break for us. Joe Mullen came along too but otherwise all my old buddies were left behind. This leaves me as the least experienced member of the outfit tho of course not the youngest.

How is the flying coming along? At least I expect you have done some by now. In your last letter you mentioned that you expected to go to Nashville soon for classification. I hope you make pilot training for I think you would enjoy that more than just riding.

Wish I could know all the places you will be going for in many cases I might be able to arrange for you to meet some nice people. I should have gotten some information from Dallas Jones for his home is in Nashville.

A letter from Burt arrived this morning dated Oct. 4. He said you might get home for Jan's wedding. Wish I could make it but am afraid the seats on the next train going east are all reserved. Haven't had a letter from home in nearly a month but have sort of gotten used to it now. I guess I don't write nearly as many now either.

Got the letter from the central Farm Bureau office with your bit of ballyhoo added. It was a nice gesture on someone's part tho – looked like Fred Morris' work. Guess I should drop them a line sometime.

I saw Jim Young of Angelica and also Coleman Petrie who graduated with us. They both took advanced drill and have been in the army ever since the reserves were called in the fall of '41. Also saw Elwin Willett who was working with Prof. Salisbury and did some instructing – knew Burt quite well. We got together several times.

I'll call this enough, Ted. Let me know how things are going. I'm sure you will like some things about the south – especially the people. See all you can and never miss a chance for some extra fun. Have a bit for me.

As always
Bob

Shirley updates Ted on high school events and proves that she does indeed have the "gift of gab."

October 25, 1943

Dear Ted,

Marian and Mom just said someone ought to write to you and they set me to work because Marian said I had a gift of gab. (Isn't that an awful thing to say!)

We got a letter from Burt today telling us that you and Peggy are coming with them Friday nite for sure. Gee are we ever glad! Of course we'll more than welcome Peggy. All of us are guessing what she'll look like, etc. Of course our brothers are pretty good picker-outers.

Beside the letter from Burt we got a letter from Bob today. He is at this new place and is with a couple guys from Cornell and some of his pals at Jacksonville and Atlanta. He says that the natives are not so highly-civilized, but can understand some English and they manage to understand each other pretty well. He says they're having spring there now. He must be quite a bit below the equator then, I should think.

We're having quite a time lately with our painting. We've painted and papered the kitchen, painted the dining room and downstairs bedroom floors and the front stairs. Every once in awhile we find a cat track in the paint. I don't know whether I told you or not that I have a new cat.

Johnny gave me a grey tiger, part angora so we call him Johnny. He's an awfully smart cat. He looks around all the while for something to play with. He tried to help Marian paint today. The two cats together get a lot of mice.

We'll have to get our puppy for Bill pretty soon. I can hardly wait. Teen's going to let us keep it down here to train I guess.

I got all my seven-weeks test marks now today. I got 95 in Biology, 90 in S.S, 91 in both Latin and English, and 76 in Geometry. Darn if I'd had a decent mark in Geometry I'd have had a ninety something average. I got best marks in all the classes except Geometry and one of the boys that's taking it over got the best mark in it. I'll just have to study it like sin. It isn't easy for me tho either.

The other night at a dance at West Leyden school Bob O'Brien asked me for your address and I told him you expected to come home this week-end.* I guess he's going to be able to go back to school this year because he's a vet student, but Bud Kent will probably be called soon so he's not going to try to go back.

Gee, Ted, if you didn't have a girl there's the best-looking and nicest Home-ec teacher at school this year who stays at Aunt Mary's.** She's just swell and enough to knock your eye out. Peggy is no doubt equally as good tho.

Well, it kinda looks like paper is growin' short. Be seein' ya.

Love,
Blondie

---

*Another Bob O'Brien.
**Evelyn's sister, Mary.

Jan's wedding is only five days away, and Ted still isn't sure if he will make it!

October 25, 1943

Dear Folks,

It still is uncertain whether or not I can get up for Jan's wedding. I am playing my cards and have high hopes of getting there if at all possible. Within a few days I'll know more about it and will let you know.

It is quite likely that I'll bring Peggy with me if you think the house will handle an extra lodger. Peggy is very anxious to meet you folks and I am anxious for you to meet her. Peggy is a nice common ordinary girl like the rest of us. Don't put yourself out for her because she isn't the kind who would want such doings.

I have hopes that we can leave here on the 4:00 PM bus which will get us into Ithaca at 8:15 PM. From Ithaca we could probably catch Burt and get home Friday night. If I can't leave post soon enough to catch the bus we will have to take the train which would get us into Syracuse at 10:30 AM Saturday. If we have to resort to the train could someone meet us in Syracuse?

I hope that things will work out because I have an awful urge to get home. It has been over six months and if I can't make it this time I'm afraid that it will be another twelve months.

I'll try to drop a line later in the week.

Love,
Ted

At the very last moment, Ted was granted a weekend pass. He and Peggy met Burt and Melrose in Ithaca and made it to the wedding.

Jan and Johnny are pelted with rice as they leave the church. Don McGovern and Shirley – best man and maid of honor – laugh behind them in the church doorway.

116

MISS JANICE E. MARKHAM TO WED

Daughter of Turin Couple to Be Married to John F. Klossner.

Turin, Oct. 30.-The marriage of Miss Janice Elizabeth Markham, daughter of Mr. and Mrs. Ernest Leonard Markham, and John Francis Klossner, son of Albert Klossner of Constableville, and the late Mrs.Klossner ,wil be solemnized this afternoo at 2 in the Methodist church with the pastor, Rev. Lyndon Paul Harris, as the officiating clergyman.

Preceding the ceremony, Mrs. Clifford Wendt will sing "Because" and "At Dawning ," accompanied by Mrs. Otto K. Was-Muth, an aunt of the bride. Mrs. Wasmuth also will play the wedding music from "Lehengrin" by Wagner as the bridal party enters the church, and Mendelssohn's wedding march at the close of the ceremony.

The bride will be escorted by her father who will give her in marriage. Her only attendant will be her youngest sister, Miss Shirley Ruth Markham, and best man will be Donald F. McGovern, of Constableville. The ushers will be Frederick J. Klossner, brother of the bridegroom and A/S Theodore W. Markham, Wiliamsport, Pa., a brother of the bride.

The bride will wear an afternoon dress of powder blue wool with a matching velvet hat and veil and carry a bouquet of white pompoms. The maid of honor will wear a two- piece dress of dusty rose wool with a matching flower hat and carry talisman roses. The bride's mother will wear a navy blue afternoon dress with matching accessories and a corsage of red roses.

Following the ceremony a reception will be held at the home of the bride's parents,after which the couple will leave on a motor trip through the Adirondacks. On their return they will make their home on the farm near Constableville, operated by Mr. Klossner and his father.

Miss Markham attended the local school and the Constableville Central High school from which she was graduated in June, 1941. In May, 1943, she was graduated from the New York State Agricultural and Technical School at Canton, here she majored in clothing. Mr. Klossner was gra duated from the Constableville Central High school in June, 1938, and since then has been engaged in farming.

Miss Markham was guest of honor at a personal shower given by Miss Marion Regetz and Miss Marion Long.

Relatives from out of town who will attend the wedding are Mr. and Mrs. Burton H. Markham and Miss Linda Markham of Ithaca; Mr. and Mrs. Rudolph Klossner and Miss Patricia Klossner of Sodus; Mrs. Clark E. Markham of Richfield Springs; Mr. and Mrs. Joseph H. Rowe, of Syra-Cuse; Mrs. Marian Markham Dewan of Old Forge; Mr. and Mrs. William B. Holmes, Utica; Mr. and Mrs . Hobart E. Wasmuth, Mr. and Mrs. Lee W. Wasmuth, and Miss Jane R. Wasmuth, Watertown; Mrs. Claron E.Markham, Mr. and Mrs. Robert O'Brien and son, Billy, Lowville; Mr. and Mrs. Howard Klossner of Boonville; Mr. and Mrs. Otto K. Wasmuth and Miss Mary Wasmuth of Castorland; Albert Klossner, Miss Clara Klossner, Mrs. Edward O. Anken, Mrs. John Markham, Mr. and Mrs. Albert J. Miller, Constableville.

From the Watertown Daily Times.

The wedding is over and Ted is already back on base in Williamsport. It's Monday night, and he's had a gut-wrenching day in the air.

November 1, 1943

Dear Folks,

Peggy and I arrived ok last night, and everything worked out fine. I am pretty tired tonight, but I certainly had a wonderful weekend. Peggy said she also had a wonderful time, and I am sure she did though she seemed a bit timid and unaccustomed to the great times we have.

I had a pretty stiff day at the airport today. There was a strong low pressure wind blowing into a high pressure area north of here together with new maneuvers which gave me all of the air I care for today. First of all the air was all I could contend with, and secondly I spent the period doing spins and stalls. I felt sick as a dog, but I kept my dinner inside. It was a hell of a sensation to force yourself to the new work while you sit with the cold air blowing in to help keep away that cold sweat which was pouring out. The more I fly the more I realize the strenuous effort required of a pilot. Certainly it requires good food, lots of concentration, and high physical condition. I am beginning to realize that there is nothing glamourous about flying; on the contrary, it is a tough task.

I will have to quit now, for I have a thousand and one things to do tonight.

Love,
Ted

Two weeks after the wedding, Ted received an unexpected weekend pass and he and Peggy made another trip to Ithaca, where they stayed with Mr. Baxter and Marian. Ted is worried about Bob in his next letter.

November 15, 1943

Dear Blondie,

It seems that it must be your turn to get a letter this time. Don't tell me that the whole family is so excited over Willie's ability as a huntsman that they can't write anymore. Congratulations Willie, I had "buck fever" when I saw my first buck.

Peggy and I had a swell time with the folks in Ithaca last week end. I never dreamed that I could get a third pass until Saturday afternoon I found that several other fellows in our squadron were getting passes. The whole thing came to me on the spur of the moment. I got the pass at 3:15 PM, then we packed and caught the 4:00 PM bus. We got back at 11:00 last night and figured that we had had a swell time.

If you haven't sent me Ray's address, don't fail to because I surely hope to see him in Nashville. I hear by grapevine that Don Van Waes, an AZ man, is in Nashville now awaiting classification. I hope that he stays long enough so that we can lock horns when I get there this week end.

Speaking of letters, I had a letter from Bob the other day. He was a bit blue because he seems to get only about one letter from home during a month. Certainly six cents for airmail postage and a few moments time are only too little to afford for the pleasure he seeks from a letter, aren't they? Isn't it a bit selfish for you, who don't write, to enjoy yourself at something else when Bob has little else than mail to look forward to?

I guess that this is all tonight, Blondie. Write and get the rest of the family to, will you?

Love,
Ted

P.S. We'll probably ship next Saturday.

Ernestine is feeling better and writes of an early snow in Lowville.

Nov. 16, 1943

Dear Ted,

I must write in a hurry about a couple of thing while I still know your address.

I meant to write before to tell you how glad we all were that you could come home for Jan's wedding and how much we liked Peg. We wish we could have had more time to catch up on our visiting with you and to get acquainted with Peggy. Everyone was so busy and excited we sort of neglected her but we hope you'll bring her again and we'll go all out to entertain her.

Billy is very proud of his new "Are Corps." He will have it on his snow suit and one left over for next summer's clothes.

We're proud that you have completed your first ten hours flying. Have you soloed or are you just ready to?

Did you get over being air sick as you got used to the plane etc? It sounds like being pregnant except the results are a little different.

I think I'll do my solo the first week in April and bring back a daughter. I'd just as soon have all boys but Bob & Billy ordered a girl. We would appreciate suggestions for a name, too. You might send a few.

I talked to Grandma about socks and she has time to knit some for you if you'll still want some. When you have time send me a note of your size and the length you prefer.

Mother got Ray's address from Aunt Mary yesterday and I'm enclosing it. I hope you can locate him.

Marian & Hank Springfield came Sunday to get Alton and take him to Boonville. Clyde came home very suddenly and only for a few hours. His days in the U.S. are numbered. He's had his second batch of inoculations.

We had our first snow this week and there was quite a lot some places, tho not much here. Traffic was blocked around Copenhagen!

Billy loves it! He's been looking for snow for a month or so and was some excited the morning he woke up and saw the ground white.

Cindy* acts wild in it, too. She couldn't quite understand it at first, I guess, but soon was rolling and romping with Billy. She puts her nose in the snow and blows, for all the world like Patsy did.

Baroness has a new baby – a heifer. She's little but so nice. All fawn colored and so pretty. Billy loves her but can't figure out where Baroness got her.

They have twenty-five head of cattle in the barn now. It looks pretty full for us.

I suppose you've heard all about Will's buck. I'll let him write you about it.

---

*Cindy was Billy's puppy, a cocker spaniel. Ernest and Evelyn were still housing Cindy for "training."

Autumn 1943

Marian called last night to wish Alton "Happy Birthday." They enjoyed having you and Peggy for the weekend. I suppose Mr. B. outdid himself entertaining you. Was Peggy thrilled with Cornell?

I must finish this and mail it.

Hope to hear from you soon.

Love from all,

Ernestine

Will also writes about the harsh weather. He is pretty proud of his first buck.

November 22, 1943

Dear Ted,

We have some real winter weather up here now. Last night it snowed about eight inches and last week the temperature got down to zero.

Saturday we had a raising at Uncle Teny's* and got all the frame up but the plates and rafters. It's too bad he couldn't have had some more good weather so he could have gotten a roof over it anyway.

I shot a deer up at Mr. Baxter's just two weeks ago today. He weighed about 125 lbs. and had four points.

Baroness freshened and had a nice heifer calf, not bad huh! 100% [i.e., all heifers]. Marie slunk today and wasn't due until the first part of January. Would it be best to have a blood test right away to find out if she has abortion or what would be the best thing to do?**

I suppose you know that Uncle Lee*** now lives in Lowville. I was up there today to get the truck fixed and I went up to the drug store to see him and I don't think I have ever seen him looking so good. He likes it a lot there and says they are nice people to work for. He says he at least has room to stretch and that is something he didn't have in Watertown.

Teen and Bob are trying to find a place in Lowville to live but as yet have not decided.

The hay went pretty fast at first but isn't going as fast as it was. We sure got the barn full and it keeps it quite warm down there.

---

*Augustine Freeman was married to Ernest's sister, Ruth.
**A cow has miscarried. Will asks Ted for some advice.
***Lee Wasmuth, one of Evelyn's brothers.

121

Dan McGovern got a spike horn last Thurs. or Fri. that weighed 95 lbs. Guess I have just about run out of news.

Willie

Bob cautions Ted that the life of a pilot isn't all fun or glamorous. As usual, Bob thinks a lot of home and wonders how things are going on the farm. He wants to hear all about the wedding.

Nov. 25

Dear Ted,

You may be in Nashville by now as your last letter is Nov. 8 and you guessed it might be three weeks. I'd like to go there sometime, in fact the more I get around the more I wish I could get around and there are lots of things I'd like to see that I hadn't thought about two years ago. Maybe it's because it seems easier to travel now.

Glad you could get home for the wedding and wish you could tell me more about how things are there. I have done a lot of wondering but haven't had any real news about the things that interest me a lot. Mother writes that the financial situation is good but I have wondered just how good a job Willie is doing and if he has been having good luck with the herd. I hate to ask too much tho. Guess I'm just happy when I don't worry about it but get to wondering every now and then tho.

Wish I could tell you more about what we are doing for I know it would be interesting and might give you some fairly good ideas of what may be ahead of you. Most of it goes pretty slow and is rather drab. Having been around the way I have has kept me from doing very much good tho as far as I can learn I was the first of my original class to fly over enemy territory. That is just a coincidence for some of them have considerably more time and flying experience.

Right now we are taking it easy for awhile. Most of the men and planes have earned a rest but I haven't earned one and don't need it. Still get a plus sixteen on the Schneider as of this morning. Pretty good for an old guy but it really doesn't mean much as far as I can see.*

---

*The Schneider Index as a test of pilot fitness was discontinued in 1947.

Perhaps you won't believe yet that flying can be monotonous or boring but you certainly can get sick of looking at water and clouds. I haven't had a lot of it yet either compared to a lot of people. We still get a lot of satisfaction from flying these planes and get away with quite a bit of playing around that would be frowned on back in the states.

Don't know where you got the idea about my life in night clubs but it's a good idea anyway. We do have a little fun even when we are so far from "state side" luxuries.

Let me know how things are going and have all the fun you can while you can. Glad you found a nice girl like Peg. The folks liked her a lot apparently. There are still lots of nice girls and a fellow can't be too choosey. I'm convinced of that.

Good luck
Bob

Ted writes to the newlyweds on the hill that he doesn't think much of his new situation. He finds some humor in describing his "top kick" in great detail.

Squadron F-1, NAAC(AAFCC)
Nashville, Tennessee
November 27, 1943

Dear Jan & John,

I presume that this writing paper meant a gentle hint; so here is a little coming back to you. I hope that I can write a letter a bit different from the one home so that it won't be too boring.

We were shipped from Wmsport Nov. 20, and after a long dirty train ride, we arrived here late the next night. The duration of our stay should be for about five weeks for the purpose of classification (Pilot, Bombardier, or Navigator) before shipping to Pre-Flight.

I am a bit worried about washing out here because of my susceptibility to have colds. They are washing a lot of boys out here, so you can see my feelings do not rest. If I am disqualified they will send me back to take basic and the same old nonsense again despite the rigid training which we have already had. If I do make the grade I don't really care which of the three capacities are assigned me. I rather think I'd like to be a pilot, but I think I'm a bit better qualified for navigation.

This is one of the worst holes that I have yet been in. There isn't enough for us to do; so they give us lots of KP and guard duty when we aren't "goofing off" elsewhere. The post is filled with soft coal smoke, cinders, and soot which make it dirty as sin. You may think this is the sunny south for this time of year, but it isn't. It is a lot colder here, right now, than it was back in Pensy. All of the boys have colds, and the mess hall is a filthy place to breed the infection. Excuse my beefing so much; I guess if I had more to do I would think less of it and pity the boys sleeping in muddy foxholes a lot more.

Our organization is surprisingly good for this sort of place. We have a swell young lieutenant in charge of us who has a top kick (1st sergeant) to help him. We get a kick out of this old top kick. He is a card to look at as are many of these old top kicks. He walks around as stiff as a poker, he is bowlegged, toes out, and I actually think he is knock kneed. He extends his elbows sideways (against the joint) and swings them precisely six to the front and three to the rear. When he bellows, it is evident that his underjaw is too long, and he is underbitten as badly as I'm over-bitten. His tongue is as pleasing to listen to as the snarl of two wildcats fighting. Man can he swear and go through all of the actions which should scare someone. You see – at the beginning of the war, cadets came right from civilian life instead of having basic and college training to contend with. This sort of stuff went over big with them; but most of us have had several months with these old boys, and it doesn't phase us a bit. We have something to entertain us whenever he opens up, so we honestly look forward to his froth and foam. Really he seems to be a heck of a good man though, and I have seen few better men for his position.

I imagine by now that the love birdies have started building their nest and getting used to the inconveniences of getting from Highmarket to the West Road.* I'll bet that you feel pretty old and accustomed to married life and that the whims and whams of the younger generation are positively exasperating by now. Well, maybe the lights of Highmarket are not so alluring, but we all know damn well that there are many others in

---

*The Klossner's farm was in Highmarket, about six miles from the Markham's home on West Road.

the world at present which are too alluring for human duration. Anyway, I hope you're damn happy.

It is nearly time for chow; so this is all for now. Drop me a line when you can.

As ever,
Ted

Burt writes that they may move to Elmira. So far, the possibility of being drafted doesn't seem to have entered his mind.

---

varna apartments
ithaca, n. y.

m e l r o s e , b u r t , a n d l i n d a s a y :
Sunday P.M.
Nov. 28, 1943

Dear Ted,

I've meant to write before but I thought I'd better wait until I knew your new address. We were glad you could get up this way. I'm afraid you found us rather tired out. You probably knew that Mel had been away Friday and Saturday and that I'd had several night meetings that week. We would have liked to have you come here but I guess we were too tired to suggest it.

We've had quite a touch of winter this last week. We had quite a bit of snow early in the week. Roads were plenty icy and snow drifted in places. It's mostly gone again now.

I don't know whether I mentioned it or not but there's a possibility we may move to Elmira. The fellow we have over there is quitting Dec. 15 and as yet we haven't found a replacement. Ethel Selden's husband who works out of Cooperstown might be interested but if he is it would be only in Ithaca & that would mean we go to Elmira. We aren't fond of the idea but may have to.

I imagine you've heard from the folks saying that they have found out where Bob is. Shirley wrote & told us that it was the Ellis Islands.* If so, he's probably in plenty of action.

---

*Ellice Islands in the South Pacific.

125

We haven't had much excitement around here. We stayed home for Thanksgiving. You probably read that Prof. Savage is dead & probably heard Harrison is leaving. I don't know who is taking their places.

As ever

Burt

Evelyn writes of putting up a lot of meat for the winter. She and Ernestine have been canning chickens and venison.

MRS. ERNEST L. MARKHAM
BOX 143
TURIN, NEW YORK

Turin, N.Y.
Nov. 28, '43

Dear Ted,

It was good to get your letter and card on Friday. We felt quite sure you had moved. No doubt things will be different at Nashville than you found them at Williamsport, but we hope you might like it there too.

Thanks for the little picture. It is very good. The larger ones also came. We will keep them for you. Since Aunt Helen is clamoring for a picture, perhaps (this pen is awful) you could send her one of those. Minnie Hart has a whole mantel full of local boys' pictures. I've a notion to give her that little one tho we hate to part with it. She is very interested in all you boys and writes to and receives letters from quite a few. She has asked if we could spare some of you and Bob. Since the wedding we've been just awfully busy. Teen and Billy were here until a week ago. She got to feeling somewhat better and we certainly had lots of fun with Bill. Between him and "Cindy" they kept things lively. Teen bought some old big hens from Millers and I helped her dress and can them. We also canned some of Willis' venison. Our men have drawn down a lot more wood and cut and put in some of it.

Thanksgiving Day was a busy day with no special celebration except that we butchered a hog which we had bought of Watsons. It is a nice one – Dad thinks near 200#. It isn't cut up yet – that'll be next job.

We went to Lowville Wednesday so took Grandma down and brought

126

Jane* home with us. She stayed till Saturday and had lots of fun I guess. We have had cold weather and the skating was good. We have told you haven't we that Lee's folks live in Lowville and he is in the Snyder Drug Store.

Grandpa spent a week with us. He had seemed particularly unhappy lately and Aunt Clara** thought a change might help. He seemed to enjoy being here and we were glad we were able to have him just then before winter. We had quite a bad storm while he was here and he didn't get out much except one day there was a "bee" at Teny Freeman's to raise his barn and Dad took Grandpa over for part of the afternoon. Willis has helped Teny several days taking down a barn on the Hathaway farm. Thirty five or forty men turned out for the raising and they got all the beams up. The weather has not been very favorable lately but if it warms up a little they hope to get it enclosed. Everybody wants to help. He needs it badly.

Grandma will move over for the winter this week – maybe tomorrow.

When I wrote Bob awhile ago, I suggested a code by which he could tell us where he is – by beginning his letter "Dear Mother, Dad and _____", the third name to tell or suggest the place as "Caroline", "Georgia", "Gilbert" or "Harriet" suggesting Hawaii. Back came his letter, starting, "Dear Mother, Dad and Uncle Ellis"! Ellice Islands! He seemed to be there for a few days' rest, and was going back to work soon. Plenty of work, we imagine – maybe in the Gilberts. It was written Nov. 6th. He was the censor. We have written rather regularly but I guess the letters have not always got through very fast as he has moved about so much. Hope he gets them all eventually. We've sent him several X'mas packages, including your picture.

Bob's sea chest and navy suit case came last week. He sent all his warm clothes, three white uniforms, one blue one, some shirts, pants, notebooks, pictures, and lots of things I suppose he could do without.

We wonder whether you have located Ray Miller. They (his folks) had not heard lately. They have sent him your address I think. I'm sending your new address to the Boonville Herald.

Have you heard of Prof. Savage's death? Must close now, with love from all,

Mom

We were glad you all got together at Ithaca. Marian wrote about it.

---

*Jane was Evelyn's niece.
**Clara Markham was Ernest's sister.

Ted is hoping for a farm furlough. He is nervous about the possibility of washing out and what he will do if that happens.

U. S. AIR FORCES

December 2, 1943

Dear Folks,

I just heard a rumor tonight which leads me to believe I can get a furlough out of here. It seems that some of the farm boys here in camp have been able to get furloughs in order to go home and help on the farm. You see there is little for us to do here but wait, and you must have a good excuse in order to get out of here. Maybe I'll want to get a discharge anyway if I am eliminated. Anyway if it is possible I'll probably need a letter from home and one from the county agent in order to swing the proposition. I'll have to wait a few days to learn the results of my classification and to time things just right for Christmas. If it is possible I'll write you folks and Joe telling of my success and telling the sort of a letter I need.

Tomorrow I'll finish my final physical examination, and within a few days we'll be notified of the results. I'm pretty scared because they raised the standards again, and we know of at least two definite eliminations from our bunk already. We thought that our percentage of wash outs would cease when it reached 20%, but now it is moving toward 25%. Most of the fellows were eliminated on their physicals and aptitudes. Westcott my best friend probably got it on aptitude because he was slow in math, but he was certainly one of the best flyers in our group. We sure hate to see him leave us.

If I am eliminated, I don't know what I'll do. It will be hell to go back to take basic again. Not that it is so hard, but so utterly foolish and monotonous. Maybe I'll try to get out then if some good farmer would want me badly enough to take the necessary steps.

I have been amused lately by Mom's clever way of learning of Bob's location. Pretty smart, huh Mom? I have been trying to think of such a code in case I am ever sent to such a place. Maybe we can work out a couple of codes to use.

I guess I told of the surprise Ray gave me the other night, or did I include that in Teen's letter? I am quite certain of getting a pass to spend a week end with him.

It occurs to me that I never said anything about the pictures I sent home for you to keep. The one of course was that of our squadron as we left Wmsport, while the second was that of our graduation dance as we finished the grand march. We were marking time and singing the Air Corp Hymn, so it isn't very clear. In the other picture I might mention a few of my closest friends: Verne Westcott, Dick Baier, Jim Pearce (washed out of Naval Cadets), Jim Thaxton, Bob Kelly and others too numerous to mention. The officers are probably self-explanatory except that our tact-officer, the one we thought a great deal of, was away to a school, and this Lt. Owegua was sent to substitute for him.

I guess this is all for tonight. After I find the right way and time to ask for this furlough, I'll let you know if you can help.

Love,

Ted

Marian hasn't been feeling well, and she's worried about how she will get home for Christmas.

Dec. 7

Ithaca

Dear Ted,

I'm sorry I've put off writing so long. We were on the gad until last week. Then I got sick and now I'm just plain weak. It's hard work to even do the dishes so I don't get much else done. I guess the house just won't get cleaned this year. If I can get somebody to brush down the cobwebs, I'll just hang the curtains and put down the rugs and forget it. I've got nearly 3 wks. wash and I hope the woman that cleans for Mrs. Wiegard can do it tomorrow. We've tried two other women and I guess it's impossible to get help. Mr. B. does K.P. and we get along.

Tonight's paper had an announcement of Mrs. Marion Smithling's death on Sunday. The funeral is on Thurs. a.m. in Dryden. I'd like to go if I can. I knew she wasn't well but had no idea it was serious.

I haven't gotten you anything for Christmas yet. Could you tell me what you'd like, or would you prefer money?

I hope to go home. Everyone asks me how. I may walk (if I feel better). It'll probably be by bus and ahead of the rush. Last year I missed my brothers' cars. This year I won't even have one to carry my suitcase.

Sorry you don't think much of Nashville. Shirley wrote me that you were probably just missing Peg – said she would. She hadn't had much to say about Peg – as much as she usually does. We all liked Peg a lot. It was swell to have you two come up to Ithaca. Neither of you should have fussed about imposing on us. We like it that way. Seemed good to have you here. I miss you.

I found some O.D.* buttons and Mr. B. came home with a sewing kit the other day. Note the inscription on the back when you get it. Will send them with Xmas package if you let me know right away. I found a dime under bed after you left & will send that. This isn't much of a letter. Will write more when I can. Meant to write Peg but guess I can't tonight.

Love,
Marian

Shirley says "Cindy" the pup, has grown physically and mentally. Prof. Savage died – couldn't find clipping.

---

*O.D. = Olive drab.

Ted writes that at last, he has been classified as a pilot. However, the washouts continue, and he is unable to get a furlough home.

U. S. AIR FORCES

December 8, 1943

Dear Folks,

At last the glad tidings came through tonight. I have been classified as a pilot, though I wouldn't have been disappointed so long as I was made a cadet. Many of our old gang haven't heard yet, and many are in question. Up to now seven of our seventy have been eliminated and more will wash out before the returns are all in. Among those already eliminated was Dick Baier, one of my closest buddies. The eyes were awfully closely checked, and he among many others have gotten the gate for that reason. Of my three best friends, two have washed out and the third has been appointed as a navigator. Many of the fellows have washed on their psychomotor tests. You can see I was worried and now feel pretty tickled.

I had no luck in applying for a furlough. It seems that they were dishing out furloughs to farm boys, but since crops have been harvested, the practice has been discontinued. I had hopes of getting home to help Willie get things in better shape, but now it seems impossible.

This weekend I hope to get out to stay with Ray if we can make transportation connections and I can get a pass.

Last night was the first open-post we have had here; they give up open post on Tues. and Thurs. nights from 5:30 to 11:00 PM, but not on weekends. Nashville looked like a pretty dirty city from our first peer at it. Maybe it would be better if viewed during the day.

I have had to have more dental work done. I have had two large fillings put in and will need at least one more. In Miami, you know, I had five fillings put in. The Army dentists are a great deal quicker to put a filling in than civilian dentists. I can't quite understand why I have need of so much work because Dr. O'Brien gave me a thorough check-up last April. Maybe he is unable to detect those needs or maybe he is hesitant, but it seems that he should have done something with at least three of my teeth. Army dentists seem to do excellent work and they certainly have the best equipment to work with. They are far from painless though. It seems that they are more free with the silver and more apt to drill away more of the cavity.

I must close now and write more letters. Everyone write, particularly Willie to let me know the outcome of Marie's [the cow] abortion.

Love,

Ted

Marian writes again with the news that she is planning to take a bus home for Christmas.

Wed. Nite

Dec. 15

Dear Ted,

This is just a note because I've got to get to bed. It's only nine o'clock but I ironed most of the day and I'm tired. In fact I fell asleep reading the paper before supper.

Was glad to get your letter – told Burt – and good news. Got a note from Peg today with a card. I wrote her a note with mine and it went out Mon. a.m. An answer back in that time is pretty good for the Christmas rush.

Altie will be thrilled with the insignia. It will be by far the best Christmas he gets. Even Bill treasures his "air corp".

I'm glad your eye is O.K. now. Probably some kind of infection. Hope you don't get the grippe everyone is having. Have decided it was something like that I had because suddenly I felt alright.

We did get to Mrs. Smithling's funeral. I think it pleased the family – both Griswald & Smithling. Loretta came over Fri. afternoon and stayed to supper. She nearly talked our ears off. She's been on the go night and day. She had undulant fever spots* on both sides of her neck. I never saw it so bad. I told her she ought to go to bed for a week but she said she couldn't afford to. She certainly has grit.

---

*Undulant fever is a brucellosis infection.

I went to a Home Bureau meeting last night and enjoyed it very much. They are all young women but a little older than I. It was a lesson on fitting clothes and was very welcome. It stressed new shoulder line and sleeves, so now I'll have to bring my wardrobe up to date. Some is pretty ancient. They want garments to work on next time and will I furnish material!

The meeting was out the Etna Road and we didn't know the exact place but found a woman walking along the road. Mr. B. stopped and asked if she was going to the meeting. She was, and it was Mrs. Stanley Warren. I told her you boys appreciated what Prof. Warren* was doing for A.Z.

Nice you could be with Ray. Is he still griping about everything in sight?

I haven't read "Suez to Singapore"** but have wanted to. I got Mr. B. Ernie Pyle's new book "Here is Your War".*** I read a little in it today and I know it will be good. I got Mr. B. reading his column and now he wouldn't miss it. So I asked him if he'd like the book for Christmas and he was thrilled to pieces. He's reading a lot more lately. Seems good to see him enjoy it. Lillian could hardly believe her eyes Thanksgiving the way he sat down with his nose in a book. She said he usually was on the jump when he was there.

Mr. B. has been doing a little insurance work. Yesterday he went to Newark Valley and today to Binghamton. Yesterday he sold one case and came home with over $1400 in his pocket. Now maybe we'll have enough to eat till spring anyway.

I finally decided I'd be foolish to try to get you anything so I'm sending a money order. If you get a furlough it will come in handy. If you don't maybe you could use it to paint the town red (pink anyway). Don't save it – it's to have fun on.

Shirley sent me the annual Xmas list. Nobody wants anything but Dad. He wants light wool socks and slippers. Guess he thinks I'm the only one who can buy his slippers. He hasn't had any in ages I haven't got.

---

*Dr. Stanley W. Warren, a Cornell College of Agriculture professor, was the first recipient of the "Professor of Merit" award in 1948.

**Suez to Singapore by Cecil Brown (1942).

***Ernie Pyle was an American journalist and a well-known war correspondent of WWII.

Oh yes, Altie wants wool socks for skating and a billfold. Must be in the folding money class now that he won $3 shooting snaps. Mr. B. had to get the billfold and put new $1 bills in it.

I'll put the outdoor exercise and writing oftener on my New Year's resolutions.

Love,
Marian

I am having a permanent in the morning, 9 to 1. Expect to leave Mon. or Tue. on bus. Am taking one case.

Evelyn is responding to a letter from Ted (not included here) in which, in a bad moment, he criticized what he perceived to be Willie's poor herd and farm management. He wanted the cows to be milked on time, and he wanted Willie to be paid for his labor. Evelyn understands the underlying cause of Ted's criticism: his loneliness, boredom, and frustration. At the same time, she supports Willie completely.

Dec. 16

Dear Ted,

No doubt you are feeling anxious because we haven't written. The days go by so fast because there is so much to do all the while.

We are all glad and proud of your acceptance for pilot training. But we aren't surprised. Willis has said, all along, that you would make a fighter pilot. I dread to think of it though, and I think Dad does. He doesn't say much.

Dad is sick in bed just now. It seems to be the grip. Lots of people are having it, but we've been lucky so far until now. When it once gets in a family it is hard to keep from spreading it. I've somehow felt that it wouldn't take much to throw Dad off balance. He hasn't looked or acted right for a long time. I've often wondered whether he could keep on the mail route until time for his retirement two years from his coming birthday.

I wish you could be here for a while without too many others around. I think Dad and you and I could work out some things, but if you can't be here, you must just trust us, as we do you, to do the best we know how. Your father has not the point of view or the training you have and there are also some of our situations you cannot realize, because you have never had a family. In the first place we started with nothing (neither of us even graduated from high school) and had about four times as many children as we could afford. Trying to do justice by you all has often gotten us into jams, for as you know you are eight different personalities and sometimes it seems that you all have different personalities and sometimes it seems that you all have different aims and ideals and expect your parents to agree with each one of you. Until you have the same experiences, you can never know what it takes to see one of our children through school or getting married or some other big venture. We are not complaining nor would we change it if we could, but please be patient with us tho we are growing old and stale.

Willie is just an inexperienced kid, much like the rest of you at that age. He does some things as well or better than some of you and some not as well as he might if he had a more mature point of view. All his friends seem to be going into the service and he wishes he were too. It is hard for stay-at-homes to feel important. He thinks he gets no appreciation, but I don't know what we would do without him. He's pretty sweet, usually.

I shall keep trying to pull things the right way, and praying all the while that whatever comes, we shall at least keep our faith in one another and harmony in our home. There are four generations of us living here and that means many small adjustments to be made.

I scribbled this off thinking to copy it over, but W. is going over to the office now and I'll send it as it is. Will try to write more very soon. We do hope you can come for Christmas. Bob thinks he will be coming in February, maybe.

Heaps of love,
Mom

Winter 1943

Shirley reports on all the news of Christmas Day including the gifts that she has received. She has a not so subtle way of conveying her opinion about certain gifts.

December 26, 1943

Dear Ted,

Well, we had a lovely Christmas – of course not so nice as tho you three boys were here, but as nice as you could expect otherwise. All of us said "Oh dear I haven't a thing hardly" but there were enough gifts for the community, almost. Aunt Mary, Uncle A.J., and Helen came over because they didn't have a very big family either. The two families put their food together and we had roast chickens, dressing, roast pork, squash, Harvard beets, mashed potato, salad, pickles, relishes, apple sauce, prune bread, suet pudding with hard sauce, cranberries, mince pie, and milk. Beside this we had lots of oranges, apples, fruit candy, hard candies, chocolates, nuts, and tangerines. You see we fared pretty well.

Some of the presents I got: Ernestine, Marian – a lovely water-proof, wind-proof impregnable jacket (red); Marian – an undie set & material and pattern for a red blouse; Mom – a pretty red plaid skirt & Mom's & Dad's picture; Jan & Johnny – a lovely smelling box of bath powder & some extra special present I haven't seen yet up at Klossners'; Burt & Mel – a complexion brush; Linda – a powder brush; Altie – an Indian pin; Grandma – a box of hankies with a lovely pearl pin; Aunt Mary – a lovely box of hankies & sachet coming; Janey W. – a Tangee lipstick, rouge, powder set; Joanie R. – a pin (beer bottle, two glasses) and her picture; Dotty M. – a nice string of wooden beads and cute little south-sea-island gal with grass skirt; Mr. B. – $4; Aunt Helen – $1; Miss Miller – this writing paper (drew my name at school); another girl at school gave me a stink set, as I call them, that has perfume which smells like something she might have gotten from the barn, talcum powder like chalk, bath crystals like cow salt or something the sort; three little bottles of perfume at church; Marion Clark gave me a box of bath crystals.

Billy is getting to be quite a boy. Friday nite when they came down about the first thing he said was "Lou ought to see your coat" to me. Of course he knew all about it and wanted everyone else to know too. He told Willie that Santa was going to bring him a horse-ball. No one had said anything about it. He said he got it down at "Wooie's" (Willie's) barn. He'd told his Grandpa O'Brien that "Lou know– Wooey goes everywhere I go when I'm down at Markhams."

Cindy's quite a dog now, too. She has grown awfully fast. Her hair is starting to wave now. Teddy's really beginning to be rather scared of her. She isn't afraid of the devil himself. Every time she picks on the cats and expects a chewing she turns around so they claw the back side of her where it doesn't hurt quite so much. You should see how cute she is about coming in the living room and such things she knows she isn't allowed to do. She comes just to the threshold & sometimes lays half – on the rug there. She certainly is fully as smart as Patsy [a deceased cocker] altho I don't want to say anything against Patsy.

I don't know whether you knew or not about the flu epidemic we've been having around here. There have been a lot of people sick. There were lots of kids in school that either stayed home or came and gave it to the rest of us. Of the teachers, Mr. Kaskela, Mrs. Jackson, Miss Snow, Miss Mandray, Mrs. Crane, Miss Churchill, Miss Wilber and Miss Frost were sick. Three (last ones) came but were so dopey they couldn't do much. Dad and Altie had it here and I felt a week ago Thursday as tho I'd been up nites for a week but that was all. Maybe it wasn't that. Uncle Albert was sick with it and Uncle Hugh is in the hospital with something wrong with his ear that looks like a mastoid.

Marian came home last Monday nite on the bus from the north. It has been nice to have her here. She doesn't expect to go right back. She hasn't set any date yet when she is going back to anyone or herself either. She decided the only way to have a vacation was to take one. Since she has come home we've straightened out quite a few of our family misunderstandings. One night Willie was feeling kind of blue because he didn't have any money and so on. Marian talked to him and Dad and Dad gave him $25 as soon as he got his check cashed. They both feel better about it and we haven't heard so much blaming of the opposite. Willie was so tickled that he had Christmas money. He went to Lyons Falls and bought Pyrex ware for all the women.

That same morning Dad gave him money Willie went over to see what Uncle Teeny wanted him for the day before. He got over there and

Uncle Teeny had a check made out to him for $15 for helping him so much.

Willie's an awful good kid to do most anything if you get on the right side of him but he has an <u>awful</u> flashy temper he uses too frequently. You can't tell him anything and make him understand it's right no matter how you try if he isn't in the mood. Just now it would be good if he were away at college or in the Army. He gets things too much his own way. Everyone is more or less afraid of him and therefore it makes him think he can get away with murder. I'm determined to think, tho, that Bob or maybe Burt are the ones that would make him settle down. You tell him things that would be good for him if he would only listen but you're about his age and you've worked with him more. Every time you tell him something (rather some times) he loses his temper and gets stubborn. I don't mean that you're bossy or anything like that – I don't think you are at all but he does because he doesn't stop to think. Lots of time too he says he won't listen and gets mad but we notice he does do what you suggest. I just don't pay any attention to his blustering and hot temper because I'm in a situation where it wouldn't do any good. He knows that I'm not afraid of him tho so doesn't pick on me much anymore because I did get really mad at him last summer one time. I don't very often get mad at all but this time I was so mad I just shook and he couldn't budge me. If it weren't for Jan I'd still be there fighting. Oh well, I suppose it's awfully hard for him to be staying home here when all other boys are flying planes and doing things he wants to do and he hasn't anything to be here for other than working on the farm but I think now that Dad is paying he'll do different. He gets feeling blue over that girl Kate Kraeger who went up on him. Don't you mention any of this to anyone. I don't want to make trouble. I just thought you would like to know. I'm pretty certain your letter did some good anyway. We've been getting around early at nite. Right after I get home from school we have supper & then they milk and everything is usually finished by seven or half-past. They get up earlier in the morning too.

Well, it kinda looks like this will be all for now.

Love,
Blondie

1944

Winter 1944

1944 would see some of the bloodiest and hardest-fought battles of the war, including Monte Cassino in Italy, the D-Day invasion of Normandy, the battle for Saipan, operation Market-Garden, and the Battle of Leyte Gulf. The year ended with Germany's last big offensive of the war, the Battle of the Bulge, in the Ardennes Forest region of Belgium, France, and Luxembourg.

Five million young Americans volunteered for military service following Pearl Harbor. Before the war ended, ten million more were drafted. The Markhams began the year with no warning that the war would take more of their family away.

Evelyn begins the new year with a memory of the first Christmas she spent alone.

MRS. ERNEST L. MARKHAM
BOX 143
TURIN, NEW YORK

Jan. 5, 1944

Dear Ted,

Just as I was about to write to you, Dad brought your letter, written on New Year's Day. [letter is not included] It has seemed quite a while since we heard from you excepting the Christmas cards which you sent to all of us.

It was so near Christmas when we learned that you were not coming home to hang up your stocking, we were afraid to send off a package to you in all the rush and jam. We were also afraid you would have moved before a package could reach Nashville. So, it is still here and I think it better to wait until we get your new address. It is too bad. It will be a rather "warmed over" Christmas when you get it. This was your first Christmas away from home. I remember the first one I spent away from my family. I was nineteen. It wasn't bad tho, for I was at Aunt Emma Davis' and I spent New Year's Day at Trainor's, just before closing my first term of school.*

---

*With only two years of high school credit, Evelyn taught at a one-room schoolhouse in Houseville, NY.

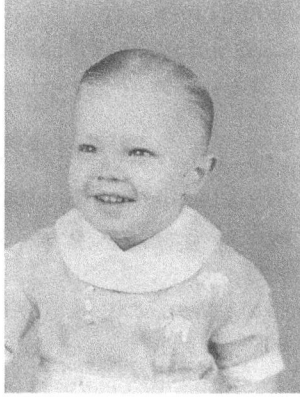

Billy O'Brien

We sure missed you and Bob and Burt's folks on Christmas Day, but we did have a lovely time though. The rest of us, including Grandma, were all here, also Aunt Mary, Uncle Albert and Helen – 15 of us.

Shirley is quite a faithful reporter, so probably she told you of our principal presents. It was a picture Christmas for us. We had your picture, Billy's, one of Mary and Albert and Janice and John's wedding pictures.

Marian came home on Monday before Xmas and was here until yesterday. It did us all a world of good to have her here. Teen and Bill were here a few days, too, and I think they will soon be back to stay for a few days again. Teen is feeling better than she did when you saw her. Her doctor speaks quite encouragingly and we feel that she is going to be all right, or at least that she will come through safely.

Billy has a big time when he is here. Cindy is so crazy about him that she is almost too much for him. She grows like a weed, is so full of pep and mischief and so intelligent and affectionate! We all have fun with her.

The mail piled up like mountains in some places, it seems to be pretty well cleared out here. You must have gotten a letter from me telling of Dad's sickness. He had the flu, I think and took a little over a week's sick leave just before Christmas. He really was quite sick and Alton had a touch of it too but lost only a Friday from school. The rest of us have been fortunate because it has seemed as tho everyone was having it. Many had a terrible intestinal condition with vomiting and fainting spells. Hugh's trouble settled in his ears and they took him to the hospital about three

141

weeks ago. I think he is going home today.* Albert and Terry were sick too. Many public gatherings were called off and some schools were closed because of the epidemic. It seems to be dying down now in this section at least.

Aunt Grace** sent us a Christmas card and told us she was at the hospital in Utica where her father had pneumonia. Some days later, (X'mas Day) Mary brought a news clipping about his death saying the funeral would be Dec. 26th at Grace's home. Dad, Marian and I went. She had written several times to several of us but the letters or cards had not got through. No other relatives were there except Gladys, Ray, Mary and a brother of Mr. Burdick's from Philadelphia. Poor Grace! She feels pretty broken up. She has no one left now but Gladys and hardly knows what to do with her home. She will sell her father's of course, at the first chance. She has a good job at Remington Arms in Ilion and has been going back and forth. I had a letter today saying she was back at work and had taken a room in Ilion for the present at least.

Everything here at home is going well. Dad seems to be feeling better than he has in quite a while. They have cut and hauled quite a bit of wood lately. We have almost no snow except less than a foot in the woods and that is quite hard and dry. The wood handles clean and nice. I went up with Dad yesterday afternoon just for the fresh air. It was fun!

Well, I'd better ring off and get Willis to write a few lines.

Lots of love,
Mother

---

*Hugh was Ernest's younger brother, father of cousin Pete.

**Aunt Grace was the widow of Ernest's older brother, Clark. Gladys was their daughter and Ted's cousin.

The Tarawa Atoll, in the Gilbert Islands, was liberated by the U.S. Marines in November 1943. Bob writes from an island airstrip, where he is hoping to be furloughed soon for a long-awaited vacation at home.

Evelyn and Ernest in 1943

Tarawa

Jan. 8

Dear Ted,

I was plenty glad to get your letter of Dec. 20. No doubt this will have to be forwarded to you as you expected to be moved on about now. You didn't say what your classification is but a letter from Jan said the folks have word that you are to get first training.* I guess that's what you want isn't it?

Glad to get your picture of things at home too as I had done a lot of wondering. What you say is about what I expected tho. It's probably best that we just forget about it for the duration.

Got your picture just before Christmas and think it's good. I know the folks think a lot of theirs too. Also I was very happy to get the picture of Mother & Dad tho it isn't especially good. I have wanted one for a long time.

Guess I won't say much about our Christmas and I can't say much about what is happening. I am hoping there will be a chance for us to get

*First training = pilot training.

together in a few weeks and I can tell you all about it. If you go to Santa Ana it might be fairly easy. I told Ernestine I might be able to help her celebrate her birthday. That may be a little optimistic. I'll call home and find out where you are as soon as I hit the states so keep them informed. There isn't any point in writing to me for I'll be hard to catch.

I'll get in touch with you as soon as I can. Good Luck.

Bob

Ted writes next from Columbus, Mississippi, where he will be stationed until Pre-Flight Schools open up.

U. S. AIR FORCES

CAAF, Bks. 801
Columbus, Miss.
January 8, 1944

Dear Folks,

We shipped out of Nashville last night and arrived here at about noon today. We are at an Advanced Training Field where pilots get the final touch before graduation. Oh no, that doesn't mean anything for us though. We aren't sure of what is in store for us yet.

It is quite logical to believe that we are to wait here until Pre-Flight Schools open up. Meanwhile we will probably get details such as KP, plane scrubbing, or general yardbird activity. I guess this is the best that can be done by us even though the details don't seem too tasteful. It seems logical that this will be a good opportunity to have an excuse for a furlough.

I hope that if I wash from Pilot that I can get into Navigation or Bombardier. I qualified for both as the qualifications now stand. Required qualifications were 5 for Bomb., 6 for Nav., and 7 for Pilot. I got 9 for Bomb., 8 for Nav., and 7 for Pilot. You see I just hit the line for Pilot and got it only because I preferred that. Without stating a preference I would probably have gotten one of the others.

Training will really tighten up at Pre-Flight. They really get onto your neck for every little thing, such as a button unbuttoned or clothes not hung up or any other little thing. If we have the class system, we will have an upper class jamming it down our throats for four weeks.

This seems to be a nice clean camp so far. We have a good, warm, two story barracks with a foundation and heating system. Unlike Nashville, it is possible to breathe a bit of fresh air devoid of smoke and soot. Our barracks is quite crowded, but we have an inside latrine which helps a lot. Chow seems to be swell so far; even though we have had only two meals here the mess hall seems to be on the ball. (An Army Mess which is on the ball can really turn out some excellent meals). What ever we have to do here will be a lot more pleasant than Nashville even though there was little to do at Nashville and jobs may be a bit distasteful here. Pilots are badly needed in the Air Corp even though we are held in reserve training. The Air Corp still seems to have "growing pains"; you can see that the Army expects a lot more fighting than our public realizes is necessary. It seems as if all I have done is to wait, through Basic, CTD, and Nashville, but really you can't blame the Army for holding so many in reserve.

This is an AT10 base. This is the type of ship which Chet Freeman is flying at Freeman Field, Indiana. We walked out on the line tonight to take a look at the field, and we gaped in wonder at the countless AT10's tied up. Imagine that on a good day the runways are plastered with planes and pilots. There are also a few Dauntless and Brewsters here. It is quite a field.

We haven't been able to learn much about the camp here. We are told that it is about ten miles north of Columbus. The land around here seems to be as poor as the poorest land of the South. It is badly eroded or else it is water laden sandy clay. There are a lot of swamp pines through the section. The camp has a lot of pine to shade and beautify the place though.

Janice sent me a nice box of cookies the other day and Johnny included cigarettes. I haven't written to thank them yet. The cookies didn't last long after the boys caught sight of them. Whenever they get pkgs. like that they pass them around too. It works pretty good because they come quite often, we don't eat too much to make us sick, and nothing gets stale on us.

I have grown awfully lazy lately because we haven't had enough to do. If I lived like this much longer I would need servants to wait on me.

Well, this is all for now. How about dropping me a line?

Love,

Ted

Evelyn writes news of the whereabouts of several local boys. In a letter not included in the collection, Ted had asked her to appeal to the Red Cross in order to obtain an emergency family furlough for him. She writes that she is unable to do that since Ernest has recovered from the flu. The Red Cross routinely assisted families in obtaining furloughs for servicemen.

MRS. ERNEST L. MARKHAM

BOX 143

TURIN, NEW YORK

Jan. 16, 1944

Dear Ted,

We were glad to know that your expected move had not taken you so very much farther and now we hope you will get your mail all right. We have sent that much belated Christmas package and hope you still may enjoy it. You do not seem to be getting our letters very well.

You sound as if you are not very busy and that gives you time to get homesick, or bored. It would be nice if you had a chance to get a furlough but there wouldn't be much use of us trying to get it because Dad seems perfectly well – in fact better than for some time before he had the flu. Couldn't you get a leave, yourself?

I have written to the Herald to have your address changed and will do the same for your Reader's Digest.

Before I forget, I want to say that I received the $10 you sent and the bill for subs. was $6 so I will put the $4 into the bank for you. I explained about it in another letter. Hope you have gotten it. You know that Shirley, Willis and Alton sent the Digest to you?

In that Christmas package, the shower soap was from Ernestine, the buttons, etc. from Marian. Shirley cracked butternuts for the candy.

The receipt for your life insurance came and I put it away with your policy. I've just taken care of Bob's. He had his checking acct. put in his name and mine, so I could draw checks and attend to such things for him. He sends allotments or money orders direct to the bank.

Uncle Hugh came home from the hospital three or four days ago. He has had a bad time with both ears. They had letters from Pete written New Year's but I guess they are pretty anxious since the last big raid was reported, with so many bombers lost.

We have a letter from Bob written Christmas night, telling of a nice Christmas dinner. He had gotten our picture and a letter, which we sent together first class airmail, just in time for Christmas. He received two packages from Teen, one from me with your picture in it; a letter and picture from Rosemary opened Christmas, too. Other packages we knew about, he does not seem to have received unless since Christmas. His letter was about 2½ weeks coming. He gets the B. Herald from one to two months old and a bundle of magazines and clippings was a long time on the way. Some of our letters never seem to have reached him.

Chet Freeman is home for a few days after graduating and before going to Pensacola. Len Ackerman must have gone across as his family has not heard since X'mas. Link is in the latest draft and "Denny" is in the marines at Parris Island. Harry Mathis is across. Phil Freeman is in Labrador, I think, and so is Howard Chapman. Mick F. is over the pond.*

The O'Briens came today. Teen and Billy are going to stay a few days.

Must close from lack of room.

Will try to write again soon.

Love, Mom

---

*Ted's friends and classmates from Constableville and Turin.

Ted writes that he has received his Christmas package, for which he is very appreciative, but the lack of activity is getting him down. He has a preference for what kind of planes he might be flying.

U.S. ARMY ✈ AIR FORCES

January 19, 1944

Dear Folks,

As I start this letter I believe that I should wish Willie a happy birthday, for it will be his birthday by the time this letter arrives. It is hard to believe that Willie is nineteen years old when I feel no older than that myself.

Frankly I guess that I feel sort of homesick tonight. A little too much free time and a chance to think of so many minor things have been getting me down lately. Things build up on a fellow like this when he lives in such inactivity and believes that in all logical reasoning he should have a chance to get a furlough. They don't know what to do with us here, nor do they have facilities of any kind.

When we first arrived I was assigned KP with one day on and one day off. It went this way for about ten days and then they decided to give us a week's rest before serving more KP. Well the KP isn't hard work, but it is hard to lay around and do nothing except PT or drill. I long for something to do out on the line (mechanics's work), but there isn't room enough for everyone. This is what builds up on you when you know that you aren't worth a good damn to anyone. It is so hard to reconcile yourself to the fact that you are better off than many fellows doubled up in some foxhole with shrapnel in his guts, or that you are being held in reserve for something which superiors can't be sure of. If they would only let us go home or even get out to travel about the country a bit.

The lovely Christmas package came today. I was particularly pleased to get the picture of Mom and Dad. It is so natural, as well as being handy to carry. I tried to get a couple of the fellows to enjoy the spruce gum with me, but they didn't have the patience to learn to chew it. That is one thing which I can't be accused of hoarding, and I am sort of pleased.

Last night I watched a Liberator come into the field, and the day before a Fortress take-off. It is amazing to see those hulks of power roll around and move with the ease of little ships. No Willie it is doubtful that I will ever be a fighter pilot unless it will be a two-engine ship. Most fellows look forward to fighter ships, but I believe I prefer big stuff. If I ever have the luck to get through Basic Flying, I believe that I will ask for twin-engine Advanced Training. Most fellows asking for this get it because most cadets look forward to single engine fighters even with the prospect of getting a ship like the P38 from two-engined AT's. The boys in training have claimed that 88% of those graduating from Twin Engine School get the ship which they choose, and nearly 100% get a ship in the category they choose. If I fly a fighter, I would like a P38; if it is a single engine ship, make it the P51; if a medium bomber, give me Bob's ship despite the glamour of ships like the B26 or A20; but, if you give me my preference, I want any four-motored bomber. If it be a heavy bomber, I could probably only fly a Fortress because my legs would probably be too short for a Liberator and inexperience would bar me from something like the B29. Chances of flying a transport are quite remote, but the Curtis Commando (C46) is my favorite. This is all highly idealistic, for I must first face the possibility of washing out. Washouts run high, and I'm afraid of being too slow with my flying. Ten hours of flying has shown me that I'm no hot pilot and have plenty to worry about.

This is all for tonight. I guess that you folks know how I'd like to get a furlough and how it could only be achieved from your end. If you want to do it that way, it might work. We probably won't have more than three or four weeks left to do it in.

Love,
Ted

P.S. Is Len Ackerman still in this area?

Evelyn writes to Ted with great news! Bob will be furloughed soon.

MRS. ERNEST L. MARKHAM
BOX 143
TURIN, NEW YORK

Jan. 20, '44

Dear Ted,

We have great news for you. A cablegram came last night. It was:

"Feeling fine. See you soon.
Bob."

So much in so few short words! Of course we do not know how long it will be before he arrives, but we hope you can get a furlough arranged so you can come when you hear from us again. I'll telegraph you.

I wrote you just the other day. Probably you have received it all right. We also sent that long-delayed Christmas package.

Ernestine, Shirley and Willis went to Boonville yesterday, so I sent $4.00 for deposit on your account. I have to hurry now. Hope you will be able to come soon. Wire us if you have not enough money.

Love from us all,
Mother

Ted is profoundly frustrated with the slowness of his progress in pilot training. In his next letter to Janice and John, he writes that more than anything, he has "burning hopes of getting over there where the service is the service."

U.S. ARMY ✈ AIR FORCES

January 23, 1944

Dear Jan & John,

It was small appreciation I showed you folks for the nice box of cookies and cigarettes when I lingered so long in writing you. Nevertheless, I greatly appreciated it, and I'm sure the sudden made friends who were present when I opened it, also appreciated it. As far as being so slow to write, I haven't much of an excuse. I manage to write a couple of letters each day and put off others I should write until the next day when I think I surely will write. I figured the other day that I write no less than sixty letters each month now.

As for my present status & etc., I shall not bore you by going through all of that nonsense when I presume that you have been reading my letters at home. I am just waiting until Pre-Flight schools open, and that is about all that is important.

This new gang of fellows with whom I am living are quite a little younger than most of the fellows I was with previously. Most of them are Willie's age while some are older or younger. In a way when ages are discussed, I feel like Grandpaw; but generally we all feel about the same age, regardless of birthdays. The Army is a funny organization when age and experience are concerned; it makes the young men age quickly and the older ones lose years. I guess that it is because previous civilian experience, individualism, and ability is of so little importance. Though when I first had an opportunity to see these young men when they entered the service, I saw many bad cases of homesickness; today after they have a bit of service, I highly respect the way they handle themselves and the real stuffen which they possess. Most of these younger lads are as good or better soldiers than the fellows my age or older.

Mother writes that Chet Freeman has been commissioned and awarded his wings. It gets under my skin a bit when I realize that he entered the service just after I did as well as most of the fellows from Miami Beach who are still with me. Perhaps to many it looks like a break to be held up in training like this, but after you get so much of this pure nonsense under your belt you have burning hopes of getting over there where the service is the service. When I know what Bob and the many others in his shoes are going through, I feel so worthless and no good.

We aren't allowed to be out on the line (with the ships) unless we are actually on duty, but I manage to get out there occasionally to watch the ship come in and leave. I wonder, after seeing a few of these ships get bounced around, how in the world some of these trainees got this far. I expect that if I ever get as bad as that that I won't have a chance in the world to prevent elimination. Today I had a chance to get inside of my first Liberator.* (There is only an occasional one which stops at this base). My gosh you would be amazed to see how completely the whole thing is lined with instruments & etc. There is hardly a square inch of waste space or area in the whole ship. It is a beautiful sight to see how easily their pilots lift them from the ground and how smoothly they return to earth.

The land is awfully level here. Were it not for the pines and hardwood so prevalent here, you could see for many miles. The land is no good, badly eroded and outcropped. Generally, the region is poorly drained and spotted with swamps and marshes. So far, as agriculture importance and farming goes, this region could be contrasted with the poorest land around Bramingham eroded to the extent that no topsoil was left. After seeing a good share of the eastern portion of the south, I staunchly believe that overcropping and erosion play a tremendous part in a region's prosperity.

You can always give me a hunk of land in Lewis Co. no matter if snows are a bit of a challenge. Maybe this climate is nice at this time of year, but still the south is no earthly good.

I suppose you love birds are still pretty busy building your nest, but why don't you write now and then and tell me about it?

As ever,
Ted

---

*177 B-24 Liberators were used in the August 1, 1943, raid on the Ploesti oil fields in Romania.

Evelyn writes of a 3:00 AM phone call from Bob. He is on his way home! Evelyn tells Ted that she will appeal to the Red Cross to help in getting Ted home.

MRS. ERNEST L. MARKHAM
BOX 143
TURIN, NEW YORK

Jan. 26

Dear Ted,

Your special delivery letter [not included] came tonight. It made better time than mine did.

Now, we all want very much to have you come and we think the occasion of Bob's visit is a good enough reason for you to get a furlough.

Bob called us on the phone from San Francisco last night at three o'clock. He seemed to have just arrived. Had come on some sort of ship from Hawaii. We could not understand very well but it sounded like Bob. He asked where you were. Said he might be able to see you. We understood that he would be flying east over the southern states. Said it might be a week before he gets here but would stay about a month. Wants us to have some good weather ordered.

Now, perhaps Bob can stop and find you and get you off somehow or we will try our best with the Red Cross. By the way, do you know that Dr. Vadney is in the navy and Lyons Falls has one of the refugee doctors? We do not know him yet. Uncle Hugh had him a couple of times, then went to the hospital under Volovoire's care. He has had quite a time, but works some again.

Grandma has gone to Watertown for a little visit. We do not know just how long she will stay. I am sure it will be nice for her as well as for us just now. Ellis called her on the phone one evening just before she went. It did her a lot of good to hear his voice.

Ernestine and Billy have been here since a week ago Sunday. Teen is pretty well now and Bill gets rosier and better natured in a few days here because he goes out to play so much more here. He is not very crazy about Cindy because she is too crazy about him. He has gone home with Jan and John tonight. They have talked about it before and he was eager to go.

Clyde came Sat. and took Alton to Lowville for the week-end. Merrill was home too.*

You asked about Len A. The family had not heard since X'mas until a few days ago. He had arrived in N. Africa. Lincoln goes in the latest draft, also Bob Kornatowski, and Donald Hume. "Denny" Doran is at Parris Is. Janice & John have had a couple of letters from Phil F. in Newfoundland. Howard Chapman is there too. Mick is in Ireland.

Love,
Mom

―――――――――

*Clyde was Altie's father; Merrill was Clyde's brother.

―――――――――

Jan writes that she is excited about Bob's furlough, and she wants Ted to know how wonderful married life is for the newlyweds.

―――――――――

Sunday
Jan. 30

Dear Ted –

I don't know why you should apologize for not writing to thank us for the small bit of Christmas we sent you. At the time I meant to write and tell you it was coming, etc, but there was so much put before me at that time I missed fulfilling my intentions.

I'm awfully glad you and "the hungry wolves" you must live with enjoyed the cookies and I wish I'd filled a bigger box for you. I made five different kinds of cookies 2 different afternoons and there still are some in the house. They are staler than all get out now. Family tradition – blah!

As you probably remember to-day (I think) is Dad's birthday. I should have called up home today but either I've been busy or someone has been listening to the radio. This evening Clara and I went for a walk down to Markham's (Claron's, you know) and stopped in at McGovern's. The sun set up beautiful to-nite and all day the sun has been bright. It seemed so good after the foggy and rainy weather we've had this past wk.

Last Wednesday night Johnnie and I went over home to get "all the dope" on Bob's furlough. Golly – it's almost too grand to be true but we expect he'll be coming anytime now and I certainly hope he'll be able to find you on his way home. There are a great many things for him to tell us – I imagine – but whether he will or not is another matter.

Dad and Willie expect to have his car in the best working order and are getting the license before he arrives. Johnnie has some extra gas coupons and Dad too, I guess, so he should be able to travel quite a bit if he chooses. If I know Bob he'll be on the road quite a bit. It's too bad Chet Freeman's furlough wasn't a little later so he & Bob could have gotten together.

Have you had any news yet about your furlough? It certainly seems to me that this is the logical time for the army to want to hand out furloughs. Isn't your C.O. a good guy? Couldn't I send him a box of fudge or cookies with your compliments? Ha.

You asked how we love-birds were getting along. Johnnie and I get along fine and have loads of fun and think every young couple that doesn't marry certainly misses a lot in life. It certainly is an awful mark against the governments & nations of the world that they can't give more young people the opportunity we have, the chance to make a decent life of our own. Must close now. Will try to write again sooner.

Love,

Jan

In some brotherly advice, Bob tells Ted that he needs to get a "mental adjustment" in order to deal with what feels like training inertia. Bob is going to try to get that furlough for Ted.

Turin

Feb. 4

Dear Ted,

Yes, I'm home again and it certainly feels good. So far I haven't been able to accomplish anything except sleep a lot and visit with everybody. Mother showed me your letter of Jan. 24. They haven't quite known what to do about your situation and have asked me to decide. I'll go to Lowville this afternoon and see the Red Cross people and let you know if anything develops.

I'm sure I know how you feel tho I probably never had to take quite that much. We had a couple of spells down in Atlanta when there was nothing to do and everybody was ready to go over the hill.

I personally think you would be ahead to see it through tho and be on hand when things do happen. There will be a lot of waiting in any type of military organization while you are training. It has been nearly two years for me and I'm just beginning to be useful. The fellows who can take the most and eventually do the most good are the ones who find something that's fun wherever they go and forget the things they left behind. It's pretty much a problem of mental adjustment. Do all you can to get mentally and physically ready but don't let it worry you.

You know that you want to get home, but the traveling would take most of your time and energy and in the long run it wouldn't be worth it unless you could get a couple of weeks at least.

I'm not saying we won't try for you but that's the way I see it. I'll make a definite effort to see you when I head back west so if you don't get home be sure to keep me informed of your location and the chances I would have to see you. I am due back in San Diego on the 29th and will try to fly. I'll leave here plenty early. If you go to Santa Ana I'll have an excellent chance to see you. If you go to the central or northern Texas it won't be too difficult and I might even be able to get somewhere near Mississippi.

From S.D. I might go to Alameda to reform the squadron or possibly to Washington again – we can't be sure yet. I hope to get back into 137 and fly the PV.2 and I have a fair chance of doing that.

I'll give you the details on my leave later and in the meantime we will see what we can do for you. It won't be any fantastic story tho for that wouldn't help you in the long run nor make you any happier.

So long for now
Bob

There is a one-month gap in the letters now. Ted was able to get a lengthy furlough, spend time with Peggy, catch up with Bob, and relax at home. He and Peggy stayed with Marian and Mr. Baxter for a few days while they were in Ithaca.

Ted, Peggy, and Bob at Cornell

Ted and Bob at Cornell

Bob at home, February 1944

157

The furlough is over, and once more, Evelyn has had to say goodbye to her soldier sons. Burt has received a questionnaire from the draft board.

MRS. ERNEST L. MARKHAM

BOX 143

TURIN, NEW YORK

Turin, N.Y.

Mar.3, '44

Dear Ted,

We found some more of your things, so I am sending them today along with some cookies, etc.

We hope you had a nice time at Williamsport and a good trip back. Have you gotten rested again?

And we hope it did you as much good to get home as it did us to have you here. The memory of your being here will cheer us through many a long day – how well you looked, what fun you seemed to have with the youngsters, the dogs, milking the cows and even cutting wood!

Willis drove Bob to Syracuse on Saturday evening and made a safe return though there was a fine rain, freezing on. We had a card back from Bob from Chicago, nothing since, as yet.

Burton received his questionnaire a few days ago, so he and Mr. Petzolt (spelling?) came up to see the draft board. Melrose came too, leaving Linda with Marian. They came just before supper time Wednesday, the men went to Lowville that evening, all went again next morning, back to lunch and then were off before twelve-thirty. There was not much time to visit but it was good to see them. Burt's number has not been called and he does not know the outcome of his visit, as yet.*

Mr. Klossner is sick again. They had the doctor Sunday and he said it was almost pneumonia. They sure have had a bad time with colds and grip. It seems that some of them have been sick all winter. Shirley went up to help Janice what she could on Monday, Tuesday and Wednesday nights from school. Dad and I must go this evening if possible.

---

*All men registered for the draft were issued a number. Draftees were called by number in the order of a random lottery system.

The mail takes Dad a little longer these past few days. The Brenon road is not plowed and the sun has made it bare in many places. The concrete and other hard roads are nearly all bare.

Hope we'll hear from you soon.

Love, Mom

Marian writes of playing cards, feeding the squirrels, and helping Mr. B shop for a new house. In a rare complaint, she does some venting about the difficulty of collecting child support for Alton.

Mar. 12

Dear Ted,

I'll write tonight but may not mail it for a couple days. I have the film I took pictures on when you were here down to be developed so may hold it. I wrote Peg and enclosed the pictures she wanted and will wait to send some to her. I just remembered I only ordered one print (I'm a dope) so I'll send your pictures separate.

I guess I haven't much news – we don't do much. I had my last wisdom tooth out this week. This one seems O.K. and I'm afraid I'll live.

Week before last Burt, Mel & Petzold went to see Lewis Co. draft board. Burt was put in 1-A.* Mel's feeling pretty bad about it. Guess the reason I don't have much patience is because the war is nearly 3 yrs. old for me. Believe it or not I finally got a check from the gov't. I got one last year and then Clyde's rank changed and it stopped. I guess 1st Sergeant's pay is supposed to be enough to take decent care of a family. I'd like to know how much it is. Could you find out for me?

Enough griping – don't mean to. Anyway while B & M went up home Linda stayed with me. She was awfully good. She likes it here anyway – is always teasing to come. Now she teases to go Mamie's house – have bubble bath. She still calls Mr. B. "Grandpa." She invited him to put on a "tie-tie." And in the afternoon invites me to put on "pretty dress." Guess it would do me good to have her all the while.

---

*1-A = most fit to be drafted status.

Mon. A.M. I had to stop and play pinochle last night. We've kept score since we came down last fall and the last few nights, Mr. B. has been sneaking up on me. He got 2 games out of 3 last night.

I had a letter from Teen the other day. She said Bill is singing "Maresy Doats." I'll bet that's good.

If this sounds mixed up, it's because I stop to feed the grey squirrels. There's one that comes when I call him – even up the side of the house to our window sill. He took a nut right from my hand the other day.

We enjoyed having Peg & you and Bob come. I hope Peg's mother wasn't shocked that she stayed here with you boys. Neither Mrs. Weigard nor Mr. B. could see anything wrong. Mrs. W. said folks that make anything out of situations like that have nasty minds.

I must get dressed to go out with Mr. B. & a real estate agent to look at houses. The moths are driving me crazy. The latest things they've picnicked on are my velvet dress and the blankets I'm using on my bed.

I'll mail this and send your pictures later in the week. I'm sending some clippings. You might pass the one about Joe Taylor on to Bob.

Love,
Marian

Burt writes that they are all "up in the air" over his unexpected classification and the possibility that he will be sent to war.

---

varna apartments
ithaca, n. y.

m e l r o s e , b u r t , a n d l i n d a s a y :

March 13, 1944

Dear Ted,

Plenty has been happening around here since you were home.

I got another "questionnaire" from the draft board about a week after you were here, so Mr. Petzold thought we should go & see them about a deferment. We didn't get very far & I got my 1-A a few days later. Mr. P. has appealed the case & I go for a physical next week. They sure aren't wasting any time. I don't know how long before my case comes up to the appeal board but I imagine it will be in about two weeks. I made an inquiry about a commission in the navy but my eyes aren't up to it.

Went all up in the air about the whole affair and don't know when we'll get our feet down again. They may turn me down next week on my physical. Frankly it wouldn't hurt my feelings in the slightest to be 4-f.*

Not much news around these parts except what I've already spilled. We were glad you could be here for a couple of days but wish that we could have spent more time with you.

Burt

Evelyn assures Ted that his February visit was wonderful for them all.

MRS. ERNEST L. MARKHAM

BOX 143

TURIN, NEW YORK

March 17

Dear Ted,

As usual, you've been better about writing than we have. We received your third letter [not included] since you went back, also the two money orders.

Didn't I tell you that you need not pay back what we sent for you to come home on? And we have not received any bill for the phone except to Wmsport, which was only $.85. It was worth fully that to us to have you come home.

In one of your letters, you said probably you had not been very good company when you were here – "pretty demoralized", you said. Of course you were tired when you first came, and we had known you were fit to be tied from having nothing to do. Who wouldn't be that way? And when an aggressive youngster like you thinks he is getting nowhere, – why if he does not get homesick and maybe worse things, it wouldn't be human nature. It just did us good too when you talked about it and sort of got it out of your system. You were just our own Ted come home to us and

---

*The 4-F draft classification eliminated many for physical defects.

we love you all the more for your frankness and for just being yourself. I can still see you in my mind's eye, milking the cows, playing with Billy, romping with the dogs and always with your old happy smile. You did us all worlds of good, really and truly, and we just somehow feel more hopeful and cheerful about everything lately. Dad, Willis and I seem to have lost some of the old tension and apprehension and we seem to have better understanding and teamwork. Willis is surely feeling different. He and Johnny are talking over plans for helping each other with the coming season's work.

By the way, Mr. Klossner is better than he was, but not very fit for work. They all seem to be as proud as Punch of the little calf.* They say she is growing nicely. John calls her, "Theodora." We must get her registered.

Willie had to go to Boonville today to help Fay get a car home, so I had him deposit that $10.00 you sent.

Grandma expects, any day now to go to stay with Mrs. Ward. Mary Lee lives with her mother, you know, and she wants to go to Evelyn's to stay a couple of weeks or so while Evelyn goes to the hospital. By the time she leaves Mrs. Ward, Mother hopes to go to her own house.

It has been raining lately and the snow is like a wet sponge. The robins and killdeer haven't come yet but we expect them every morning. Don K. has tapped his trees but has not boiled.

Had a letter from Burt. Guess he will go unless Petzold's appeal succeeds. But I guess it won't be a calamity. We must just keep all our chins up. All will be well.

Love,
Mom

Willis has his deer head home. Nice job. The wood shield was made in Williamsport, Pa.

You know, don't you that Bob's address is the same as before. Probably you've heard from him. Please send on this clipping to him.

Phoebe has a little bull.

---

*Ted gave the Klossners a calf, born to a cow that he owned.

Ted writes that he will be shipped again, this time to Maxwell Field just a few miles away from his current location.

C. A. A. F.
COLUMBUS, MISS.

March 19, 1944

Dear Folks,

I should have written a couple of days ago. There isn't much news to relate, but what I have may be of some consequence.

I expect that we will be shipping out of here about the time you get this letter, so it will be best for you to hold my mail until you hear from me again. We expect that we are bound for Maxwell Field. It will be a relief to ship only a few miles instead of several hundred. Troop trains often get a bit monotonous to ride because they are considerably slower than other trains.

I wonder what has happened to my Boonville Herald. I believe Dad told me that it was a year's subscription. It hasn't come since the week I went on my furlough.

Have you heard from Bob? I have anxiously awaited word from him but I guess that he must be pretty busy.

I wonder what has happened to the letters from Willie, Blondie, and Altie lately. It seems ages since I have heard from them, except Blondie's valentine. Do I owe you letters? I don't have a very accurate system of keeping track of who I owe letters to at home, but I do keep track of letters from others than those from home or I would forget a lot of them.

The next few months are going to be the toughest of my training days, I believe. Pre-Flight and Primary will be days of pretty hard work and many disappointments. Since they reduced the size of this cadet program, reports have been reaching us of boys actually quitting and requesting a washout in these places. Washouts in these two phases of training have

163

been running at about 50% lately. I shall never quit but realize that good luck must be with me in order to prevent elimination. Pre-Flight is a period of academics, military training, and flying.

It was a year ago today when you informed me that my notice to appear for active duty reached you.

Love,
Ted

Spring 1944

Ted has finally arrived at Maxwell Field for his Pre-Flight training. He writes of some interesting accommodations.

U. S. ARMY AIR FORCES
MAXWELL FIELD, ALA.

March 24, 1944

Dear Folks,

We arrived here at Maxwell Field early this morning. Since that time the upper class has been riding us so fast that we haven't had much of a chance to get a note off to our folks. Maxwell Field, for your information is at Montgomery, Ala. Along with another air base, Gunter Field. It is headquarters for the Eastern Training Command, has Pre-Flight for pilots, navigators, and bombardiers, and also has a transition B24 flying field. Before Nashville (NAAC) was established cadets were classified here as Pete was. Before the war it was a permanent camp for tactical flying training, and as a result we find many of the buildings here of stucco construction and of Old Spanish style. Since the war, new temporary buildings have been erected resulting in a more crowded and dustier camp than was CAAF.

We are all pretty tickled to have gotten here, though we realize that these nine weeks here will probably be as tough as any phase of our training. When we ran abreast with the upperclass as we stepped off the train this morning, we realized that we had not been misled when told that this place is rough. The training here will dwell on military training and academics in more concentrated form than we had at C.T.D. It is going to be rugged, and a lot of us will never get through, but it will be so much better than waiting.

Again I have left a lot of buddies and have new ones to make. None of my three roommates did I previously know. However our squadron and barracks is full of fellows whom I know from Williamsport and Columbus. We have also run into some of the boys classified as Nav. in Nashville who have completed their training here and are ready for shipment.

You have probably read in the past few days of the Air Corp returning men from their ground forces and cadets to the Infantry. I guess that we just got in under the wire for a pile of fellows behind us will be getting the gate for reasons beyond their control. I guess it will mean cadets from basic training, CTD, and even fellows whom we left behind in pools. I sort of wonder what Willie has heard from Howard Cutter, and if he was unlucky enough to be caught by this order. From a broad point of view it is probably an asset to winning the war, but it is tough on the boys who have anticipated this training.

Our barracks are of wooden construction and we are presumably divided up into rooms by studding without the boards to effect a wall. It is comical that we have this studding without the sheathing and that we must treat the studding as a complete wall. (That is we cannot commute through the studding and must leave and enter the room through the doorway.) Chow is good but we cannot enjoy it, for the upper class is riding the devil out of us at all times to make sure that every movement is strictly at attention. (You cannot imagine the rules and faults found at a meal such as we have here.)

We had our hair cut short again today. It is comical to see all of your friends and buddies running around looking like clipped monkeys. It has to be cut short each week, not more than an inch long.

Well I must quit for now, for I seem to be running out of ideas and nearing the time for lights out.

Love,
Ted

Ted has written that nineteen of the men he started with in Williamsport have "washed out." Evelyn, as usual, looks for the positive in his long wait for training.

MRS. ERNEST L. MARKHAM
BOX 143
TURIN, NEW YORK

Turin, NY
April 1, 1944

Dear Ted,

It was good to get your letter telling where you are. I suppose you are rather relieved, though you will be much busier and may see many times when you will wish you could have saved up some of that leisure which became so monotonous. There is an old saying about everything having its virtues, so maybe that long period of waiting was to train your patience. Anyhow, we all hope for the best to come out of all these things.

Grandpa has been quite sick. He really should have been taken to the hospital but was so helpless when we realized. Ethel took over as nurse (She knew what to do from having done it before). Hugh and Dad were strong to lift and turn him. I could do the washings, make broth, etc., and Clara took care of him when the rest of us weren't there. It was the old kidney trouble.

He is better now, so he can get out of bed with Clara's help, but was as helpless as a baby.

Grandma went, over a week ago, to stay with Mrs. Ward for a few days. Then she will go to her own home. I think she will be happier because she will get out and see more people and will be more independent. She has failed more mentally than physically since last year.

Have we told you that Gladys has a son, William Raymond, born March 18th at St. Luke's? He weighed 9 lb. 11 oz.! Some boy! They will all be very proud and happy, including Grace.

Ray Miller was home from Monday night, I think, until yesterday morning. He came to see us Thursday evening. His face is as round as a full moon. Looks fine.

166

Spring 1944

The Anthony Kraegars have bad news. Bob is missing in action – over Rabaul, they think.* We can only hope they will get good news again as the Websters did.

No word from Claron** lately, but no news is supposed to be good news and there are several boys from Lowville in the Eighth Air Force and no news is coming from any of them.

We have not heard from Bob since that letter when he first reached the coast. We are also awaiting the news about Burt's appeal and physical exam.

Marian wanted Shirley and Alton to visit her during Easter vacation but I guess they are not going. Shirley is going to help Ernestine a little and Marian will be coming in a month. Teen and Bob have leased a little house, partly furnished on Lanpher St. in Lowville and are moving in. They were here last Sunday – all looking fine. I expect to go to Boonville Monday. Will give your new address to the Herald. Did you notify the Reader's Digest of the change?

Dad says to tell you that Belle has a fine heifer a week ago and Doc is working on Cymbie.

We are trying to make a little syrup but the wintry weather hangs on. Only the roads are bare.

Robins came a week ago, but disappeared.

Love from everybody,
Mother

---

*Robert Kraegar, a classmate of Ted's, was killed in the southwest Pacific when Allied forces attacked a Japanese base on the island of New Britain. His sister, Kate, was Will's girlfriend.

**Claron = "Pete" Markham.

Ted is still at Maxwell Field, and Jan writes of goings on at home and on the farm. He has given them a Jersey calf, and she wants him to know how much they appreciate it. She has some sisterly advice concerning Ted's love life.

Sunday night
Apr. 16

Dear Ted,

I've been wanting to write you but waited for your new address. The folder you sent was nice and the buildings look much stronger and more comfortable than most. I noticed your Headquarters Building resembles that at Rome a great deal but the others at Rome don't begin to compare.

Pop, Johnnie and I went over home for dinner today. We had a great visit. Bob, Teen, Billy & Shirley came just as we were ready to eat so we set some more places and all stuffed ourselves. We had sugar on snow for dessert and it sure tasted good. Mother has boiled down over 20 qt. of syrup this year and it certainly is nice. Everyone seems to be having good luck with it this year but are having such a time getting help. Bob O'B. said a worker gets $6.00 a day for boiling syrup. (P.S. that is a laugh about your worry over our wanting the calf. It's a pride to us. Pop thinks the world of it & it grows like a weed.)

Johnnie is busy working on mastitis lately and just got some of the blotter recently and today Dad gave him some of the liquid you brought home with you. Blue Test you know. To-night he has put drops of the Blue Test liquid on a regular blotter & to-morrow will try it & see if it works that way as well as in a test tube, although he also has recently bought test tubes. Johnnie wants me to ask you if you know where he could get more of the brom-thymol liquid after his is gone. Also he wonders if you could give him some references at Cornell to write to for information on mastitis. He's been reading & trying everything he ever heard of.

I'm so glad you finally got to Flight School although of course we realize they are snapping fellows out of such for the infantry all of the time. But hope your luck turns the other way. Willie has been deferred again & probably his status is pretty certain now.*

Everyone at home seems to be feeling so good lately. Altie is getting fat as a pig & Billy, too. Mother says Altie is much better natured too. So perhaps his appetite is doing away with his sensitiveness.

---

*Men in occupations considered essential to the war effort (e.g., farmers) were often exempt from the draft.

Dad took the truck to Watertown yesterday P.M. & came back on the bus. He is going to stay at home for a few days & help Willie get caught up at home.

Shirley was up at Teen's in Lowville this vacation to help her scrub & get settled. I suppose you know Teen & Bob found a house. Friday Johnnie & Don had business in L'ville & so Marion R. & I went along to visit Teen. They have a nice little house that has been fixed up cleverly but was awfully dirty. (Furnished)

Marion R. has a teaching job in West Leyden next year. Kindergarten & 1st grade + music in all the grades. It will be hard but nice that she is so near home. One of the girls she has lived with while in school has a job here at C'ville teaching primary. I know her quite well.

Ted – you hinted in your last letter about an engagement for you & Peggy. It's probably very true that most girls who are really in love like some definite proof from the other party that she isn't just wasting her time but Ted after all perhaps there are other ways you could show your appreciation without such a great step as a ring, etc. It is very true there is really no great hurry to settle down and there are many things to talk over & make plans for before such a step. You never can talk about your families too much because they are there and can't be shaken sometimes.

Well enough of this. Take this advice or forget it – that's up to you.

Love,
Jan

Marian writes about her busy life in Ithaca. She is not only Mr. B's housekeeper but his social hostess as well. In keeping with Jan's sisterly advice, Marian has some suggestions for Ted concerning his romantic life.

Sun. Nite
Apr. 16

Dear Ted,

I owe you so many letters it's awful. For some reason or other I keep quite busy. This last week I've hardly sat down. A week ago Fri. a.m.

Bob Neill came on the bus. Then the two Harolds came for lunch.* The boys stayed all night and Bob left on the afternoon bus. Mr. Fain (Mr. B's C.P.A. from Roch.) came on the 6:08 bus, he & two Harolds here for supper. Only Mr. Fain for overnight and next day (Easter).

Harold Jr. is on furlough. They discontinued training meteorologists and put him down in Amarillo, Texas. He was there about two weeks, then transferred to Air Transport Command at Los Vegas, New Mexico and a 3 week furlough before reporting. He stood for 16 hrs. coming home. Then an elderly couple with a compartment let 4 fellows sleep in their upper berth. Mr. B. bought a plane ticket to Chicago for his trip back. He was advised not to try it all the way.

To get back to my program last week. Monday I ironed (week before I couldn't wash 'til late because Mrs. W. used laundry). Tues. p.m. went to town, had my hair done, shopped, ate down to Joe's and went to see "Snow White".

Wed. a.m. 7:30 we left for Rochester to see Aunt Em. She has angina and isn't a bit good. She's lost about 20 lbs. and is very short of breath and can't eat. Her eyesight is about gone now. It rained most of the way up and turned to snow so we started back about 2:30. Mr. & Mrs. Savocol were with us and went to see his sister. There was about 4 in. of wet snow when we started home. Mr. B. stopped at the Sagamore Hotel and saw the two Harolds. Then I wanted to go to Strong Memorial Hospital to see Mother Dewan. She had gone home but I saw Geraldine a few minutes. Said Mother was getting along all right. She had skin grafts from both legs and 18 Xray treatments.

We got in town about 6:30 and went to Joe's to eat. The Savocols are good company.

Thurs. I cleaned and Loretta came that night. The next a.m. took her downtown to meet Henry. Then we shopped for groceries, ate at Joe's and I shopped some more while Mr. B. had a dental appointment. I got a pinafore and a white wool skirt. I'm so pleased with the skirt. It really fits (as no other I ever had did). It is size 9 and I'd always had size 12 before. No wonder they didn't fit. We stopped at Stuarts' a little while on the way home. Mr. B & Mr. S. had a little pinochle. Mr. S. expects to go on duty soon in quartermaster on the hill. He's pretty tickled. Fri. night I went to

---

*Mr. B's son, Harold, and grandson, Harold, Jr.

Home Bureau. Sat. we went to Stuarts' for dinner and the afternoon. Today we went to Elmira, met the Tates at the Langwell Hotel for dinner and then over to his brother George's for a little while. He is pretty sick with ulcers of the stomach. Then we went to their son's a few minutes and on home.

Maybe you can see how I can be busy when a few meals, a little sewing, mending etc. are sandwiched in. Tomorrow I've got a whale of a washing; Tues. 2 dental appointments. I should start tearing things apart this week to leave for the summer. Mr. B. wants to leave in about two weeks. I'll step some if I make it.

Burt had his physical in Syr. a week last Wed. His urinalysis had albumen so they kept him overnight. (You don't suppose he was out the night before?) The P.C. had a meeting there day before and he stayed up. They (exam board) put about 12 in a room at the Onondaga with one coat hanger among them. He came in on the bus the next p.m. pooked. I'd talked with Mel the night before. She was sitting feeling bad for them all. She called the next day to say Burt was back and had been classified for limited service because he has only 10% of vision. She was quite smug about the fact he'd probably be deferred. I laughed when she said Burt was pooked and said to tell him he couldn't take it. That made her mad. As for my impressions of Peg, I like her very much. I think she's very sweet and sincere. Of course the short times I've seen her haven't been enough to get acquainted with anyone as quiet as she is. But I definitely approve. You said she meets your specifications. In my opinion you don't need to look any farther. I have only one comment. Don't tie her down till after the war. She wrote me something about going out with some other "war widows". That's no life for a girl her age. Maybe it's her preference now but it will get pretty dreary. You'll believe me when I say I know all about it. There are a lot of things a girl can't do without an escort. So, I think you should urge her to have a good time. And you do the same.

Thanks for the information about 1st Sgts. I've gotten $90 for Alton now and am in hopes it will continue. I feel quite rich. I knew Clyde was getting more than he ever had but the law wouldn't let me do anything about it and he has no sense of honor or responsibility. He knows I'll do what he doesn't.

I must get to bed. I guess Bob is on the west coast – he's Lt. J.G. now.*

*Lieutenant Junior Grade.

Forgot to mention it first time. By the way, I'm anxious to get my silver wings (to wear on my black dress with silver buckles). I'm going to be busy so don't expect a letter.

Love,
Marian

Mr. B sends his best.
Aunt Em wanted to be remembered to you.
If Burt goes in the army, Mel is going home.
Mr. B thinks Peg is swell and she'll always be welcome with us.
I'm looking for a new niece any time. [Ernestine's big event is coming soon.]

Bob writes from California where he has been enjoying the perks of being single, at the same time wishing he could see more of Rita, a Lewis County girl and Chet Freeman's sister-in-law. He met Rita while on furlough in February.

U. S. NAVAL AIR STATION
ALAMEDA, CALIFORNIA

May 3

Dear Ted,

I have meant to write sooner but somehow I haven't gotten around to writing much since I got back out here. We seem to spend all our time working together or fooling around together.

I don't know how much you know about our new setup. Jack Porter who was our executive officer before is now the skipper of the squadron and there are eleven of us who came back to the squadron with him. We were all second pilots before except two and the gang was picked by the skipper so we know we can all get along together. It was a good break to be one of the gang for some of the people who were dropped by the wayside aren't too well fixed at present. The "Old Man" was willing to do a lot for the people who did their job right but he was plenty rough with the others.

Of course we have a lot of new people now – enough for 18 crews and we are beginning to work pretty much like a squadron. There are some senior lieutenants who have been instructors so that those (jg)s who have had fleet experience will have to be second pilots for awhile at best. We are all getting training to qualify as pilots tho and I think I have a little edge over three of the new men. It doesn't worry me anyway.

We have been able to do quite a bit of flying tho our new planes are awfully slow in coming through. These light training planes seemed awfully funny at first but they really get up and go and it's more fun to scoot around here than it was to run patrols. It doesn't look now as tho we will get the PV.2s but there is still a possibility. They are coming off the line now and I had a chance to look them over when I went through the plant a few weeks ago. Saw one take off and land too. They are somewhat longer, have nearly 10 ft. more wing span and larger tail surface but mainly they have been changed to make them easier to fly. We aren't too sure they would be better except for night work or instrument flying. They are a little slower than the 1s (ones). We expect to have a chance to try one in a couple of weeks. We will have some new equipment that leads us to believe we might do a lot of night work and for that I think we would be better off with the more stable plane.

Have had quite a bit of fun since I came back out here. Spent a couple of days in Hollywood with those gals I knew there when I first came out. They met us at the plane in the middle of the night in fact. Went back down for a weekend last month too. They were a lot of fun and I really saw the sights in LA, Hollywood and Beverly Hills, then saw the Lockheed Plant. Of course I was in San Diego to check in before coming to Alameda and saw a lot of old friends there.

We really have a great gang and four of us who are single have had a great time. I find however that I'm not as rugged as I was once and have to take it pretty easy sometimes – lost some weight while on leave and have a bit of trouble keeping in condition. Of course now we are out in the valley east of Alameda at a small auxiliary station so there is little to do except fly. There is lots of sunshine too – in fact it's getting to be pretty hot and dry.

Rita Schoff, 1944

This is a pretty rich agricultural valley tho everything has to be irrigated. They grow quite a bit of fruit, alfalfa, and beans. Also some of this plant they get rubber from – I've forgotten the name of it. There are quite a few cattle here too for they can use the hilly slopes for pasture in winter and keep them in feed lots or irrigated pasture in summer. There are some fairly good looking dairy herds too.

We are near a little burg called Crows Landing which is about the size of Turin or smaller so the base is named after it. Most of the villages around here are strictly rural but quite different than around home for the people are largely Portuguese or Swedes. Quite a combination.

I haven't heard from home recently, probably because I haven't written much. Had a letter from Marian saying that Burt will probably be called soon. Thought from something Mother had said that he might be deferred a little longer.

I have heard from Rita quite regularly but she is so busy she doesn't have time to dig up much gossip. Darn if I really wish she was out here. We could have a good time. She is a pretty nice sort of gal in case you didn't know it. I had several nice times with one of the gals in Hollywood but she has gone back to Illinois now.

We can usually fly over to the city for our day off and mostly we are free to come and go as we please as long as we do everything that we are scheduled for and keep the work going smoothly. It's not such a tough life even tho there is little around here that is really interesting.

Write when you can and I'll try to be more prompt next time.

As ever
Bob

Burt and Mel's hopes for a deferment are gone now. Burt is on his way to Fort Dix in about a month. He writes to Ted about the difficulties of leaving their apartment, but most of all, he is worried about saying goodbye to Linda.

varna apartments
ithaca, n. y.

melrose , burt , and linda say :

May 9, 1944

Dear Ted,

It's been quite a while since you wrote and a lot has happened since then. I've had my physical, been accepted by the Army, marked for a "special assignment" (whatever that is) and am going about the middle of June. I'll go from Ithaca and I suppose to Fort Dix for induction. From there you know as much as I.

As yet I've not definitely made up my mind what I'd like to do but I've an idea the ground forces of the Air Corp might interest me. There's not much choice about the matter now I guess since they have abandoned many of the training programs.

It seems there are a thousand little things to take care of before I go. I guess the longer you have a family the more there are. We plan on moving our things out to Fillmore as soon we hear the date.* Mel and Linda are staying there. I'll work up to the last minute for a couple of reasons but mainly so we'll have that much more of a financial reserve.

This moving thing has its problems. What to keep, what to sell, what to give away & what to throw away. We're selling our refrigerator after much debate and some other things that are hard to move. We're going to Lewis Co. with some things this week-end & say our good-byes.

They hired a fellow today to take my place. He's a little past sixty but there's not much to choose from. I have the assurance of my job back when I come back and the whole bunch, directors & all, are giving us a party next week.

---

*Mel's family lived in Fillmore.

I think the hardest part about the whole thing is leaving Linda. It isn't that I don't care for Mel as much as ever but she can understand and Linda will be just old enough to know I'm gone but not old enough to understand where or what.

She's getting to be quite a girl now and worse than ever to handle. This morning about 4 o'clock I felt something crawling around the bed & a little girl crawled in between us. I guess she decided she wanted a bed fellow. She can get out of her crib now so we have to put her to bed about 5 or 6 times before she goes to sleep.

Burt and Linda at Jan's wedding.

Well, this is getting to be quite a letter for me but I guess I've kind of run out so I'll say good bye for now.

Burt

Ted writes to Evelyn telling her that he will be thinking of her on Mother's Day.

U. S. ARMY AIR FORCES
MAXWELL FIELD, ALA.

May 10, 1944

Dear Mom,

I'm over my head in business tonight, so this will have to be short. I'm awfully sorry that I don't have a card to send you for Mother's Day.

It seems that they didn't have any at the PX, and I forgot to get one when I had an opportunity to buy one in town last weekend. I hope that you will understand just the same and feel that I at least had good intentions. I want to say that I'll be thinking of you regardless.

Our training has kept us jumping pretty hard lately. The routine has let up a lot, but the miscellaneous subjects and requirements have flooded us lately. We're getting pretty well caught up though and feel that we have definitely accomplished something here and see a light ahead.

We just finished our Gunnery School today by firing the .45 Pistol on the range. (The same as that which Bob had home with him.) It was really my first good chance to fire for an official qualification, even though I had fired most of the small arms previously. I qualified for "Sharpshooter" with the pistol and frankly feel as if I know how to handle it by now. It is no great feat but rather a measure of your experience and familiarity with the weapon. Most of our boys made at least "Marksman" and one shot is high as 96%. (He wasn't from Texas either.) That is some score for a fellow who has handled the gun so little. There are only two or three highly experienced range instructors who have even beaten it here.

I finally got a letter from Bob last week. He seems to be at a nice base and has pretty nice privileges. The lucky devil can watch the agriculture of a Calif. Valley this spring.

I must quit now and hope to get a bit of work done before taps. These studies are sort of a pain-in-the-neck because they amount to little but yet must be done.

Love,
Ted

Evelyn writes to Ted with the welcome news of the birth of her fourth grandchild. Her grandchildren are her "greatest joy and comfort now."

MRS. ERNEST L. MARKHAM
BOX 143
TURIN, NEW YORK

May 18, '44

Dear Ted,

It was so nice to get your letter for Mother's Day. It means as much to me as any of the other cards, letters and gifts I received. That day reminds me how very rich and proud I am.

Melrose, Burton and Linda were here from Friday eve to Sunday afternoon. It was such a pleasure to have them only Burt is going away in a month and this was his last trip home. They will move the most of their belongings to Fillmore about June first. It seems hard, but we must just hope for the best. I think it will be good for Burt, physically, anyhow. Mel is looking like her old self again and Linda is just a lovely child.

And now we have the great news! Billy's "little sister" has arrived but is a boy.* Bill still says "she". He was born Tuesday morn at 5 o'clock at Mercy Hosp. Watertown. That's all we know as yet except that everything is O.K. Bob told me over the phone that he had heard nothing yesterday which was supposed to be good news and he was going down last night. Harold O'Brien is laid up with one arm in a sling which gives Bob about three times as much as usual to do. Teen has been very well lately and I have expected she would be all right.

Billy was here nearly all last week and is at O'Brien's now but we expect him back here soon. He is growing to be a very self-reliant little guy and I might fill a book, if I had time, with his original speeches. Oh, Ted, these grandchildren are the greatest joy and comfort to us now. Without them I don't know how we could bear these days. Altie is such a grand little sport. He is growing fast this spring and getting sturdier. He takes such pride in caring for the calves and yearlings. Do you know that he is raising Ellen's calf for his 4H heifer? He has been saying for some time that he is not going up to Old Forge to stay this summer. He is going to "stay home and help hay it." Marian seems resigned to the idea.

---

*David O'Brien was born on May 16.

178

Spring 1944

The cows and heifers (20 in all) went out to pasture this morning for the first time. The crazy things! We have left Bernice, Baroness's six month's old calf; Alton's calf, Eleanor; Billy's calf, heifer two months old (unnamed); Nell's little heifer, spotted, which Alton calls Norma. She is not such a hot looking one but her mother is doing well. We may sell her though. Yesterday we sold Phoebe's bull, 2 months old to Chris Beller of Croghan for $25. We get two full cans of milk twice a day.

It is so nice to hear what you are studying and doing. We finally had a letter from Bob written on his birthday and another short note for Mother's Day. He'll be going out on the Pacific again in a few weeks. Doesn't say much.

I banked the $50 for you the other day. I received one bond, just after you were home, but none since. It probably will come soon. Alton just got one.

I've finally got my dental work finished, I think, except to check up in a few days. It has taken a lot of running and fussing. It consists of two rather large pieces of bridgework and will, I think, serve me better than the partial plate we tried and found unsatisfactory. It is a lot of gold and probably will cost plenty though. Willis went with me and had an abscessed one pulled.

Spring seemed slow in coming but came all at once. Nearly everyone has finished oats and seeding. Ours has been wet ground but will be done soon. Corn ground is plowed and Dad is breaking up a piece in the pasture just above the north meadow. The apple blossoms are just coming out. We are having parsnips, greens, and rhubarb to eat.

I must close and try to write to Bob. Will let you know more about Teen and the baby soon.

Love,
Mom

Ted writes from Decatur, Alabama, that he is beginning primary training.

AIR CORPS TRAINING DETACHMENT
DECATUR, ALABAMA

May 25, 1944

Dear Folks,

We arrived here at Decatur last night. I can't spend but a minute to dash off a note but perhaps I can do better later in the week.

This is primary as you already presume. It is not strictly Army flying but rather a civilian organization which has an Army contract to teach us during these first 60 hours. Of course the immediate organization, administration and tactical dep't is Army – much as it was at Williamsport. This is the most critical phase so far as preventing elimination goes. The last class had 50% washouts and the class before it 55% while our present upper class has lost 20% already. However this doesn't defeat a one of us but rather makes us more anxious to try hard.

The surroundings make most of us feel about the same as I felt when I was shipped from Miami to Williamsport. The post is quite an ideal little post with most sorts of nice facilities. It seems just small enough and ideal enough to relieve us from the army atmosphere of most posts. It is far enough from town so that a thousand and one civilians aren't pestering us. We are about five miles north of Decatur on the north side of the Wheeler Reservoir which is a part of the TVA.* (I'll have more to say about the TVA for I hope to learn as much as I can about its activities before leaving.) The town looks as if it is not badly crowded with soldiers and everything in general looks quite pleasing. I'm sure going to do my best to be lucky enough to complete these ten weeks.

I must try to write later but this will at least serve to let you know of my whereabouts.

Love,

Ted

For Willie and Altie – I will probably fly the PT17(Stearman) or PT23(Ryan) or both.

---

*The Tennessee Valley Authority is a federal agency established during the Depression to construct dams and power plants in the Tennessee River basin. It brought electricity to thousands of rural Americans for the first time.

Ted with a PT-17, or Stearman

Ted writes that he met the local County Agent while he was still at Maxwell Field. He is worried that his progress in the air is too slow.

AIR CORPS TRAINING DETACHMENT
DECATUR, ALABAMA

June 4, 1944

Dear Folks,

I'm sorry that I haven't been able to write much of a letter in the past three weeks. We've been pretty busy during that time.

It's good to hear that spring's work has been going so well. I'm quite interested to learn what fields have been planted and how they were fertilized and seeded. Mom spoke of plowing up west of the north meadow. Did you plow up a chunk to lengthen the rows of that field? I'm particularly interested to learn how the Ladino clover is coming and how the alfalfa is competing with it in the seeding. Did you plant some this year, Willie?

It's also good to hear that Altie is growing such good calves. Keep at it Altie! You have got some calves there that should stand with the best in the barn or show ring. Have you definitely enrolled in the 4-H and are you going to keep records on how you feed Eleanor? Belinda sounds like a good name for Belle's calf.

About the nicest thing which has happened to me in a long time was a visit with the County Agent at Montgomery before leaving. Just as at times when I felt these people indifferent I found these people very, very hospitable. It was the Sunday before we left Maxwell when Clyde Hart and I set out to look up the County Agent here. He took us to his home to meet his wife and two sons and then proceeded to have a good bull-session about their extension programs here in Alabama. They took us out into the country and showed us a good herd of Herefords and the general lay out of their agriculture as it has descended from the plantation system. We really learned a lot about the agriculture in that immediate region and got a good idea of what progressive southern agriculture can be. They drove us around for most of the afternoon and then took us home with them for supper and more visiting. We simply had a very nice time and just couldn't get away from their over-hospitality until we had to get back to camp. It was the nicest day which I have yet spent here in the south.

With that tour and the train ride up here I have seen quite a few things about southern agriculture which I have never had a chance to see before. It is peculiar to see some crops being harvested and others just being planted. Flax, oats, barley and wheat have all been harvested or are ready for harvest now. Cotton and corn (their major crops) are just piercing the ground. It is queer that the corn is probably behind some regions of New York State. The best is only six or eight inches high now. Near Birmingham we saw several good peach orchards where the peaches were being picked already. Some places good looking dairy herds are found with some good looking Jerseys too. Jerseys are as universally kept here as Holsteins are in NYS because they can stand the heat of the summer and cold of the winter best. Yes, "cold of the winter" for the cattle are seldom shut up in the winter and have to endure weather that we wouldn't dream of. This is a good farming region right here for there are several good fields of alfalfa and wheat bordering our field. There are few fields of alfalfa here but where it will grow we find the south's best land. Easily ¾ of all of the land here is plowed each year to grow their cash crops – cotton, corn, flax, wheat – and it's only on dairy farms where we find much sodded land. Diversion ditches and terraces are very common because even a very gentle slope is badly eroded with so much fallow land and such downpours when it rains. However the farms which are doing well are those which are shifting to a system of crop rotation and try to grow some legume like alfalfa, vetch, crimson clover, lespedeza and pasture land. Vetch and crimson clover are the most common legumes for hay crops. In the pastures we find White Dutch Clover, Yellow-Trefoil (they call it Black Medic), California Burr-clover, Hop Clover, and several grasses, such as Dallas Grass, Brome Grass, Johnson Grass, and some Ky. Blue Grass. Their common weeds are often Dallas and Brome Grass, Yellow Dock, Primrose, and a daisy which they call Buttercups.

This is an unusually nice post here. We are north of Wheeler Reservoir about five miles from town. Practically everything here is under control with the Army even to the extent of our living quarters and mess hall. Chow here is absolutely the best that one can imagine. Unlike the sloppy, poorly prepared food which we've been so accustomed to, they take this dollar a day allowed for rations and put on a feed absolutely unequal to anything less than the Home Ec Cafeteria back at school. This establishment grew with the war, but instead of taking on an atmosphere of a military post, it is planned to turn to a civilian flying school after the war. It is owned by Southern Airways.

This flying is coming pretty slow for me. I have 5½ hours in here and can't at all be optimistic about getting through. It isn't that I couldn't get it eventually but rather that it now seems to be coming a little too slow to keep pace with present requirements. A few months ago, they needed pilots bad enough to spend more time with us but now you simply have to get it fast. These planes are Stearmans (PT-17's) or the same as that which Bob stands next to in the first picture he had taken in his flying togs. I'm trying hard though so perhaps it might start breaking differently.

Ted shows off his new haircut at Maxwell Field

I read of Len Ackerman's misfortune in the Boonville Herald.* I hope that it is no worse than that. Lots of times it seems that our Army is pretty slow but they certainly aren't wasting life if there is a chance at all. I have long been convinced that our generals are leaving no stones unturned when it comes to saving those boys, and our medics are almost super-human in their ability to save them when there is any possible chance in the world.

I'm sending a few pictures taken back at Maxwell. They aren't very good but may give some small idea of our activity there. Incidentally, that is a "G.I." haircut. Sometime when you are sending a package to me I wonder if you would dig out my snapshot album and send it. I don't know where to tell you to look for it.

I must quit now and try to write some more letters.

Love,
Ted

P.S. Could it be that Willie, Shirley, and Altie as well as Dad have forgotten how to write?

---

*Sgt. Len Ackerman was wounded in combat while serving in Italy.

Ted writes with some exciting news.

June 11, 1944

Dear Folks,

I'm sending a $45 money order to be banked if you would. It sounds like quite a little with last month's $50, but I drew out $30 from last month to help out one of my friends and to get me through into this month. It's sort of foolish to send money to be banked and then withdraw it like that but sometimes it's worth it to help out a friend and make sure someone doesn't steal it. It seems as if my bond from April should have come through and May's by this time.

The big news from me is the fact that I soloed yesterday. It was quite a feeling and quite an inspiration after having a whole week of uncertain progress. I was pretty down in the dumps before yesterday morning because I just couldn't seem to progress and was afraid of elimination had it continued for a couple more days. Yesterday wasn't a terrible big break in making progress, but it did seem awfully significant in comparison with previous days. Soloing is just one milestone and by no means a big one but it gives me another to look to when the 20 hr. check comes along. I have 10 hrs. now and will have a lot of hard work to get by the 20 hr. check.

It is a great feeling to have the instructor unbuckle his safety belt, jump out, and point his thumb skyward. Yesterday we flew over to one of the auxiliary fields to short landings and take-offs. I was pretty determined and set the plane in three times and take off without fault. After the third landing he grabbed the controls and began taxiing like mad for the side of the field where he jumped out and gave me the high sign. He didn't have much of a chance to get out of the "prop-wash" before I had jammed the throttle forward to taxi down to the runway. Then was the time when I made three more landings and take-offs with the most precision that I

185

After about 10 hours of dual instruction in Primary School, the instructor tells this cadet to fly off on his own, his first solo in a naval trainer. Instructors constantly practice, so they will be ready when needed for combat.

This picture and its caption, published in National Geographic *during the war, illustrate the moment Ted has just described.*

ever had. It's quite a feeling to listen to those 220 horses beat away at the air without anyone in the forward cockpit. Whether or not it is of any importance it certainly uncovered two faults which have hindered me. I haven't been confident enough, and it has been too easy to feel that he would correct me no matter how well I flew.

I've just felt like a happy kid since yesterday. It isn't because I want to fly so badly but because I felt some improvement after a lot of hard discouraging work.

I forgot to tell you last Sunday that we saw Donald Nelson here the previous week. It seems that he must have been touring the war industries about TVA and sought our mess hall for a banquet. It is a remarkable place for us to eat and probably the best to be chosen around this vicinity. Anyway they held their banquet in one corner while we ate our chow in another.

Spring 1944

The news this past week has been more encouraging.* Most of us were eager to hear it because it seemed to be something which sounds more progressive.

The news from Lewis Co. has been pretty sparse lately. I haven't even learned the name of my new nephew after nearly a month's time. I thought maybe Teen would write, but she hasn't. If it wasn't for Mom I wouldn't hardly know that the Markhams still existed. My brothers and sisters are uniform anyway; they're all poor at writing.

Love,

Ted

---

*On D-Day, June 6, 1944, the Allies invaded France.

Marian writes from Old Forge where she is back at work. She has just returned from Lowville, where she spent some time helping Ernestine with the new baby.

Sun. A.M. 8:25

June 18

Old Forge

Dear Ted,

Mr. B. had me read the letter he wrote [not in the collection] and it made me ashamed I hadn't written since we came up.

Of course I've been busy. Am not thru housecleaning yet. As Mr. Baxter told you, I took time off to help Teen. She didn't have anyone. She didn't ask me – I just went.

David is a lovely baby and Teen is fine. He weighed 7lb. 8oz. when born and the day he was three wks, weighed 8lb. 9oz. Bob said Billy wasn't so scrawny. Both Mom and I thot he'd forgotten. David was all wrinkles and I said – loose skin a well pup. Teen said that's what the doctor said. He's awfully strong. I never handled a small baby that was as active. He held his head up alone and steady. When he lay on his stomach he'd lift his head up three or four inches and look all around. He fussed a couple days and both of us thot he acted hungry and not like a stomach ache. We

187

wondered if he needed to eat oftener and then Teen remembered that the formula should be increased (in strength) according to how fast a baby gains. He was gaining about 2oz. a day. So she added a couple oz. of milk and decreased the water and he shut up in a hurry. He's an awful good baby.

The first morning he was home we were giving him his bath. I washed his eyes and forgot to warm the boric acid and it made him cry. So Billy got a fuzzy and tried to give it to him. Wasn't that cute?

One of the first things he wanted to know was why Mommy didn't get a big baby. He wouldn't let me say anything about the baby. If I said he was nice – he was jealous for fear I'd like him too much. If I said anything against him he was insulted.

One of the first mornings the baby was home Bill went downstairs and got in bed with Teen. She was trying to wake David up to have his bottle. Teen said he was a lazy, good-for-nothing baby. Bill said, "Yes, but Marian can't have him." I hadn't mentioned any such thing. Before I came home something was said about baby girls – Bill said Marian can have the girls. So I guess he's satisfied. Shirley wasn't! I think Bob was disappointed too. I told him better luck next time.

Shirley & Alton went to Lowville when Mr. B. took me down and Shirley just couldn't go home without seeing the baby.

In some ways Shirley is so grown-up and in some ways she's such a little girl yet. She only weighs 142 lbs. now – more than Willis, Bob O. or Johnny. She giggles about it.

She says Johnny is swell but he's so silly. Jan says he acts foolish just to hear her laugh.

Jan is awfully thin – 98 lb. (I weigh 105 now. Fat!) And she's working hard. Girls just starting out don't realize how much work there is to running a house. It's a big job and always more to learn. There's always more work to be done.

From all reports Jan is a good cook. She doesn't get time to sew. That's too bad. She had good training and ought to keep at it. I guess I do as much sewing as the other girls. Teen still does the nicest sewing but it drives her crazy.

I just killed a mosquito. They drove Mr. B. out of bed at 4 o'clock this a.m. and woke me up at six. I bet I killed 50 in my room before 7 when I got up. All the bugs are here in full force. Some of the lumber camps had to close they are so bad.

While I was down to Teen's a "Weekly Reader" magazine arrived for Alton c/o E.B. Baxter, Old Forge. He'd said he wasn't coming up – he'd have to help with haying. I told him the magazine let the cat out of the bag and he giggled. He is changing so much. He's so grown-up. And he's getting quite chunky. His legs are nearly as big as mine but just like Clyde's. And he has so many little mannerisms just like Clyde. He gave me to understand I couldn't lick him anymore. I didn't have time to demonstrate then but no doubt I'll have the dare again. I was beginning to wonder if I could. To hear me talk you'd think I pounded the child. A couple little swats were usually sufficient for him but he always knew who was boss. I've always realized I had to finish the job myself. So far I've kept on top. It sure takes some quick thinking and strategy to stay there sometimes. A child with a mind like Alton's is a big responsibility. Hope I can keep him steering in the right direction. So far I don't think he's too spoiled or conceited and has a pretty fair disposition. Teen says the latter is from the way I've handled him. A big compliment!

Enough bragging about my son. Bob says I'm conceited about him. How is Peg? I haven't heard from her lately.

Must close. Suppose Bob will be going out soon. No word from Burt but he's probably in by now. They expected to move June 1st. Thanks for pictures. They were swell.

Love,
Marian

Let me know how the flying goes.

Summer 1944

Shirley has just finished her sophomore year of high school. She has lots of things to write about: the frustrations of school, her new nephew, Teen's neighbors, and more news of family and friends.

June 23, 1944

Dear Ted,

You probably will wonder who this is writing to you. You see it's like this, I've had lots of studying and getting ready for tests. The teachers (some rather) have been dawdling us around most of the year and just woke up about six weeks before tests. Then did they pile it on!! Our social studies teacher didn't give us any review and we had lots of reading to do for assignments right until tests. I guess the test was different from anything we'd studied in class anyway. About half the class didn't pass and I got only 80. I was figuring on getting nineties in most of my subjects so that I'd be heading toward a good average. I wonder if there is such a thing as a good social studies teacher? I haven't struck one yet!

Our geometry teacher got us through the book by Easter and we've gone thru the review & then some. If we didn't pass that it wouldn't be her fault. I got 84 in that which was the highest. The regents seemed quite difficult on the last part or parts and I was getting cramped for time and all muddled up! I only got one wrong on the first part.

Billy came down with Mom and Willie the other day to stay for awhile. He went to school with Altie this morning. Altie had to go only a few minutes to get his report card and he wanted Bill to go so we let him go. He's been having quite a time.

Teen and David are coming down sometime soon to stay. My but David is growing fast. Last week-end Teen said she thought he weighs about 9½ lbs. She has the same trouble with him she had with Bill. He can't get enough to eat. She says David it seems is even quite a bit stronger than Billy. He held his head way up even when they first came home. I don't know whether you know his name or not but it's David Robert. Isn't that nice? He has dark hair & quite a bit of it; his nose is quite big, long arms and legs; and Bob thinks he's homely. He said Billy was never so skinny, scrawny, homely, etc. as David. David weighed about 7½ lbs. when he was born. He's very good when he gets enough to eat. Billy thinks he's just the thing. The first morning they were home, Teen was washing David and he was crying. Bill felt so distressed that he went and got him one of his fussies. He would like to hold him, touch him, give him his bottle and everything, but he wouldn't want to hurt him. Marian was down there to stay with Teen, you probably know. Teen came home on Saturday before Mem. Day. Mr. B. bro't her down & he had errands in Lowville too. Marian told me to get ready and go too & I could come back with Mr. B. Marian bro't flowers, etc. & when we got down there I couldn't come back so I stayed and helped Marian open up & so on. When Teen and the baby came it was all aired out, flowers around and homey. Marian stayed down about 2 weeks. It was nice for both Marian and Ernestine that she could go down. I don't know what Teen would have done, although she said she didn't need any help, she was feeling fine.

Ernestine has awfully nice neighbors. They live up on the corner of Sharp & Lanpher. They are somewhere in their thirties, I would say. When Clint was making garden this spring he had some manure there and when he spread it, he invited Bill to come over and help him. Billy was working away at it as he could. Teen went over pretty soon and Billy said, "It's just like being on the farm over at Cwints." Clint and Madeline have quite a time with Billy. Clint fixes Billy's toys and lets him follow him around. I don't know which has more fun. Billy's always telling, "I and Cwint made garden" or "I and Cwint fixed my tricycle" or something. Madeline offered to take care of David last Saturday night so that Teen could go uptown. They keep pretty close track of Billy for Teen and wouldn't let anything happen to him for anything.

Phil Freeman was home until last night I think. He was home since about the 1st of June. He got married!! The girl he married is or was my Latin teacher. She's nervous anyway, but wait til she finds out what kind of a silly guy he is! I suppose I shouldn't say that, but that seems to be in everyone's mind around here.

Janice and Johnny are alone up there for awhile. Mr. Klossner is having some kind of an operation on a funny bunch on the side of his face near his ear. He had it removed Tuesday, I think. It broke & ran and he's scary about such things anyway.

You ought to see that calf you gave them! They all baby it so that you can't get near it but you have to pet it and fool around. It's about as big as their calves. Mr. Klossner said it hasn't had a speck of dirt on it since it was up there. Johnny's anxious to get it registered, etc.

Well, I've taken time out from doing my housework & it's about time for Uncle A.J. so I'll call it quits. Sorry I have neglected to write for so long. I hope it isn't so far between the next one.

Love,
Blondie

P.S. We got those proofs of you. They're good. Does Peggy want one? Willie also got the picture of him & me the other day. I can't say so much for that.

Evelyn writes to Ted with worries about the state of things at home. She is feeling overwhelmed, but at the same time she is comforted by the nearness of her children and grandchildren.

MRS. ERNEST L. MARKHAM
BOX 143
TURIN, NEW YORK

June 23

Dear Ted,

It would seem that all of us have forgotten how to write. Day and night I carry you boys on my mind and in my heart and all my striving is a continual prayer for you and the winning of this war. But each hour seems to bring more things than I can do, so I stop only when my hands get so tired and stiff I can't hold a pen. If I could only have the strength and power of accomplishment I would gladly do ten times as much as I now can. I worry most about Willis – for fear he will be demoralized by this everlasting <u>pressure</u> to keep the farm running almost by himself. The mail route seems longer than ever and Dad seems to have more and more difficulty keeping up with it all. It is just the same old story, that's all.

I do have some comforts and distractions though: Ernestine and her babies – they make me live over my happiest days again when my own

little ones were in my arms. I am so thankful Teen has come through her
trial safely and has such a lovely little son. Billy is here for a few days and
maybe Teen and David will come soon for a few days. Twice I've spent a
day with her in her cozy little home.

Marian comes whenever she can though seldom ever free to be
herself. She spent nearly two weeks with Teen and the old lion got pretty
"roaring" before she got back.

Janice and John come to see us quite often. It is a great pleasure to see
them apparently so happy, so serious about their responsibilities and so –
well balanced, I guess. John is a real live guy, I think.

Your April and May bonds came all right. You now have 4. We have
received three class booklets, etc. which you and Peggy have sent us.
They're great.

And great, too, is the news that you've soloed. But of course you
would make it. We always knew you would. When a fellow means to do a
thing and works as you do, nothing can stop him.

The news of late is surely heartening, though we realize the cost is
immense.* Perhaps it will even be over in a few months.

The Ackermans have a recent V–mail** letter from Len. He seemed
well again, spoke of marching through Rome and said, "if you want to
know where I am watch the headlines." They think he's in the Fifth Army.
Alair's husband is in the Eighth. Was in England recently. Lincoln is at Ft.
Blanding, Fla.

Your proofs came. It is hard to choose between them. I think we'll
order a half-doz. Shall we get one for Peggy? I must write to her. She's
a sweet girl, I am sure, but I did not get much acquainted with her. She
must have thought us an awful rabble when she was here at the wedding.

That roll of film you asked about – Willis filled it out, it was sent
to the drug store and sort of forgotten. They found and gave it to Dad
recently, so Shirley sent your pictures. Do you want negatives?

I guess I'd better stop this scribble. I am finishing this on Sunday. No
company except Billy. He and Alton have big times together.

---

*The Allied casualties of the Normandy Invasion, from D-Day on June 6 to the liberation
of Paris on August 25, are estimated to be 226,386: 72,911 killed or missing and 153,475
wounded.

**See footnote on page 300.

Please do not let this get you down. I somehow feel that you need to know and that everything will come out right someday. I guess our souls as well as bodies must have "growing pains" sometimes.

Your letters are wonderful and we are all so proud of you!

Love,
Mother

Ted writes that he feels more confident about his flying. He has just passed a twenty-hour check.

AIR CORPS TRAINING DETACHMENT
DECATUR, ALABAMA

June 28, 1944

Dear Folks,

I feel a little guilty about beefing in my last letter [letter not included] about news from home, especially after getting a nice letter from Blondie yesterday and another nice one from Mom today.

I had been wondering what happened to the pictures which they took of us here some time ago. Evidently they figured that our parents were bigger suckers than we so sent them to you rather than to show them to us. I want you folks to get one for anyone who might be interested in one and you may take the cost out of the money I send to be banked. Yes, I wish that Peggy may have one if possible. I would sort of like to see one too, but I guess I can wait. I don't want one to keep anyway.

No, I guess that Peggy didn't think us an awful rabble while she was home with me for the wedding. She was pretty thrilled over my family and has said many times since that she has quite a weakness for everyone. It wasn't a very good opportunity to get acquainted, and Peggy isn't easy to get acquainted with at first. She is pretty quiet and quite self-conscious until she is acquainted.

My flying has momentarily improved. I took a twenty hour check

Saturday, got by that and then was put up for a progress check yesterday. Well it didn't bother me badly and I beat them. Today I was back on routine flying and working for the forty hour check. I'm sort of pleased because usually after an instructor puts a student up for a progress check he starts slipping right along through three others until he is out.

Momentarily then it is more promising, but I have a lot of hard work to meet the forty hour check which is only twelve hours away. As it stands tonight we have lost 21% of the original group here through the phases which I have just completed. I still don't feel very confident about the whole thing, but I'll just try my best. That is all that can be hoped for.

I flew three flights today for a duration of one hour each. Consequently, I'm pretty darn tired tonight. We've just started a few elementary acrobatics and it is physically tiring to be tossed around in the plane like this. It's a lot like going over the knoll by Mathis'es to land squarely on your bottom from a ten foot height for a whole flight's duration. After this continues for long one starts to get nauseated a little, but I'm pretty lucky in not having it bother me the way it did Bob. If it did they would have eliminated me long ago. I haven't tossed yet. About the most tiring flight of the three is the hour spent with my instructor. Boy these civilian instructors chew you so that you hardly know whether you're coming or going and still expect precision flying. My instructor is an artist at it and tries his best to get you all mixed up. I'm getting used to it though.

I was glad to get those pictures from Willie. I had wondered if they wouldn't turn up, but it wouldn't have made a difference. They don't amount to much. If you have a chance, I wonder if you could send my album of pictures sometime.

I visited the county agent Sunday afternoon and found it quite worthwhile. He, along with his wife and two sons, were very nice. They asked me to come back next Sunday for the whole day, and I believe I will. It seems to be a good way of having a good time and to put this traveling to some educational use. I must quit now.

Love,
Ted

P.S. I think Peggy would enjoy a letter from you very much. Here is a picture of the B-29. It is a magnificent looking ship.

Evelyn writes of chores and events typical for a summer month. Most of the jobs that need to be done are collaborative efforts, shared by family members.

MRS. ERNEST L. MARKHAM
BOX 143
TURIN, NEW YORK

July 4, 1944

Dear Ted,

This is the Glorious Fourth and we are celebrating as most people seem to be by digging in at our everyday work. Dad is at home today of course and they had expected to clean up the last of the hay – maybe they can even yet. John has been down to help Willis parts of four days and Willis has been digging in like a good fellow. Dad usually does chores with me to help and Willis mows or draws hay. Saturday he worked by moonlight till ten-thirty to finish what he wanted to do. It was cool and nice then and we have had some terrifically hot days lately. One of them was still and humid so some people were overcome with it. But there hasn't been a drop of rain on the hay, and it is nice. It doesn't bulk up so big in the barn as last year's but there will be more to cut later. The ladino and other clover look fine.

Just now Dad is repairing some part of the loader and Willis has gone to Klossner's with the side rake on the wagon hitched behind the truck. Shirley went along to watch.

The strawberry season has been a short one. Most people had only a few and they have sold for $.40. The Riebennacht's berries were quite good and Shirley has been picking for them. We bought ten quarts and put the best of them down in the freezer. So when you come home, we'll have shortcake!

I forgot to say that Willis is going to help John and take up several tools that they do not have. Rudy came home last night to stay several days and help too. Mr. K. had a cancer removed from his face a few days ago and still goes to Utica for radium treatments. Janice came down twice with John. Once she brought her ironing and helped do mine and

196

yesterday she helped fix the berries and I gave her a few. Now Shirley or I can go up to help her sometimes.

Lee, Beulah and Jane came out Sunday morning on the bus.* Lee spent the day at camp, Beulah and Jane stayed at Mother's. Yesterday Lee had to be at his work but is at camp again today I think. He is looking very pale and thin. I wish he could be outdoors more. He does have a garden this year though. Jane came over here yesterday and we took her back today just after dinner. She is just the same old Janey but she's "sweet sixteen" today.

Helen and Joe were up Sunday. Janice and John, Dad and I went over to Clara's to see them for a short time. They are looking well. Guess they won't be up to stay at the old place this summer.

Marian was here a little over a day early last week and took Alton back with her. Mr. Baxter went to Binghamton to see Bob Neil graduate and brought him and his girlfriend back for a two-weeks' stay. Bob goes into service soon I think.

Billy stayed with us about a week and a half and never said a word about going home until they came after him. I think Teen and the little boys will come down soon to stay a few days. We can save her some of the washing, etc. and it will be a big treat for all of us. It does Dad loads of good to have the little tots. Bill is such a little dynamo and I guess David will be too, he is very strong and bright and so sweet. I just wish you and Bob could see him now.

Bill Healt has been home but I guess he has gone again. They say he looked fine. We told you didn't we that Phil Freeman was home and got married? Len Ackerman writes that he marched through Rome. Sent home his purple heart and the piece of shrapnel that just missed his jugular.

We had a nice letter from Bob Saturday, the first in over a month. Says they probably won't go out for another month, can't get enough planes. They are getting a good lot of night flying.

Burt went last Friday, we think. He said, on a Father's Day card, that he expected to.

Your letters have all been so nice, the recent ones especially

---

*Evelyn's brother, Lee; sister-in-law, Beulah; and niece, Jane.

interesting. We know you are sticking to it "like death to a dead dog."
Of course you'll make it.

Everything going well here.

Love,

Mom

Dad mowed the south pasture. All done now but a few weedy corners.

Ted writes with some news. He is looking forward to moving on to his future options.

AVIATION CADETS
AIR CORPS TRAINING DETACHMENT
DECATUR, ALABAMA

July 6, 1944

Dear Folks,

I don't like to write this letter, for I have to admit failure. I washed out today even though last week I beat them on a check. I don't feel badly though for I tried my best and now it is just water over the dam as far as I care. It wasn't because I couldn't fly but rather because I just couldn't take it fast enough. I was washed out because of lack of progress. It just seemed to be something which I couldn't do much about. My check rider today told me that I could get by very easily if I had even five less hours. I could feel badly about it, but it is useless and the wrong thing to do. They have just narrowed down this program to where they can't spend time with we who are just a little slow. Of the group who arrived here about 1/3 have been washed out tonight and it seems quite likely that the figure will be more than 1/2 in a few more days. They have been eliminating no less than six a day for several days now. Less than half of our original group from Wmsport have survived thus far. It just means that they're closing down the pilot training program as fast as possible and some of us just can't make the grade.

198

I haven't officially washed out yet but for all practical purposes I have. When I go before the interviewing board for re-assignment it will then be official. I believe that I'm still just as well off perhaps much better for I believe that I can be assigned as a navigator or bombardier. Most of the boys who have qualified for either have had good luck in getting one. I would prefer to be a navigator but my qualifying score is highest for bombardier so that is probably what it will be.

I hope that this doesn't sound like sour grapes when I say that I should probably have taken one of the others in the first place. I've never been very crazy about flying anyway and often thought it better for the boys who hope for a future as pilots to get through. I can do just as much as a bombardier and be just as well satisfied after the war. I have enough time and skill to get a private pilot's license after the war in case I should want such so why should I care. This is a pretty common day occurrence around here so why should I let it bother me when others have more reason to be disappointed. I'll probably have just as good chances to get a commission as quickly this way.

The news has sounded quite encouraging lately. We are a long way from any real decisive battles, but at least it seems that we're maneuvering for such. Our successes against the Japanese have been amazing to anyone that has any concept of how slowly such warfare can be carried on.* Our war of position seems to be quite well timed to the time when our fleets and supply lines can be turned into China. Maybe we can make landings and get a decent volume of supplies through the western coast of China before the year is out.

Well I must quit now and try to write later in the week. I hope that you folks don't feel that I'm very disappointed over this. I've been reconciled to any such thing for a long time and as far as it bothers me now, it is water over the dam. It'll probably be a couple of weeks before I ship out of here and I'll probably continue to be an A/C.

Love,
Ted

---

*American forces continued leapfrogging across the Pacific and, in July, had taken control of Saipan and Tinian, two islands in the Marianas. We now had the capability to strike the Japanese mainland.

Ted was shipped next to the Moody Army Airfield in Valdosta, Georgia, where he immediately hoped to be given a farm furlough. Evelyn writes next to tell him how proud they all are of him. Once more, she expresses concern for Ernest's mental and physical state, finally writing what must have been troubling her for a long time. They might have to give up the farm if Will is drafted.

MRS. ERNEST L. MARKHAM
BOX 143
TURIN, NEW YORK

Turin, N.Y.
July 20, '44

Dear Ted,

For several days I have been feeling that I ought to write to you, but thought it might be better to wait and see if you had a new address.

Please believe it when I say that none of us are disappointed in you because you did not come through as a pilot. We are immensely proud of you for having put your very best into it, and that you are resigned to being a bombardier. Each man gives his best in the service to which he is best fitted. And now you are again playing the waiting game – in a pool, which is tedious.

How we wish you were stationed somewhere near home and could get some time off! It would be a help and a comfort from some of our worries.

This summer has brought many things to do and fewer people to do them. John came to help Willis get in our hay and now Willis is helping John. They have such a big haying to do, we will be ready to get our second cutting and then it won't be long till grain harvesting and then corn harvesting. Dad wants to get the wood supply cut this summer and put in while it is nice and dry because it would go farther. Do you know that last year we did not buy a bit of coal but burned all wood in the furnace and cook stove? That helped make a good payment on the old farm this spring. Dad keeps plugging away, but doesn't get around from the mail trip very early and that leaves Willis to do the work mostly alone which seems at times rather discouraging for a youngster. If he had some

The Markham home

of the training in agriculture that you, Bob and Burt have had, it would be different. We all expect more of him than his experience warrants.

You have asked me to send your snapshot album and I have kept thinking I would find it. I seem to have looked over all the possible places even among Bob's books and pictures. If I ever do find it, I'll send it. I think I told you I received the express money order. I sent ten dollars of it for pictures and banked the rest. Another bond has come.

Marian is having a week of vacation and spending it mostly with Ernestine. Mr. B. has gone on a fishing trip to Canada with the Savocols. Bob N. went too.

Ernestine and the boys spent the most of last week with us. It was such a treat to have them! David is growing well and is so bright and sweet.

A letter from Melrose a few days ago said Burt was still watchfully waiting, at Fillmore, painting her father's house.

Bob's most recent letter came on my birthday. They were training with the new equipment and getting very accustomed to night navigation. Expect to go out on Pacific soon.

All the family and relatives are well as far as we know and everyone is working hard. Even Grandma has a good garden.

Will write again soon.

Love,
Mom

Dear Ted,

Since writing this letter, and saying I wish you could come home, I have thought more about it. Do you suppose you could prevail upon your officers to let you off for a time? I've been very worried about Dad some of the time. He seems fairly off his base, mentally, – the long hours, the strain of doing his regular work and then trying to keep the farm running with inexperienced help, or if Willis should go in the service, we might even have to give up the old home you boys look forward to returning to. If you were here a little while to help do some of the work and get things in smoother running order, it would help Dad's morale a lot – yes, Willis' and mine, too. You know having Dad like this is harder for me than hard work. Don't worry about it if you can't come. We'll do the best we can and keep hoping and praying.

Love from all of us,
Mother

Ernest writes next with news of the farm.

Thursday nite

Dear Ted,

Your most welcome letter came today. Have looked up on map to see where you are located & find that you are not very far from Thomasville Ga where Mrs. Ireland is with a large herd of Jerseys. Imagine that it is hot there for it was six years ago. Too bad that some of the heat you encounter down there could not be utilized up this way in Jan & Feb then I would not have to worry about how I will be able to get fuel for the heater. It seems quite a task. And slow. Somehow the old grey mare isn't what she used to be. It seems to take longer on the route than it used to. I don't know whether there is more work or I am getting slower altho I leave the office about three, sometimes it is later when I arrive back. I know I am handling more pieces of mail & more stamps, more money orders, more

Ernest in front of the Turin Post Office

pkgs etc. and driving slower on acct of tires,* etc. so it does not give me more time in the P.M. before milking & supper.

We had a fair crop of hay and put in the barn without a drop of rain on it. Only two loads was over dried that was mowed on Saturday & put in barn on Monday. All in the barn before July 4th. Second cutting looks fair. Corn is shoulder height at present. We have had a nice rain today so corn & second cutting will be bumper.

Am going to try & cut wood enough in the next month for two yrs but wish I had a little more time & help. Have clipped the South pasture am going to try & clip the middle one soon. Have been to Watertown two days lately with the truck. Had some work done on it, first since I bought it 3 yrs. ago. Valve job, new rings & wrist pins, new bearings in rear end, brakes and some minor work. Walt is pecking away with Erwin & Harold. Bill Sampson has been up there a few days the past week but it is pretty slow.

We had two weeks of beautiful hay weather, no rain & hot just like Southern Ga., 100+ every day but the hay cooked ok. Must close or will have to pay double postage on the letter.

Dad

---

*The Lewis County rationing board issued certificates for tires and tubes. Even Ernest's position as a mailman didn't allow him adequate tires.

Ted writes that he is unable to get a furlough, and once more will be shipped to another field, in Panama City, Florida.

August 16, 1944

Dear Folks,

You have probably been so mixed up because of the hopes I had for a furlough that you sort of wondered what became of me. I too have been mixed up and uncertain so I have hesitated to write. I finally know just how the score stands so I can write.

The hopes for a furlough are gone now. I had hopes of getting the farm furlough and did go through all of the necessary red tape in order to get it. The request was approved through channels at this field but I had to send a letter from here through channels to the commanding general of Eastern Flying Training Command at Maxwell Fld. This morning after waiting exactly two weeks it came back disapproved. That didn't bother me at this point because I am alerted for shipment and would like to ship and get out of here before they turn us all back to an enlisted status. That's the way it stands so I hope you can appreciate that it isn't best to want such if I could get it now.

How utterly foolish it often seems when it takes a general's approval in order to get a furlough in addition to the red tape and wasted time. Of course it wasn't the general but an aide who was asked. It just shows how little power even the colonel of one of these posts has. The important thing is the fact that we have nothing of any importance to do around here except to have a little shavetail chase us around like a flock of sheep. "Junior" is a little shave tail who is only about twenty and can't seem to find much success in preventing the boys from goofing off on him. He sweats and puffs like a steam engine when he starts chasing the boys for a detail. Sometimes he has to chase a hundred or so before he gets a couple of men. It's just like a game of chess.

It is a pretty good rumor that this sort of a pool is going to be dispensed with and cadets with it. That is the big reason why I don't want a furlough. Already the radar cadets have been reverted to an enlisted status. Most of the radar cadets were boys who washed out of the latter phases of advanced flying and couldn't qualify for nav. or bomb. Some had only 24 hours of flying before their commissions, but at least we fellows have the consolation that training requirements are met even if we are disappointed in our personal ambitions.

This is a day later and I have some news. I'll be shipped to Tyndall Fld. at Panama City, Fla. on Monday. This will be gunnery school where we train for six weeks before shipping to bombardier school in the Southwest. I believe that Chet Freeman is there flying a B17 for gunnery training. Would you find out and let me know?

We are all pretty happy to hear of the successes in France.* It is something to be really proud about but something to try and prevent over optimism about. It would do the public worlds of good to see some of the movies of the real war as they have shown them to us. It sort of makes us realize what a terrific struggle lies ahead and to make us want to keep on working even more than before these late victories. Our American buddies are winning but what a hell of a fight they wage to win. You would realize what I mean if you could see movies of a few air battles as well as action of the infantry. It is going to be plain hell for both sides if the Germans start putting gas bombs in those robot planes. Bob Hope once said that it is a good thing the American boys have a sense of humor. That is one of our strongest weapons because it gives spirit and a chance to maintain a clear means of thinking.

I'd better call this quits and try to write as quickly as I can at Tyndall. Everyone write.

Love,
Ted

---

*General George Patton and the Third Army were advancing toward Paris through a gap in German lines.

This next letter from Evelyn crossed with Ted's previous one. She writes that Bob once more has gone out on active duty. His belongings have been sent home in a parachute bag. Burt is still waiting to be activated.

Mrs. Ernest L. Markham
BOX 143
TURIN, NEW YORK

Aug. 18, '44

Dear Ted,

We've been looking and listening to hear from you, and of course we are still hoping that you may come.

Monday we got a short note from Bob, the first in over a month, with the expected news that he was just going out on the ninth, just a year from the day he went last year. A parachute bag came Tuesday with his belongings, but we haven't received the key as yet.

Pete reached home night before last. We went up to see him a little while last night. He looks fine, except heavy, and he has that tired look in his eyes.

Burt is here. He blew in last evening and can stay till Sun. He doesn't hear anymore about going.

This is Lowville fair week. Shirley is at Ernestine's and Uncle Lee's, I guess. Alton went to Lowville and then, I guess, to Boonville with Clyde.

Clyde and Viola, Merrill and Elsie have all been home lately.

The boys have gone fishing taking Barney Felshaw along. He has been home a couple of weeks. He hopes you'll get home.

Lincoln Ackerman is home.* He is a full-fledged paratrooper now. Has his wings and boots.

Dad is going to take me to Boonville to the dentists, so I'll have to cut this short. If you don't come soon, I'll try to write again soon.

Love from everyone,
Mother

---

*Lincoln (Linc) Ackerman enlisted in February 1944 and trained as a paratrooper at Fort George Meade, MD. He was sent overseas in October 1944.

Ted writes next from Tyndall Field, Florida, where he has been shipped for gunnery training. He is dealing with some unwelcome "blood transfusions" in the middle of the night.

August 25, 1944

Dear Folks,

We pulled in here Monday night after spending the whole day riding a couple hundred miles in one of these filthy cars which southern railroads oblige the government with.

We won't start school until next week so this week doesn't amount to anything. School lasts for six weeks during which we have two weeks of ground school, two weeks of skeet-shooting and range, one week of gunnery from a B-24, and one week of camera gunnery from a B-17. The skeet shooting should be quite interesting and very good in developing skill. We start out with ordinary skeet shooting with shotguns and then get into .22 cal. and finally wind up with .50 cal. machine guns mounted on a moving vehicle. This is the same course as regular aerial gunners take. It lasts six weeks but it will probably be eight weeks before we ship out. From here we will probably ship to Texas, New Mexico, or Calif. for Advanced Bombardier School.

I'm not overly impressed with this camp but probably can't expect much. It is about as full of soldiers in training as any I've yet seen: The last few days we've spent trying to reduce the numbers of bedbugs and cockroaches in our barracks and particularly our room. Finally the Corp of Post Engineers exerted enough initiative to let us use their sprays so that is what we've been doing this morning and early afternoon. After using the spray, chasing them out of corners and cracks, and using roach powder we hope they won't be so numerous. My roommate's name is Roach* (an Irishman from Detroit) so we have good fun getting bloodthirsty toward his "cousins." Now we'll just try our best from getting too many blood transfusions in the middle of the night.

This field is located on a peninsula or really an island in the Gulf of Mexico. It is the same hot weather as that at Moody.

*For a picture of Roach, see page 263.

I've found out where Chet Freeman is located, but haven't been able to reach him. I think that I can make connection perhaps tomorrow. I believe that he is flying a B-17 for gunnery students.

We've seen quite a few new P-63's around here. For Willie and Altie they are new improved P-39's with a 1500 HP Allison engine and high altitude characteristics. It is claimed to turn with a zero and that means plenty of maneuverability. Looks as if it should come close to being a match for the P-51. They sure whistle around here plenty fast.

Some day I hope you can see the engineering accomplishments found in most of these ships. It is little wonder that we lost one to the enemy's four.

I've been wondering what has happened to Willie, Shirley, and Altie when it comes to writing. How about a note now and then?

Love,

Ted

Evelyn writes to Ted at Tyndall Field that Willis has had an accident. She believes that the war in Europe is nearing an end, but victory in Europe wouldn't happen for another long and bloody eight months.

MRS. ERNEST L. MARKHAM
BOX 143
TURIN, NEW YORK

Turin, N.Y.

Sept. 2, '44

Dear Ted,

We were glad of the letter with your new address. I will give it to the Freemans, just in case you haven't found Chet yet.

Eddie Woch is also at Tyndall Field. I am sending his address. I will also send yours to him.

Guess I have not told you that your pictures came some time ago. They are good. There is one large (8x10) hand tinted, one in a large folder, and 6 3x4 in., I believe, in folders.

Shirley and Willis each claimed one of the small ones as they did not have one of your other pictures. Shall I send the large one to Peggy or did she have a large one before? Who is to have the others? Shall I send one to you, give one to W.B.* and one to Grandma and keep one?

I have received another bond and put it away. I had the notice of your ins. premium and was not sure where you would be, so paid it. It was sent back to me because you had also paid.

Bob's extras were all sent home in a parachute bag, among them all his pictures. Guess I'll send a few to you and you can send them back again. My, he has a lot of clothes here now! Five pairs of shoes this time, navy blue uniform and top-coat, the light topcoat, raincoat, flying jacket, gloves, and green pants. Only hope he'll use them one day.

Yes, it looks more as though we are nearing the end, in Europe.** May the Lord keep those who are in the midst of it. It is hard enough for even those of us who only read or hear of what is going on.

We told you Pete was home. He has to report at Atlantic City Sep't. 9th. He has been resting and looks just fine. We saw him the other night when the band played in Turin and an honor roll was dedicated – a very nice one!

Sep't. 4   Since I started this, I have had interruptions.

The O'Briens brought Marian and Alton and Shirley home yesterday. Mr. B. came down and took Marian back, also Pearl Walsh who is going to work for Mr. B. Marian is going to show her the "works" and come home again soon.

Willis had bad luck in baseball yesterday. Stan Paczkowski tripped him, he fell hurting one thigh painfully. The boys took him to Dr., then to the hospital then came and told us. When we got there it was late, he had been put to sleep, so we didn't see him. X-ray showed no fracture, only bad bruise but he suffered much from shock and was given hypos. Today Dr. reports him better. Says we can bring him home tomorrow night.

Silo filling is about to start here. Walt has his corn about all down and Fay will cut ours tomorrow. We are the first.

I'd better send this to mail. Dad isn't carrying mail today but going over to town.

Love from all,
Mother

W.B. spent last week with us. Adriel is sick – heart trouble.

---

*William Markham, Ernest's father.
**As of September, the Allies had freed France, Belgium, and Luxembourg. They then moved east into Germany.

Marian writes that she hasn't been feeling well and is leaving her job with Mr. Baxter. It's time for her to move on.

Old Forge, N.Y.
Sept. 5, '44

Dear Ted,

I sure am ashamed I've taken so long to answer your letter. I just haven't had ambition for anything. Ernestine was quite flattered last week to get the change of address card sent to your regular correspondents. Me, too.

Perhaps Mom has written you I've been on the shelf. I had a blood count of 60, taking iron and liver & iron shots & still losing weight so I got orders to get off the job. I went down to Teen's and was down there four weeks. I had two or three shots a week and osteopathic treatments. The last few days I've felt better but haven't gained much strength. The Dr. said he thot I'd been down so long, it would probably take quite awhile. Dr. Lindsay told me I should do nothing for a month but I found it wasn't especially easy to do nothing. I had to change David's pants and do such things.

David is awfully cute (of course). He's going to be a rascal. He's laughed out loud since he was two months old. He watches your face and when you smile so does he. Shirley was down last week and he squealed at her. Even Bob has admitted that he's more alert than Billy. He has big eyes and we think they'll be blue. His hair is dark – what he has of it. The last few weeks it's been funny. It started coming out around his face. For awhile he had a few hairs for sideburns and was bald all around them. Now he has light fuzz on top and real dark and rather long fringe around the back. The back of his neck and the shape of his head is like Bob O. I think he looks like his Dad. He's got big hands and feet and long arms and legs. And he's long. When I hold him he stands up on my lap and sticks his head over my shoulder. I never had anything to do with a baby as strong. He weighed 15 lb.10 oz. Sunday. And does he like to rough house!

The other day David was in bed asleep when Teen sent Bill up for his nap. All of a sudden David yelled right out so she started up. She

The Hotel Parquet, built in 1796, circa 1950. (Image courtesy of Peter Hayes, Constableville Historian)

heard Bill scamper back to his bed and when she got there he was sitting in the middle of his bed and he told her, "David hasn't any teeth yet, but he's going to have. There's a hard place next his tongue." He sure gets disgusted with me when I propose giving David a bread crust or something. Bill says, "He can't eat it – he hasn't any teeth." Bill will probably try him out when he does get some. The other day Bill told Teen he hurt his elbow and an "electric" went right down to his fingers. Then we wondered how he knew about the "electric."

Bill's changing this summer. His face doesn't seem as round and he's stretching up.

Altie is too. He's gained about six lbs. this summer and growing tall all the time. The suits I got him a year ago in the spring look pretty short but he'll have to wear them. The dirtier he gets the better it suits him. He went to Parquets* to dinner with us one day in overalls and old plaid shirt and was as poised as anyone there.

I'm finishing this on Wed. night. I got interrupted last night. I'm getting sleepy now.

As you've probably heard I'm leaving this job. Mr. B. has looked high and low and finally got Mrs. Pearl Walsh from Constableville. She was a teller. She worked at Klossners 3 yrs. before Jan & John were married. She

---

*The Hotel Parquet, a Constableville landmark.

came up Sunday and I came back from Teen's then. I've got some things I want to get done and also show her how things go.

I don't know what I want to do from now on. I haven't any plans at all. I'll have to get to feeling different before I try anything. Trouble is I don't want to work but I do miss pay day.

I read a letter from Peg down home Sunday. I'd hoped she'd get up. Even after you gave up hopes of bringing her, I thot maybe she could come. We'd like to have her. She owes me a letter but I know she's busy.

We had the bunch down to Teen's just after Pete got home. We couldn't find anyone to invite but Markhams. Burt was home and Jan & John and Willis came down and Pete & Doris, Bob, Teen & I. I let Altie stay up and he was some thrilled. Shirley told Burt she knew why she wasn't invited – we were going to drink. When we proposed a party to Pete he said it sounded good. I said I'd gotten as far as a case of beer. When he arrived he marched in with a big box and we thot – more beer. It was gin, rye, ginger ale, Tom Collins mix and soda water. Altie mixed the last three and thot he was in the swim with the rest of us. He'd have us taste it once in a while and ask if we didn't think it was strong. The next day I accused him of getting stinking. He said you have to when you go to a party – at least that kind of a party. He pestered everyone trying to get a game of cards started. We had spaghetti and homemade biscuits.

As far as I can find out Burt is the same status as when we left Ithaca except that he quit his job, sold some furniture and moved to Fillmore. He's been painting houses etc. He looks the best I've seen him in several years and has an appetite. Eats most as good as I do.

Mr. Baxter says to give you his very best wishes. He's fine as always and as busy as always. The gardens aren't much – it's been terribly dry. The flowers have about 1/3 the usual growth. Some vegetables didn't amount to much but others made out alright. We have lots of cucumbers and tomatoes.

I'm not sure but I think Altie is going to Constableville to school this year. He's so anxious for training in music and I'd like Mrs. Wendt to start him out. I hope he can have piano lessons. There's been nobody that gave lessons in Turin since Bernice left. I told Altie he and Gram could decide it. Bob McConnell would be his teacher and I hope he'd be an improvement over his last one. She didn't get much work out of him.

I read in the paper that Rita Schoff is going to teach in Bath. She must graduate soon.*

We had an earthquake Monday night. I hadn't gone to sleep and couldn't imagine what was making my bed shake. Things shook pretty sharp for a few minutes. I guess it centered around Malone and Cornwall. It shattered windows, ruined chimneys and plaster in Malone. The paper said it was felt as far south as Virginia and west to Wisconsin.

I hear you and Chet got together a short time ago. I'll bet you had some visit. I saw Clyde a little while when he was up to the fair. He'd just brought his wife from Texas under morphine. She had a rather serious operation after she got to Rome. I suppose you know Clyde is with the engineers now. Merrill and his wife and oldest boy had come up about the same time. They hadn't been home two days when he got word to come back. He thot it meant his was going out again – Alaska he thot.

Well Bob is gone again – he said there wasn't much excitement this time. It must be three weeks he wrote he was all packed and just waiting to go on the ship. I'd like to hear he'd arrived <u>somewhere</u>.

I didn't say much about Pete. He seems about the same – plenty of pork. He weighs over 190. After he got plenty under his belt he talked a little. He had 28 raids – Ploesti** was his first and then he was flak-happy. He was over Bremen*** twice – said that was toughest – over Keil – over France (the rocket rocks). Said he was over the edge of the Ruhr valley and that was new enough. Said they aren't sent over the valley in daylight any more. I think he said there were 1000 big guns in that valley. I can't remember much more he said. He flew back – took 18 hrs. including 2 stops. When he landed in Boston he got 2 bottles of real beer and then called his old lady. He was allowed 65 lbs. of baggage and he brot mostly shoes. Then he had no clothes to wear. Sound like him?

Guess I've rambled on enough for one time. I'll try to see if I can't get at it oftener. Tho I probably wear you all out with my "books".

I forgot to tell you Mr. B's grandson Neddie (Bob's brother) who is

---

*Rita was a student at Cornell.
**Hitler's oil refineries in Ploesti, Romania, were bombed by the U.S. Army Air Force on August 1, 1943. Pete (Claron) was presented with the Distinguished Flying Cross for his role as a bombardier in the raid.
***A historical city in northwest Germany.

just 7 yrs. old, has polio. He started being paralyzed but an osteopath has worked on him a couple times a day and that seems to have disappeared. He's been pretty sick.

Must close for now. When you write Peg tell her hello for me.

Love,
Marian

As usual, Ted wants to hear about what's been going on at the farm.

ARMY AIR FORCES GUNNERY SCHOOL

September 10, 1944

Dear Folks,

I was sorry to hear of Willie's mishap. Gosh I hope that it doesn't develop into anything serious. Will it mean any lasting injury such as a sprained hip or trick knee? It certainly came at a tough time when you are rushed with heavy work like silo filling, plowing and wood cutting.

I'm sending a snapshot of Peggy which you might like. I have a duplicate so thought perhaps you should have one. About those pictures of me – you had better do as you think best. I'm not terribly enthusiastic about them because though they're equally common to a bombardier's appearance, I was still a pilot when they were taken, and then I dislike the underhand way in which this company handled the situation. (We were called out in a military formation to have what we thought a required picture for the army taken – only to find that it was just a photo company's scheme and a bigger scheme when they asked our folks whom they thought would be more likely to buy without even asking us.) Peggy only has a small picture of me and I would be pleased if she had a larger one but you might like that large one too. Peggy's birthday is Oct. 9 so

Ted in his pilot's uniform

Peggy in her parents' garden

perhaps that would please her as remembrance from the Markham's.

I haven't seen Eddie Wach yet because we've been pretty occupied – not so busy but just without free time. Last week we had night classes until ten and the week before details most every night. Two weeks from last Friday we will go to Appalachia, an auxiliary field about 60 miles from here, to stay a week and take our air to air gunnery.

Yes, I would enjoy Bob's pictures.

I must be quite a ways behind on the family news for I didn't hear that Marian was quitting. I've also been waiting to hear some of the farm news. I don't even know what cows are milking or how many calves you have now. I've never heard how well Beatrice has been doing or in fact how well any of the herd has been milking. I don't know how the corn or oats were this year or whether or not the pastures held up. I haven't heard a thing about the farm work except that haying was done up in good shape.

I'm still interested to hear a few reactions about the Ladino Clover. I've just heard that it is growing and that's all.

Chet Freeman paid me a visit last Sunday. I couldn't catch him in at the flight line so I left my bks. number, and he found me. His schedule and mine are quite different so we haven't seen each other since. He looks swell and is still Chet. He is first pilot on both B17's and 24's for gunnery practice. He, Irene and their boy live off the post and apparently it is a fairly good set up for them.

I suppose that Burt feels pretty uncertain about his expectations. I am glad that he could get home and hoped that we could get home together. It is probably a disappointment in financial terms to have to wait like that but if he can have a little fun that is the important thing. They will probably never make a fighting man out of him, but I hate to see him get stuck.

Our men over across still seem to be accomplishing the impossible. It is such a satisfaction and re-assurance when we have to see the less efficient phases of the organization at times. To me it seems right now that the Nazis have only a taste of what they might expect if they try to set up any defense line like the Siegfried Line.* Remember – we still hold a complete airborne army in England – 250,000 troops which are assault troops. "Blood and Guts" – not so tactful yet quite able to use tactics which has given the "supermen" a chance to see all of the blood and guts they care to.

Well this is all for now. How about a few lines from Willie, Shirley and Altie? Dad came through with a nice letter a short time ago so how about the rest?

Love,
Ted

---

*The Siegfried Line was a German defense system stretching over 390 miles along the German western frontier. Built in the 1930's and expanded in 1944, it included 18,000 bunkers, tunnels, and tank traps.

Bob writes from his new undisclosed location. He's having some fun but isn't very happy about flying as a co-pilot. He has some encouraging words for Ted.

Sept. 16, '44

Dear Ted,

Mom just sent me your latest address so I guess I'll hurry up and write before you move again if I can. Have been meaning to all along but don't manage to write many letters anymore. I guess it's partly because we have such a lively gang and there is always something going on to divert my attention.

Things are going much the same as they were a year ago. We are seeing some of the same scenery and I'm still putting in part of my time as copilot and not liking it too much but it's the only fair way as other fellows are in the same boat.

Mom tells me that you have seen Chet and Irene fairly regularly recently. Lucky you. Last time I saw them Jerry was only a couple of weeks old and Irene wasn't feeling so good. I'll bet they have both gained a little weight since then. I hear from Rita now and then and she tells me a little about them. Also she said she wanted to go south to visit them after graduation but might not be able to now that she is starting work. She has a job teaching in Bath.

The folks tell me you had to give up pilot training. Maybe that's not too good if you are sure you wanted it but there will be lots of chances to learn later on and maybe you can do more good some other way. I know there are lots of boys being washed out now that would be better than some of us who got thru when I did.

Wish you would let me know what you are doing now and also what Chet is doing. Of course I can't say much about what we are doing so it will have to be a bit one sided. Naturally we think we are a pretty sharp outfit and the little old Nippers better start hustlin' out of our way. Might be that they don't agree with us tho.

Tomorrow I have a day off. The question at present is, "What shall I do?" Shall I stroll in Central Park or ride the subways out to Long Island? I guess it would be easier to just go swimming or fishing. There are more choices than you might guess tho.

Well this is enough for tonight. Drop me a line when you can. Give my best to the Freemans.

As always
Bob

Ted is still in gunnery training in Florida. It has been a long, hot summer, and he's clearly frustrated by the lack of letters from some of his family.

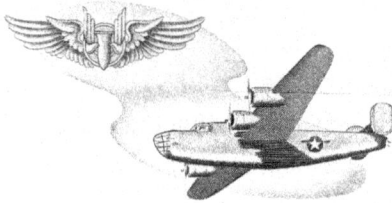

ARMY AIR FORCES GUNNERY SCHOOL

September 24, 1944

Dear Folks,

Somehow I feel selfish enough to almost say "Dear Mom" and restrict the letter from the rest. If I have hurt the feelings of the rest of the family then I would like to know about it. Otherwise I feel pretty gripey about the cooperation shown by the rest of the family. Dad, Marian, and Bob are the only other members of the family whom I've heard from in the past five months. Remember that sometimes a fellow needs a little help in order to drive away the bitterness and prejudice. Sometimes it is quite evident that only Dad and Mom have any realization of what this whole thing means.

I got a nice letter from Bob yesterday. He tried to give me a strong hint of his whereabouts but I couldn't quite understand him. I know that he has hit Hawaii and that is probably where he is now.

I didn't write last weekend because I was just too darn busy. Jerry Nuffer* came over from Keesler Field, Miss. to spend from Friday night until Sunday night with me. I fixed him up in a GI bunk and we just spent the whole weekend remising old times and acquaintances. Chet and Irene had us for supper and a swell visit on Saturday night. Their little boy, Jerry, is a great little guy too. All in all I think the good time did us all lots of good. Jerry has really had a raw deal and I know that it changed his views and helped him settle back into his old ways. We could see that it did Irene worlds of good too – she is such a trouper and a real all around woman. You have little idea of what even an officer's wife has to put up with in a place like this.

---

*A friend from home.

This week we start our air to air firing – in fact we do this afternoon. It will be firing the cal. 50 from turrets and hand held mounts in a B-24 at a sleeve drawn by a B-26. Next week we will be "firing camera guns" from 17's and 24's at P-40's and P-63's as they attack in simulated battle conditions. Last week we finished our range work by firing the cal. 50 at moving targets and shooting skeet from a moving base at stationary targets and flying skeet. Shooting skeet is really quite a sport. We were firing from the truck moving at 30MPH off at the stationary or flying targets which varied from muzzle end off to about a hundred feet. To get an idea of it just jump in the back end of the truck while someone drives you down the road at 30 MPH and try to hit a fence post with the shotgun and then imagine the difficulty in hitting a flying object. It can be done though and is really quite a sport when you get on to it.

Since I started this letter I went up on my first air to air mission. We were up four hours – quite a little time when you haven't been up for quite awhile. We were up in one of these darned 24's. They're a pretty reliable old crate but no one likes them. They are just a boxcar with wings. Our nose turret was broken so the bombardiers fired from the waist guns. This cal.50 fires enough better in the air so that I really have hopes of being able to use the gun now.

I don't know who renewed the B.H. for me but I'm pleased with it. I guess Dad must have since I heard nothing about it. It is a bit disgusting to read so much about Clara Smith visiting Flossie Jones, etc. but all in all I get enough to enjoy it quite a lot.

I meant to send this money order before, but didn't get around to it. We've had so many partial payments and supplementary payrolls lately that it has been a little doubtful to budget and save. I guess that I'll be sending some more next week.

I haven't gotten to see Eddie Woch yet but still have hopes. I've been over a couple of times but he was either out or at work. I guess that he is a mechanic. It has been difficult to even get to the PX, but from now on it should be easier to get away from our own area. I probably won't see Bob Frank for Chet tells me that he got married at C-ville this last week. I must quit now and get some more letters written.

Love,

Ted

Evelyn writes the next letter on the same day as Ted's previous one. She doesn't need to be told that letters from home have been sparse – she knows. And she has the news that Burt is finally on his way to Fort Dix, New Jersey, for basic training.

MRS. ERNEST L. MARKHAM

BOX 143

TURIN, NEW YORK

Turin, NY

Sept. 24, '44

My dear dear Ted,

It seems that we have been more negligent than ever. But really, we have been more busy than in a long time. As you know, it has been corn harvesting time. The weather, for the most of the time, has been nice. Rain came just nights at first, then finally, a big rain which we had needed so much. Now we are having nice clear weather and the silos are all filled except the Millards'. No killing frost yet. I think I told you that ours was the second silo filled, both nearly full, the corn ripe enough so it shelled off some, well eared.

Well, Burt went for induction last Thursday morning. Melrose, Linda, Dad and I took him to Lowville at seven in the morning. Mel and Linda will stay here until they are able to make other plans. She hopes she will be able to be near him when he gets just a bit settled somewhere and in the meantime we think they are glad to be here and we are _very_ glad to have them.

It has been very fortunate for me to have Melrose to help me out. When she first came there was canning to be done, and I spent one day away helping Alice feed silo fillers in return for her helping me. Then I began having a bothersome boil on the underside of the left thigh. It developed to be a carbuncle and has been very painful some of the time. I could get no relief except by keeping hot wet packs of epsom salts on it. That necessitated lying on my stomach and having Shirley or Dad or Mel change them often. Then, when I was a bit better, I sat on the edge of a stool by the stove and tended it myself. Today (the 24th) I can walk quite comfortably about. I've been to see the Port Leyden doctor twice. He is young and seems a great little doc. He hopes to prevent me having anymore of these. I certainly wouldn't choose to. Shirley must have written alarmingly about Willis' injury. It came out very luckily, we think. He was at the hospital two days, came home with his thigh all strapped up. (They had X Rayed for a fracture but it was only a bad bruise). He tried crutches at first, then a cane but didn't keep off it much. The second or third day after he was home he drove team on the corn job. Got O.K. soon.

Dad got the most of the potatoes dug while Willis was working on corn jobs. They are rather small due to dry weather, but smooth. They have drawn down quite a few loads of wood and have some buzzed. We just begin to feel the need of a little fire for warmth sometimes. The weather keeps very mild. Leaves turning a little.

I had a nice letter from Peggy awhile ago. I will send her the large picture for her birthday. That is a good one of her you sent.

A girl Bob knows near San Francisco sent me, for him, for my birthday, (but it came later) a picture he had enlarged from one of Joe Mallen's negatives. It is a sunset in Samoa with palm trees in silhouette in the foreground. It is beautiful. You will find a small print of it in the pictures which I'll send to you soon. I think I better send mostly the ones you haven't seen. Hope nothing happens to them.

Yes, your bonds keep coming, near the end of each month. There are six now. You do well to buy any, I guess.

Mrs. Freeman told me they heard that you and Jerry Nuffer had been the first guests in Irene and Chet's new home, and she said Chet may fly a little plane up home soon. (Wish you could come too.)

You knew of the damage done along the coast recently by a tornado, I suppose. It hit pretty hard at Atlantic City so Pete got another furlough home. (10 da)

And did you hear about our 'quake'? It was about three weeks ago. Nearly everyone hereabouts was wakened by the rumbling and shaking. It lasted less than a minute the first time (about 12:40 A.M.) then a slight tremor or two later, they say, but we did not notice them.

Mel and Shirley have gone to the movies with the Phillipses and will be home soon. I'd better get to bed.

All our folks are well as far as I know. I'll be all right soon, and I'll try to write oftener.

Love,
Mother

You must know that Iva R. and Godfrey Regetz are married.

Burt writes from basic training at Fort Dix where his biggest complaint is typical. It's the food. He's hoping his IQ will get him into Civilian Investigation.

Service Club

U. S. ARMY

Sun. Sept. 24

Dear Ted,

I've meant to write long before but I guess you know what I've been doing so far.

We got in here late Thurs. nite and I hope all of the camps aren't quite so bad. Except for meals today all we've been fed is s_ _ _ . We are only partly processed – have had our interviews but not our shots, movies, tags, & life insurance, etc.

I got 140 on my I.Q. so have a good chance at a fair assignment. The interviewer tried to fix it up so that I could get into C.I. (Civilian Investigation). I don't know much about it but it doesn't sound bad.

I got the afternoon off – K.P. tomorrow – my first but probably not my last. Went to church this morning (to get out of special detail) & am planning on the movies tonight. I'm learning some of the ropes & don't find things too bad but will be glad when I get shipped out.

I'll write again when I get shipped.

Burt

Ted writes about having some fun in the cockpit of a B-24 thanks to his friend, Pilot Chet Freeman.

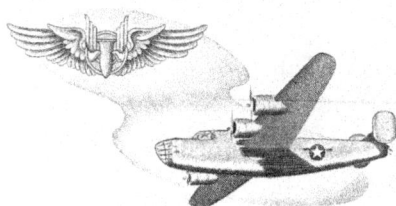

ARMY AIR FORCES GUNNERY SCHOOL

Oct. 1, 1944

Dear Folks,

Mom's nice letter came last night. It made me feel badly about that blue letter which I wrote a week ago. I would still like to hear from the others at home though.

I got a letter from Burt last week telling of his arrival at Ft. Dix. He didn't tell of Mel and Linda being at Turin, but I'm pleased that they are. It will do you folks a lot of good. I haven't the slightest idea of what Civilian Investigation might be, but it may be connected with G-2 or A-2 (Ground or Air Intelligence. I hope so, for the field may be relatively new – meaning better ratings and organization. He did well on his G.C.T. (general classifications test) so we can hope that he'll get a good break.

I'm sorry to hear of Mom's carbuncle. I hope that it ceases to be so miserable. I'm glad to hear that Willie's injury was only a bad bruise. Shirley didn't write of Willie's injury – she hasn't written me since last summer.

Yesterday was the first day for our outfit to fly with Chet's outfit, and he had it all doctored up for my section to fly in his plane – a B-24. Chet really demonstrated (regardless of my personal respect of him) the way a pilot should fly and assist the students on one of these missions. Best of all while we were waiting for an attack he called me out of the nose to report to him on the flight deck. Thereupon he asked the co-pilot to jump out of his cockpit and motioned me in. He gave me a chance to get the feel of it flying and then began showing me how it really reacted. He'd have me

223

intent upon flying and watching my instruments whereupon he'd sneak a hand down on the control block and throw a train tab or engine throttle out of adjustment. I hadn't had so much fun in a long time correcting for its reactions while out of train. This went on for about twenty minutes during which we had a delightful time though I doubt if the crew did.

That old Lib is a rough old gal to wrestle with, but quite calm when a pilot like Chet has her. Wednesday we again fly on his shift so he thinks he can get a 17 and show me how that handles in the air. Yes Chet has a flight with a BT-13 approved for cross country to Syracuse, but I couldn't get away to go with him.

Last night Chet and Irene had me out for supper and the evening. They also had Martha Frank, but Bob had to work. (Bob is an inspector in the inspection hangar.) I had a swell visit with them and stayed pretty late. Their boy, Jerry, is a great little guy – looks a lot like Herby Freeman. They are quite a lot more comfortable in their home now that they have found some furniture and Irene has scrubbed and made things like curtains, etc. Gosh I hope that Chet will be able to stay here longer now.

Everyone write when they can.

Love,

Ted

Autumn weather is arriving in Lewis County, and Evelyn writes with news of the home and farm. She seems more hopeful that life on the farm will be easier for Willis now.

MRS. ERNEST L. MARKHAM

BOX 143

TURIN, NEW YORK

October 4

Dear Ted,

Everybody else is asleep, but I want to scribble a few lines to you because I imagine you will soon be moving again.

Edith Freeman called me on the phone today to tell me that they had just received a letter from Chet telling of another visit you had made at their home. He had told before of you and Jerry Nuffer being there. Irene is a real person and a good sport isn't she? They said Martha Kelley Frank was staying with Irene until she could find a place to live.

Pete is in Florida now – Tampa, I think. Merrill D. is still at Elgin Field.

Ray Miller and Linc. Ackerman are both on their way across now, we suppose.

For all we know, Burt is still at Fort Dix. Mel has had several letters from there. He wrote that he <u>might</u> get into some intelligence work – don't tell it because I am not sure but if he does he will be a sort of investigator and live mostly as a civilian. Well, I hope he gets something that will be good for him – for his mind, I mean. Melrose is missing him, of course, but I feel sure she isn't finding it as hard as she had expected. She is brave and cheerful and Linda somehow seems to understand and not expect him back or tease for him. They both are fitting into our home life so nicely as though it were the most natural thing in the world. And it is a great comfort to all of us to have them here. Melrose lives in hopes of going to live near Burt if he gets located a bit securely, but I think that is dubious though I say nothing.

It has been fortunate for me having Melrose here. I guess I wrote you that I have been having a carbuncle on the underside of the thigh. It has been with me over two weeks and has been a miserable thing indeed. The weekend after Burt went, I was just sick and the girls had to take care of me. Then I got so I could sit by the stove and tend my hot packs and take care of myself. Dad took me to the Port Leyden doctor four times. It is cleaned out and healing now. I have a small one on my ring finger now. Trying hard not to get any more. That's a job.

I've sent your picture and a card to Peggy for her birthday.

I'm sorry I have not gotten those pictures of Bob's sent to you before now. Guess it is so late I'd better not send them 'til we get your new address. I never found your album. It seemed that I looked everywhere it could be.

We have heard from Bob just once since he left the coast. From hints he gave, I thought he might be on Midway. Said the scenery was familiar. He had just caught enough rain water to wash his hair and his underwear. The letter was longer coming than it would be from Hawaii.

Willis is finally through with silo filling. The Millards were way behind everyone else. Frost held off till last Sunday and then our garden, etc. did not show it. Last night was harder. Taters are dug, quite a lot of wood drawn down and they are cutting more in the woods. This afternoon they cut a beech with a lot of nuts. There are quite a lot of hickory & butternuts.

Willis seems to be working with more interest and spirit lately. He and Dad are much more harmonious. Maybe Dad really began to think where he'd be if Willis were not here this winter. He still says nothing about hiring Willis, but at least doesn't blow at him all the time. It has been pretty demoralizing to be treated as a kid while expected to carry a man's responsibilities. I think Burt helped him, and Mel and Linda being here helps. Dad is determined to pay as much as possible on the farm. He will pay another $500 in a few days. Well, all will go well if only Willis can keep his faith and courage. Neighbors who work with him like Willis; Mr. Kaskela is a swell friend to him and I think he is getting his feet under him. John is good for him too.

Well, don't mention these things when you write, but I know you want to hear how things are running. I feel better about everything than I have all summer. I'll try to get Dad and Willis to write to you.

Shirley says she wrote awhile ago. Didn't you get if? She works hard in school, and is having piano lessons from Madeline Hoffman. And she just goes right to town with her practicing! Gets 100 marks. Must close. I'll bank that $20 soon.

Heaps of love,
Mom

We threshed last week. Oats hereabouts are poor. Had 41 bags.

Burt writes from Fort McClellan, Alabama, after a two-day ride on a troop train. Despite his hopes for intelligence work, he will be training for the infantry.

FORT McCLELLAN, ALABAMA

Sunday, Oct. 8

Dear Ted,

Well, here I am & they're going to try to make an infantryman out of me. I understand that the training is rough here but we've got a good bunch of guys for non-coms & officers. Most of them have had overseas service, some as much as 2½ years. Our C.O. is on leave so haven't met him yet. Our 1st Louie* is a good egg.

We're still restricted to the company area but some of the fellows have gone to the movies this afternoon. I've been quarantined for a couple days with a couple of boils so I've been trying to get my clothes washed & hung up, catch up on my correspondence, & try to learn the parts of my M.1** Today is the first chance I've had to put on my uniform & wash my one set of fatigues. They would nearly stand up by themselves.

I've been moved to different barracks about five times but I think I'm all set now.

We got in here about 4:00 AM Thursday morning after two days in a troop train. It seems nice around here & will be glad when I can at least look the camp over.

I'll be glad to hear from you because mail has not been very plentiful as yet. I've had one letter from Mel so far.

As ever

Burt

---

*1st Louie = 1st Lieutenant.

**The M1 was the semi-automatic rifle developed by John Garand and declared by General George Patton in 1945 to be "the most deadly rifle in the world."

Once more, Ted writes from a new location, the San Angelo Army Airfield in Texas, where he begins his Advanced Bombardier training.

October 12, 1944

Dear Folks,

I haven't much of a chance to write tonight, but I'll try to do better this weekend. You must have gotten my card from New Orleans telling of my new destination.

We arrived Tues. morning and have been pretty busy ever since. It took us three days to come but we had good G.I. Pullmans and layovers amounting to about 30 hr. We had two good layovers of 12 hrs. each in N. Orleans and Temple, Tex. – both nice cities. N. Orleans is particularly a very interesting city with its historical sights and tradition. We had a good chance to see the high spots – such as the harbor, French Quarter, Huey Long Bridge, etc. We were there from early Sun. morn to early Sun. night so we saw and enjoyed a lot. We had a lot of fun on a shipment for a change because we had a small group and one of our fellow bombardiers – a 2nd Lt. student officer – in charge.

This is advanced bombardiering – the stage in which we hope to finish with wings* in about seventeen more weeks (the middle of Feb.) They will keep us pretty busy here and give us little free time but then that is what we're used to. Upon graduation we will also be qualified navigators for all types of navigation except celestial which shouldn't be hard to pick up after radio navigation.

Again I've been split up from many old buddies. We have about 50 of our gang from Tyndall scattered through 150 virgin bombardiers from the Central Command (virgin bombardiers are those who have come directly from Pre-Flight and haven't had the pleasure of getting the axe from flying.) They also have about half the service and time in cadets as we. Naturally it is different.

Our bks, etc. are a lot like Nashville but better insulated and cared for. We have to go about a half a block from the bks. to the latrine. This

---

*Upon completion of his training, an Aviation Cadet would receive his commission along with his wings.

The French Quarter in New Orleans

Ted's barracks in San Angelo, Texas

camp seems adequate, simple, efficient, and practical instead of some of
the camps like Tyndall which have offered us better quarters but exhibited
a great level of elaborate construction, waste, and inefficiency. This is
the AAF Central Flying Training Command whereas we were in the AAF
Eastern F.T.C. – headquarters in San Antonio instead of Maxwell.

This part of Texas is almost semi-arid with cattle and sheep predominating. Now it is fairly warm in the day but cold as sin at night. I hate the thought of another winter in these inland sections of the south. You have no idea how cold it is.

I must quit now. How about a note?

Love,

Ted

Shirley has begun her junior year of high school and writes lots of news about her niece and nephew.

October 20, 1944

Dear Ted,

Well, it's about time isn't it? You see I haven't exactly forgotten you because I'd been thinking for a long time that I needed to write to you but with Mom sick, music lessons, and so on plus school work, I haven't written to anyone. It isn't that I left you out.

Today I finished my last test of my seven weeks tests. I like chemistry very much and it isn't too hard for me, but Latin certainly hasn't been easy because we have been covering the other half of Latin 1 that last year's teacher didn't cover & we've gone so fast I haven't been able to entirely catch up as there has been enough and more besides for me to do at home. If Mom tells you my marks, don't be disappointed in Latin because I've studied all I've had time for but it hasn't been enough.

I don't know exactly what my Chem. mark is because he didn't have the last part to my test corrected, but I got 42 on the first part and he said he thought I got better on my second, if so my mark would be between 85–90 which would be the highest. I should also have a pretty good class average. I got 88 in my Social Studies test. I've been kind of slipping in Social Studies too because I didn't have time to read it all. It makes it pretty hard sometimes when you can't read fast enough. This year we have to have about 30 book reports. I'll have to do some stepping.

I don't know whether Mom told you or not about her boils. She was awfully sick and they pained her badly for about a week. Of course it hasn't been a party any of the while. She first started having them when

Burt and Mel first came which was over a month ago. After Burt went they really started to bother her. It was a good thing Mel was here to keep house and help with canning, etc. Mel and I really stepped as there were peaches, tomatoes, and pears right then too. She certainly helped us a lot.

Linda is very sweet now. She comes back with some pretty good answers for you some times. One day I was fixing hamburg & sampling it, as usual. She, of course, had to have some, too, so ups she went & got some quick before anyone could tell her differently. I said "Oh Linda I don't think that's very good for little girls." She pipes up and says "Good for you Bwondie?" Of course I had to say, "Yes."

She has to "help" me practice my music lesson every night. I'll be counting 1&2&3&4&. She'll say "and five and six too". Everything is six or 3,4,5,6.

Every night when it is nice she and Mel come to meet me when I'm coming home from school. The day her Daddy went was kind of a long one. I was just leaving when they came back that morning and she wanted to go with me, but we told her that she could come and meet me that night. She watched for me all day long. Toward the later part of the morning, I guess, she came in and wanted "Gramp's" hat (hunting hat) so her mother gave it to her. The next thing Mel saw was Linda with the two dogs, the wagon with her tricycle in it and Linda with that hat over her eyes was going to get Bwondie. She was way off on the side of the road, and too comical for words, I guess. When Mel finally caught up with her she was beyond Sampsons'. She told her mommy, "I not naughty. I just going to meet Bwondie."

The two dogs just love her and does she ever like them. The doors are busy all the time with her putting them in and out. They know perfectly what she wants of them by her quiet little voice. She'll be going out and she'll say "Come on Lad, come on Cindy" and they follow her around like her shadow.

It's been awfully nice with Marian at home too. She came about two weeks ago. She acts some different since those treatments and shots. She bustles around like everything. Mom certainly has needed her and Mel, too. She plans on staying home for awhile at least. Mrs. Wendt has wanted to get her to work for her. It would be wonderful to work over there. Her children are so nice & she also is just wonderful. Mrs. Wendt said she'd pay her $12 or $15 with every other week-end off. She could come home most every night if she wanted to. She said if she wanted to work at all she'd work there if any but she feels Mom needs her and she's gotten tired of working like she has I guess.

I was at Teen's last week end. We had Thursday & Friday off (Columbus Day) so I went down Thursday morning on the bus and stayed until Sunday. My but I had fun. Teen said I really helped her catch up and we had some good old gab sessions & I saw Jane, the Alexanders, etc. David is a little rogue. He weighed 17 lbs. 10 oz. last Sunday. He gains about 5 to 8 oz. every week now. His two lower teeth came in at the same time & we suspect a couple more are coming in on top as he drools & chews his fist a lot lately. He can almost creep. If his mother had time enough to let him down on the floor more often he probably would do more. He gets his legs right up under him and jumps ahead. He squeals every time he gets excited or wants to talk now. He's an awful funny looking guy right now with frizz sticking up an inch all over his head.

Our class is starting the Junior play for November 14. It is good. I have a part but not very long as I told them I couldn't have. We are also planning a dance for November 3 with Madeline Hoffman's Orchestra.

I have been taking piano lessons from Madeline Hoffman since school started. It's really wonderful to take from her. They cost $5 for 4 lessons ($1.25 per) but it's worth it.

We got a letter from Peggy today thanking us for sending your picture and a birthday card. It was very nice. I would like to write to her if I ever get the time.

The folks gathered 3½ bushels of hand picked Beauty apples & 1½ falls the other day. They are wonderful. We thot we'd send you some.

Things sure have been going more smoothly lately. The back yard is full of wood & quite a bit in the shed & down cellar. The fall work is coming nicely altho they haven't started to plow yet.

I guess I'll call it a letter here before I go onto another page. Sorry I didn't get to write before.

Love,
Blondie

Mel's going out to see Burt. She's going to ride with a girl from Carthage who's going to see her husband in Ala. & driving. She saw an ad in the Watertown paper & called this girl. Lucky, eh wat?

Burt writes that it took seven hours to get a call through to Melrose who is on her way to join him. Army chow has helped him put on ten pounds of muscle, but he would give a lot for a home-cooked meal.

Oct. 24, 1944

Dear Ted,

I don't know yet whether my other letter has caught you yet. I mailed it to Florida before I knew you were shipping out.

I don't have much free time around here because I'm a squad leader and going to NCO* school four nights a week. What time I've had has been cleaning my rifle, shoes, etc. I guess you know.

Melrose is coming Saturday and is planning on staying a while. Linda is staying up with Mother. She (Mel) was lucky & is "sharing" a ride with a girl from Carthage who is coming within 30 miles of here. I called her up Sunday and it took seven hours to get the call through. There was quite a delay.

Thanks a lot for the fiver. It wasn't awfully necessary but needless to say it came in very useful. I have a check bank but I'd have to go way down to the main PX to get it cashed & I'm pretty busy to get there when the bank is open.

There are quite a few hills around here and we are all the time climbing them. I guess it's to condition us & it is. I'm lame in every joint and I've gained at least 10 lbs. since I came in the army. Our P.T. is notoriously rugged here but I can take it better than most.

I've got to get to bed. The lights were supposed to have been turned off by now and we have night problems the rest of the week. I am always hungry and tired. I can't complain too bad about chow but I'd give a week's pay for a good home cooked meal.

I'll try to drop a line again soon.

As ever
Burt

---

*Non-Commissioned Officer.

Evelyn writes to Ted that she has outwitted the censors and figured out that Bob is stationed at Midway. For the first time she writes of the certainty that her youngest son will be drafted soon.

MRS. ERNEST L. MARKHAM
BOX 143
TURIN, NEW YORK

Oct. 29, '44

Dear Ted,

Things just seem to come along so fast that I hardly know what I have written about, and when.

We have had two letters from you since you have been at San Angelo. You are surely seeing a lot of the south, anyhow. Time must have passed more quickly at Tyndall Field because you have seen so many you knew there. It surely was fine seeing Irene and Chet as you have.

We had a pleasant surprise a week ago this evening when Alex Trainor dropped in to see us. He wanted to know about all you boys. Came from Camp Stewart.

The only letter we had had from Bob since he went out had been dated Aug. 27 until we got one the other day. It was written Sept. 28th, postmarked Oct. 2nd. He said he had just received one from you that had been 3 wks. on the way. He said my first guess about where he was was right. I guessed Midway. He says, "For awhile, we might do quite a lot of moving around."

Did we tell you that Pete is at Tampa? No doubt you know as much about Burt as the rest of us do. Mel left here Wed. morning on her way to Alabama. She got a ride with a cousin of Uncle Albert's who was driving to join her husband only 30 mi. from where Burt is. It seemed quite providential. She had been trying to plan and then saw the advertisement of this Mrs. Pearl Miller Young of Carthage. We had a card back from her from Carlisle, Pa. where they stayed the first night.

Linda is here, of course, and it seems best. We get along very well with her.

You know, don't you, that Marian is home? That is good, too. I can't begin to tell how good that is for me. She isn't any too strong, and

I think (or hope) the change will be good for her. She and Alton need to be together. And if Willis has to go, as I think he will before long, we will need her. I can't say or write much about this now, but God help us all!

When I went to the bank with your money the other day and asked for a statement of your account, they said you would have to write them and ask for one, Or fill in this card and make it a joint acct. and then you could have me do those things. Funny, they gave me a statement and your returned checks once before!

Willis says I should have sent this price list to you. He just doesn't write to anyone. He has been all unsettled for so long.

Weather is good to us. Snow just once, pond frozen over once. Mostly mild. We have a huge pile of wood down – partly buzzed.

Lots of love, Mother

Ted writes to Shirley about how appreciative he is of her nice long letters. He isn't afraid to say that he gets homesick. There is only one home for him.

San Angelo Army Air Field
BOMBARDIER SCHOOL
SAN ANGELO, TEXAS

October 29, 1944

Dear Blondie,

Your much welcomed letter arrived last week. I liked it so well that I had to pass it on for Peggy to read. If you would like to write Peggy I'm sure she would enjoy it a great deal – she has said that she wishes that she could hear from you.

That letter is the kind which I speak of when I say that it is nice to hear everyone's opinions or stories. Mom's letters are so swell yet it is also so worthwhile to hear Blondie's, Willie's, Dad's, Altie's, and everyone's opinions and thoughts. It is so realistic that way because after all my connection to home deals with everyone and not just one special member.

I didn't know that Teen is evidently teaching again this year. Nor did I know that Marian had gotten home and was feeling so much better. I'm glad to hear that Mel could get to Alabama as both Blondie and Burt wrote me.

I had another letter from Burt last week. It is easy to see quite a change in Burt's ability to correspond since he put on the uniform. It was the same with Bob and I as well as any serviceman I guess. Letters are golden even if it is pretty difficult to keep up with them. Physically the army seems to be agreeing with Burt. He has the same gripe about chow but the physical exertion, routine, and appetite can certainly take off the pork and put lots of beef on. We don't much like PT and other healthful requirements but we are still quite appreciative of the fact that we're tough as hell.

My past week hasn't been especially eventful – just pound, pound, and pound some more without much of a let up for anything. It isn't all hands on active except that more than ever each minute is scheduled on a rush from reveille to taps. I like it this way though because it keeps out the bitterness and makes you feel more natural in doing something worthwhile. I'm coming to realize that this bombardiering is quite a complicated duty – especially when we find it is as hard to learn to operate the bombsight as it is to learn to fly and when technical ability and background is even greater than that required of a navigator. I haven't flown yet but I feel confident that I could stick a bomb in our pond from 10,000 feet. By the way our class is scheduled to graduate Feb. 10.

It was a year ago this weekend when Jan was married, and Peggy and I were home. I guess that I shall always remember that weekend as one of the largest in my life. It's sort of useless to say that I would like the same again this weekend, but I do even more so. I guess that it is because I still get as homesick as I used to when I first stayed with Grandma & Grandpa or when Burt and I ran away from Uncle Adrial's. It's useless to try and forget it or even to disbelieve in it. There is only one home for me as there is for millions of others.

Everyone write and write Burt even more.

Love,
Ted

Burt writes to Ted about how helpful is to have Mel nearby. As an infantryman, Burt is learning a lot about weapons – especially about cleaning them.

Sun. Nite, Nov. 5

Dear Ted,

I was glad to get your letter the other day. I don't get as much mail as I did a while back – you see, Mel is here with me now. She came a week ago Friday nite and now I don't need the mail that I once did. Linda is staying with Dad & Mother at least until we know a little more about the future.

Mel is doing housework for a Capt.'s wife for her room and board and really has it pretty decent. She has her own room & bath and I can be there any time. It's only about a 10 min. walk from the company so I'm staying down all nights possible. The Capt. & his wife are nice & work not difficult.

I'm supposed to come down for Sunday dinner but missed out today. We go out on rifle range tomorrow morning and last nite they issued us new M-1's. If you've ever cleaned a new gun, you know what I've been doing all day. I also had to stand rifle inspection & be assigned target and firing order. Although it's a lot of work to clean my rifle, I'm rather pleased because it sure is a better rifle than I had before. Maybe I can qualify now. You say you haven't seen the M-1 but shot the carbine. The carbine is a bay M-1 but much simpler.* We get to use a lot of weapons here including the carbine, bazooka, .30 cal. light & heavy m.g., 60 & 80 m.m. mortars and the B.A.R.** Some of us may get to the 37mm a.T. gun & the 105 mm howitzer but that is highly doubtful.

We get four days this week with the M-1 & 2 days with the carbine. I hope I can do well because the 10 best shots among the squad leaders get to be cadres*** on the range, however, the other 10 get some good detail also.

---

*Bay = bayonet.
**B.A.R. = Browning Automatic Rifle.
***Cadre = officers and enlisted personnel qualified to train new soldiers.

I'm still going to school four nights a week and have some night problems. Last Thursday I pulled guard for the first time and they keep us generally busy anyway. I don't have much time to spend with Mel but it is certainly worth while having her here. It gives a lot of needed stability and eases that homesick feeling most fellows get.

I think I'd better get some sleep because I'll have to crawl out about 4:00 A.M. tomorrow so will try to write again.

Burt

P.S. I doubt if I'll have much chance to see the country. Understand they have B-29's at Moody now and I saw a B-32 go over here yesterday.

Ted writes next with the news that he has dropped his first practice bombs. He has a bad taste in his mouth over the Army's poor treatment of highly qualified soldiers.

San Angelo Army Air Field
BOMBARDIER SCHOOL
SAN ANGELO, TEXAS

November 12, 1944

Dear Folks,

This is sort of a lazy Sunday for me because I've been resting and doing little odd jobs for the week to come. I haven't much to write because everything has been generally the same. It has been plenty of work and effort to keep abreast lately, but I have the satisfaction that it seems to be paying off.

238

Parade formation

I had a nice letter from Burt last week telling how well he is getting on and how well Mel is getting situated. I'm glad that things seem to be working out well for them.

I also had a letter from Mr. Baxter. He said that Willie had been up to hunt for a few days before moving back to Ithaca.

I see by the B Herald that Peg Gaffney will be teaching Home Ec. in Boonville. She was a good friend of mine in school for she belonged to at least one social organization which I too belonged to and we would see her at the house quite often. She is engaged to Don Von Waes who is AZ, my class, and a pilot in Fla. now. She was Rita Schoff's roommate in school. I believe that Bob also knows her, and Marian, I believe, knows who she is. Should you ever get a chance to introduce yourselves I am sure she would be pleased.

We had a big post parade yesterday in observance of Armistice Day. Unfortunately though it was just for the post and a bit disgusting when it was carried the same as other perplexing post parades.

I may possibly be getting a new instructor soon. They have just brought in quite a number of combat bombardiers for instructors. My instructor is satisfactory but he has never seen combat so it is likely that he

Competitive drill

may be replaced. Some of us got a pretty dark brown taste in our mouth last week when we saw them make these boys with DFC's,* Air Medals, Unit Citations, and Purple Hearts drill and get treated like a bunch of rookies.

I dropped my first bombs last week and will be dropping them every day for quite a period now. With those first three I'll have to backtrack my boast of laying one in our pond from 10,000 ft, but I would have laid two of the three in from 13,000. These are of course only practice bombs with 97# of sand and a three pound bursting charge of black powder.

By the way did Pete use the Sperry or the Norden sight? I of course use the Norden which is almost standard now.

You don't have an opportunity to get any 127 film do you? I received Bob's pictures and will send them on home by way of Peggy. We saw some of them but want to see the rest.

Everyone write!

Love,
Ted

P.S. Did I write that our training has been lengthened six weeks?

---

*DFC = Distinguished Flying Cross.

Marian has been doing some writing for the local newspapers. She writes to Ted with the news that Willis has been drafted and is on his way to Fort Dix. She was the one who took him to the train in Lowville and saw him off to a life far different from the one he has known on the farm.

Home

Nov. 22

Dear Ted,

I may not finish this tonight but thot I'd get a start. I've just been writing out the dope on all my four brothers in the service for Minnie Hart to put in the paper. She says Mom isn't very publicity minded. I merely outlined where you'd all been stationed etc. You've been in ten (10) places. That ought to fill up space and make her a couple extra cents.

As you've gathered, Willis left on Mon. morning by bus from Lowville. As long as nobody else could go I went with him. We stayed at Teen's all night. He thot he was going by train so I took Bill and went to the station but then we had to walk way uptown. Of course Bill got a big thrill.

Mom got a card from him yesterday saying he was examined in Syracuse (he thot it would be Albany). Said it took some of them longer to go through so some of them were staying at the Onondaga overnight. They had a room with 7 beds and he said they were a crazy bunch. Today an official notice came that he was being sent to Ft. Dix.

I came from Lowville Mon. night with the teachers & went to P.T.A. because Altie was in a play. He paid my dues before I moved home. Last night Shirley was in a play at school and we all went. It was awfully good. Mrs. Wendt was coach. Paul Freeman had the leading boy's part.

Linda keeps things lively around here. She talks every minute. She apparently is happy and contented and it's good for all of us having her. She is highly insulted if she can't go to the barn at night. I was down last night and you should have seen the two kids and two dogs playing in the hay. She follows Altie every step. He manages her just like a big brother. He often puts on her things to take her out to help with his work.

Altie had to have Bill come down to go to the Halloween party. So I took the whole cabudle. Linda was a clown (I've got lots of compliments since) and Bill was a cowboy (Altie's cowboy hat, red shirt, overalls, bandana and gun). Altie went as a Dutch girl. You should have seen him in the grand march with one on each side. Bill was the shy one, didn't want to do anything not even eat but Linda had a grand time.

Bill and Linda have big times together. They both try to be the biggest. Bill helps her dress and even goes to the bathroom and helps her. They swap slippers, rubbers, hats, frocks, overalls and everything they can. Of course they never argue about it. I told the folks now I know what twins are like – a double dose plus competition. But I like it. Linda keeps asking to have Billy come and let's keep him.

She is thrilled with David but complains "he's big." I suppose she thinks babies shouldn't be. She holds him and I expect him to jump right off her lap. He wears us big folks out with his jumping. He weighs nearly 19 lbs. and his legs go every minute. One of the neighbors calls them pistons. He has light hair now and we call it G.I. It's about 1½ in. long and sticks straight up. His eyes are blue and kinda bug out so we call him Stupe (for stupid). But there's nothing wrong with his I.Q. He says "een nay" for his bottle and "uh" to be taken. Also says "DaDa" to get up in the morning and "MummMumm."

He has four teeth and all on the bottom so we're going to buy him an upper plate. He has a devilish grin on his face most of the time. He pulls hair nice and hard and bites like a puppy dog. He doesn't chew his own finger because it hurts. He made Johnny K. yell good the other night. He has kissed folks for months. The kisses are a bit puppy-doggish but there's no mistaking they're kisses. When a man takes him he feels of their face first thing. He'll be taking a round out of Bill before long. The O'Briens and Klossners were here for dinner Sunday and David didn't sleep hardly at all but was good natured all the time and the next day too. He doesn't see the folks very much but remembers them and grins when he sees them. Alton thinks he's pretty special. Dad can hardly wait to get hold of him. He sees Shirley and just squeals. Everybody grabs him but he's not fragile.

More Tomorrow

Autumn 1944

We went to Klossner's for dinner today. We had roast chicken with all the fixings. Jan is a good cook. Of course we had a good time.

I seem to have run out of news. Oh yes, Helen Miller was married in Hendricks Chapel at Syracuse University last night. The man's name is Paul Seiss (I guess). Aunt Mary & Uncle Albert borrowed the Plymouth.

Mom says I've just got to get my license to drive so we can go places. It might be convenient but then it probably would be a nuisance too.

I went to Ithaca Nov. 3 to get the rest of my things. I expected to come right back but Mr. B. was taken sick – he's got angina and Pearl Walsh (from Constableville) who has been working for him couldn't tell up from down. So I stayed until Nov.14 and got back for Altie's birthday. I worked like a horse but when I came back the apartment was nearly all cleaned and running smoothly. Mr. B. wants me to come back – will pay me most anything but I think I'm needed at home now. Seems darned good to be here too. Mom and I counted up and it's been 8 yrs. since I've been home for over a month. So at present I seem to be general trouble-shooter.

Just a bit more news – Len Ackerman was reported missing Oct. 27 but they have gotten letters dated Nov. 8 so we're all in hopes it's a mistake. Lincoln is a paratrooper and is in Italy now too. Len has been in the front lines in the mountains in Italy for quite awhile. Their only supplies come by mules. Said he was sick of the cold, the mud and the people. Will let you know further developments. I do the leg work for the telephone.

Must get to bed now – got plenty to do tomorrow.

Love,
Marian

Feeling good now. But I <u>wasn't</u> built for a <u>draft horse</u>. Am enclosing some stale clippings. Does the B.S. on your address mean what I think it does?

FAMILY'S FOUR SONS IN SERVICE

Last of Sons of Mr. and Mrs. E. L. Markham Enters the U. S. Service.

Lt.(j.g.) R.W. Markham   Pvt. B.H. Markham   W.H. Markham   A/C. T.W. Markham

Clipping from the Watertown Daily Times, November 27, 1944

Turin, Nov. 27.—All four sons of Mr. and Mrs. Ernest L. Markham are now in the armed services, one in the Navy and three in the Army. The last to go was the youngest son, Willis H. Markham, 19, who had his physical examination at Syracuse last week and at his request was sent on immediately. He is now at Fort Dix, N. J. He attended grade school in Turin and was graduated in June, 1943, from the Constableville Central High school. Since graduation he has been managing his father's farm.

The oldest son, Lt. (j. g.) Robert W. Markham, 27, is now overseas, somewhere in the Pacific. He was graduated from the Turin High school and from the College of Agriculture, Cornell university, receiving a bachelor of science degree in 1939. He acted as assistant farm bureau agent and also as farm bureau agent in the counties of Wayne, Alleghany and Monroe. He entered naval reserve pilot training in May, 1942, having enlisted eseveral months previously. He trained at Atlanta, Ga., and Jacksonville, Fla., receiving his wings and commission as ensign at Jacksonville. He acted as patrol bomber pilot, being stationed at San Diego, Calif., and Whidby Island, Wash. In August, 1943, he went overseas and was stationed at various points in the Central Pacific. He was home on leave in January, 1944, and then returned to San Diego, Calif., and Alameda, Calif. In August, 1944, he again went overseas and is now stationed "somewhere in the Pacific."

Pvt. Burton H. Markham, 26, the second son, was graduated from the Turin High school, and took post-graduate work in agriculture in the Constableville Central High school. He was graduated from the College of Agriculture, Cornell university, in 1941. In June, 1941, he married Miss Melrose Marriott of Fillmore. They have a two-year-old daughter, Linda. Private Markham was inducted into the army in September, 1944, and was sent from Fort Dix, N. J., to Fort McClellan, Ala., where he is now stationed. At the time of his induction he was employed by the Produce Credit Association at Ithaca.

Aviation Cadet Theodore W. Markham, 23, the third son, attended the Turin school and was graduated from the Constableville Central school. He enlisted in the Army Reserve Corps and was a junior in Cornell university when he entered the service in March, 1943. He was stationed for a time at Fort Niagara. He is training for bombardier, and has been stationed at Miami, Fla., Williamsport, Pa., Nashville, Tenn., Columbus, Miss., Maxwell Field, Ala., Decatur, Ala., Valdosta, Ga., Tyndall Field, Fla., and is now at San Angelo, Tex.

Mr. and Mrs. Markham also have four daughters, Mrs. Robert (Ernestine) O'Brien of Lowville, Mrs. Marion Markham Dewan and Miss Shirley Markham at home and Mrs. John (Janice) Klossner of Constableville. Mr. Markham is a rural mail carrier out of the Turin postoffice.

Evelyn writes that they will have to put aside their hopes and plans and regrets. There is nothing to do but accept the fact that Willis has left.

MRS. ERNEST L. MARKHAM

BOX 143

TURIN, NEW YORK

Nov. 23

Dear Ted,

Marian probably is telling you all the news, but I will just add my scribble. Guess I've been slipping quite a bit on the letter writing. It is rather like old times with me, having Linda to keep track of. When there is a youngster around, one or more people have to keep eyes, ears and brain open every minute.

Linda surely is a little chatterbox and a "busy-fingers", catches on to everything and wants to help, do everything, is quick as a wink, and has very much of a mind of her own but sweet and affectionate. She and Alton are great pals; "Dad" thinks the world of her and so do we all. She makes no fuss about being separated from her parents.

We all went to Janice's and had a lovely Thanksgiving dinner. Your sister is a "bang up" good cook – doesn't need to take a back seat for any of them.

We have been enjoying venison lately. John shot a buck when only Willis and Pete Gydesen were with him. Another day, Mrs. Gydesen shot one. There were several in the party. There do not seem to have been so many deer killed this year, as usual.

Mrs. Miller, Lottie's mother passed away nearly two weeks ago – a blessed relief from a long period of suffering. Mr. Smykla also died about the same time, very suddenly.

I received the M.O. for $40. Must get to the bank with it soon. Your Oct. bond has come

Marian has told you about Willis. I guess I can't add much. You must have realized that it had to come to be so. We just have to put all our hopes and plans and regrets aside I guess and accept the situation. I just have to say tho that we have to have Marian at home. It will be better for Willis and maybe will work out better for the rest of us than I have believed possible. Don't worry about it.

Must close and get to bed.

Heaps of love,
Mom

Willie has made the leap from milking cows on the farm to basic training with grenades, bazookas, and machine guns at Camp Wheeler. His first letter to Ted has a distinctly cheerful tone. Even his shoes that don't fit and his arm that is black and blue from shots don't seem to get him down.

CAMP WHEELER, GEORGIA

December 3, 1944

Dear Ted,

Well they finally got me. The war board was changed from 3 to 5 so George and U. Albert didn't have the majority. I had my physical in Syracuse and was sent to Ft. Dix. Dix is a miserable camp because they don't do anything but process you, give you K.P. and knock you around right and left. Nobody likes Ft. Dix for these reasons only. We left Dix last Tues. night at 9:00 and got in here Thurs. morning. It seemed as though we would never get here. Everyone was trying to guess where we were going and everyone had his own idea where we were headed for. We came down in Pullman's and all the way we tried to get the porter to tell us where we were going but all he would say was, "The same place you are." He was a good guy and we all liked him.

So far I like it, yes I'd rather be home but as long as I'm here I'm going to make the most of it. The only thing I have to kick about are my shoes, they are too big and they hurt my feet and those damn shots knock the devil out of me. The first ones gave me a heck of a cold and I haven't gotten rid of it yet. The one we got yesterday made my arm swell up and it got all black and blue and it was as stiff as a board.

We have done some marching and I am getting the hang of it pretty well but there are a lot of guys who don't know beans about it. I guess the noncoms will have to pound it into the knoggens with a sledge. The noncoms & officers here are a darn good bunch. Most of the noncoms have been overseas. Our sergeant has been in three campaigns in the Pacific.

Tomorrow they really start giving us the works. We will be issued our rifles M 1s. We will be trained in M 1s, B.A.R,* Carbines, grenades, 30 cal. machine gun, 60 mm mortar bazooka and maybe Thompson sub machine guns but no side arms. It will be about 5 weeks before we get on the firing range but we will dry fire before that. I can hardly wait till we get on the firing range.

Fred Regetz is down here in camp but haven't seen him yet. We are restricted to company area until a week from tomorrow. He is in the area until a week from tomorrow. He is in Co. D. 6thBn. I dropped him a card so he may come to see me before the restriction is lifted. Got more letters to write so better sign off.

So long
Willie

---

*The Browning Automatic Rifle, or B.A.R., became the standard-issue light machine gun of American infantry units during World War II.

The Normandy Invasion has taken the lives of three of Ted's fraternity brothers from Cornell. He will be spending Christmas Eve in a bomber.

December 17, 1944

Dear Folks,

The nice package of cookies and <u>Better Farms</u> came last week. Needless to say it didn't last long around here but that is just part of the game to pass it around. We take turns doing that because it not only tastes good but gives us a taste of home more often. I just got a nice pkg. of homemade candy from Jan and John. If her candy is an indication of her cooking I know what you are raving about.

I heard from Willie quite recently. It made me feel pretty good to get a taste of his spirit and cheerfulness. I hope that he can someway get up to see Burt and Mel. Better get a note off to him real often and help that good spirit of his. He might also find a little money handy now too for paydays don't come very often at first until your records get straightened out. I've had quite a bunch of Christmas cards from Turin and Constableville lately. Seems as if I have one from all sorts of local organizations. Quite a few people whom I haven't dreamt of getting cards from have sent them. The Harts, Mrs. Karl Benedict, and Mr. & Mr. Arthur Lee have sent them. Probably the nicest card from an organization was from the servicemen's center of Lowville. It was a series of pictures around Lewis Co. including Whetstone Gulf, the bridge and Lyons Falls, the snow of our country, Black River, and a few other pictures which we enjoy seeing.

I have also gotten an announcement of Helen's marriage and an invitation to Norm Allen's wedding on Dec. 23. Norm was my roommate and close friend while I was a junior at school. I believe that Dad met him – red hair with glasses. His brother George was another AZ who was a good friend of Bob and Burt. George died in August from polio. Norm is marrying Gertrude Dunfee whom I also know well. Gert is Art's sister. You've heard me speak of Art and working with him in Allegany Co.

I haven't heard much from Bob lately. The last he wrote me was nearly two months ago.

I see by the B.H. that Chet and Irene had been in Lewis Co. for a short visit. This was quicker than he had expected, but what he eventually expected. He has quite an admiration for the B-29 so I'm glad he has it.

Have I told you that we have lost three AZ men in France? Bill Barnum and Burt Goulko I believe you remember well. Alf Phelps was the third who was every bit as swell a fellow as either Bill or Burt. Frank Curtis had his invasion barge (he was an ensign) shot out from under him on D-Day.

There isn't much change in my daily routine. Tonight, in a couple of hours, we will begin our night bombing. The daylight bombing is for most practical purposes finished which means that we are dropping our second half of bombs now. Ground school is entirely navigation now. Since we finished ground school in bombardiering we are in a phase of skills now rather than theory. It takes a lot of work and tolerance but it seems to be coming along pretty well. We are just busy as the deuce and have to forget most everything else – even Christmas for we have no chance to shop. We'll be bombing on either Christmas Eve or Christmas night or both.

I'd better quit now and get ready for the Flight Line. Sunday is over now.

Everyone write!

Love,
Ted

Winter 1944–45

Willie writes next that he has qualified for Officer Candidate School, and he could be shipped overseas in as little as fourteen weeks. He's beginning to feel that he's been away from home for a long time.

CAMP WHEELER, GEORGIA

December 21, 1944

Dear Ted,

I got your nice letter day before yesterday. I don't know whether you got my letter or if Mom sent you my address. Just looked at your letter again and see that you did get my letter.

I guess I have myself fairly well adjusted, of course I had much rather be home but I know that you & the other boys would also. Time is a funny thing. It seems to go darn fast but it also seems that I have been away from home a lot longer than I have.

I haven't the slightest idea what I got in my I.Q. test. I would like to know how I came out in Mech. Apt. & Ratio. When we were interviewed they didn't say anything about it.

Fri. night Dec. 22

I must have done fairly good in my I.Q. test because today a list of those who could qualify for O.C.S., was read and I was one. Tonight I filled out an application but this certainly doesn't mean I'll make it.

I didn't get a copy of the B.H. [Boonville Herald] but Mom sent me the clipping. It was quite a write up wasn't it?

Yes, Camp Wheeler is near Macon, about 5 miles I believe. I have been there twice. It is a nice little town. As far as being able to see Burt I guess it is out of the question. There are no three day passes given. Here a weekend pass is from Sat. night at 6:00 to Sun. night at 12:00 AM.

I haven't seen any of the new planes yet except the B-29. One flew over us when we were out at class one day. By the way what does a B-32 look like?

I caught cold from my first shots at Ft. Dix and I still have it. We have to sit on the wet ground so darn much I doubt if I'll get rid of it for awhile. Everyone said the more shots you had the worse they got and I believed them because the first ones I got here sure were tough. My left arm swelled up and was black and blue about half way to my elbow. We got another shot last Sat. and all that happened this time was a sore spot about the size of a silver dollar on the back of my arm. One fellow had four shots in the same arm and he was darn close to going to the hospital.

This is the screwiest weather I ever saw. A couple or three nice days, then it rains after which it gets colder than hell and that wind really blows right through you. The temperature dropped to 20 degrees one night just after we got here. Almost every morning there is frost on the ground.

We got our first rifle range today, that is we had sighting exercises and different positions. That damn sling makes your arm sore after a short time. Next week we fire for qualification. I can't say much about the weapons because I haven't fired any of them yet. The weapons we have been training on are M.1's, grenades, bazooka, 60mm. mortar, 30 cal.mg., B.A.R. and maybe the carbine. I don't imagine the regular riflemen will have training with the carbine but probably the B.A.R. men will because they are much easier to handle.

Today a Lt. told us that our training had been cut to 14 weeks instead of 17. From there I expect to go overseas, that is unless I get O.C.S. which I don't expect.

Yeah that ammunition is dangerous stuff. Last week a guy that was out on bivouac built a fire and the twigs he had wouldn't stay down on the fire so he threw an 80 mm. mortar shell he found (a dud) on the fire. They shipped him home in a pine box. Then there was another kid that found some dummy 30 cal. Shells, you know the ones they fire in mock battles, he also threw them on a fire and he also got hurt though not seriously.

About this serial number business you mentioned, I can't see any similarity between them. What is the similarity? If there is some, well I guess I'm a little thick.

Well write again soon.

Your Brother,
Willie

Bob writes that letters from Ted and Burt have taken two months to arrive. He has sent Ted a picture and wants him to pass it on to Burt and Willie.

Netherlands East Indies
Dec. 22 1944

Dear Ted,

Your letter of Oct. 15 arrived two days ago and one from Burt at the same time. I wonder if I'm going to have to furnish you guys with stamps. Air mail gets thru in two weeks or less – sometimes a week from California.

Rita had written that she had seen in the Herald that you were in Texas – otherwise I hadn't heard anything. Also she says that Chet has gone to Nebraska. They were home a week on the way and Rita was going up. She is teaching in Bath now you know. I still hear from her quite regularly and enjoy it.

I looked up San Angelo on my map and see that it's pretty well out in the arid country of west Texas. It must be a good place to fly tho. You didn't say anything about the kind of planes you will work in or what your syllabus consists of. Hope you'll get all you can out of it especially in navigation. A couple of weeks ago a couple of army fighter pilots took a 25 out of here to another spot. They didn't know the first thing about navigation, not even how to estimate their drift. One of our boys brought them in here and had a chance to give them a little instruction which they seemed pretty happy about. Maybe I'm ultra-conservative but I think it's damned foolish to continue to lose planes as they do just because they expect that it's too much to expect a pilot to know how to navigate. Also I wish they would teach some of their hotshot fighter pilots to recognize friendly planes – at least ours. Maybe I sound pretty mad but you would be too if you had seen what we have. It's not easy to get away from some of the fastest fighters that are built. I know it happens both ways but recently we have had an overdose.

We have a rather nice spot here tho it gets awfully muddy and sometimes rather dusty. We have fixed up our camp pretty well so that we live quite comfortably. I'll try to add a couple of pictures to tell the story better. I live in a tent that is about 16 x 16 with three other fellows. It is screened in around the sides and has a plywood deck that is up off the ground and therefore dries. We have built some furniture and shelves out of boxes and scraps of lumber and most of us have found aircraft inner tubes and stretched strips of rubber across our cots to make them a little more comfortable. We have a front porch, a darned good foxhole and now I have a little garden started. It took a lot of sweat at first but now we are taking it rather easy. All I did today was read, take a nap and pitch horseshoes.

Had a letter from Marian and Alton yesterday saying that Willie left about a month ago. If I knew his address I'd write to him. Hope Dad can keep things going alright but don't see how he can without some help and that is hard to find I guess. Wish he could sell the poorer half of the herd and do a good job with the rest.

We are up in the air to know when to expect to get back. They have started a new system for relieving us by crews rather than as a squadron and it's hard to tell who will be first. I'm still hoping to spend my birthday in N.Y.

Please pass the picture on to Burt and Willie and then home. Write and let me know what you're doing.

Always
Bob

Melrose writes to Ted from Alabama. He had written a letter [not included] to the family supporting her wish to join Burt. She thanks him for his help in convincing the family that she should be here.

Dec. 27, 1944

Dear Ted,

It will be surprising to hear from me, but I have my husband nearly "spoiled" now. I might as well go a little farther and help him with his correspondence. Burt has so little time that I do everything I can to help. You were due for a Christmas letter but he just didn't have time to write any. He wrote to Linda on Christmas Eve.

I guess our biggest news is that the O.C.S. board accepted Burt for the Quartermaster's Corp to-day. His eyes are too poor for Infantry O.C.S. – thank goodness. You know what a break this is for us. They have even cut Burt's cycle from 15 to 14 weeks so the boys can get overseas fighting that much quicker. His name is put on a list waiting for an opening so our hope now is that some provision will be made to keep Burt in the U.S. until his orders come thru.

Burt came dashing over to tell me as soon as he had seen the board & he was happier than he had been in a long time.

We had a nice Christmas altho' we were so lonely for Linda it hurt pretty much. We were luckier than lots tho'. We think Willie was probably one of the homesick boys.

Incidentally, thank you for the letter to the Markhams that let me come here in peace. I don't know how you knew they wouldn't hear of my coming but I guess you did. Being here has been very difficult for me in a lot of ways but I'm glad now I've been exposed to an Army Camp & I know the path has been smoother for Burt. It has been rugged for him & he has "lived on the ball". I deserve his O.C.S. break if anybody does.

You probably hear as much about Linda as we do. It tears me apart to be away from her but if Burt has to be I guess I can take it for a shorter time. I expect to go home next week as Burt will be going out on bivouac. We hope to take Linda to the next Post. Q.M.C. O.C.S. is at Camp Lee, Virginia.

My 'news' seems to be about exhausted so will close for now.

As always,
Melrose

Evelyn writes that she will keep a stiff upper lip knowing that Willie will most likely be overseas and in combat soon.

MRS. ERNEST L. MARKHAM
BOX 143
TURIN, NEW YORK

Dec. 31, 1944

Dear Ted,

This is almost the end of the old year, but it has been Christmas here for us. The twelve of us had a very nice dinner and a tree with gifts as usual. We were quite a tableful and I think others besides myself in imagination saw the other five of you with us. We hope and pray that next year it may be a reality – another home coming like the one we had three years ago, all here.

The little ones have made Christmas happy for all of us. No one can see their enjoyment and not catch some of it. David likes his new toys and spreads his smiles and sweetness around but Linda and Billy are having the most <u>wonderful</u> times. Things like Linda's little dishes and a panda bear to hug, and Bill's slippers like Daddy's mean more to them now than a million dollars will when they get old and fed up like the rest of us.

Melrose is coming in a few days, we hear. Linda takes the news quite matter-of-factly, no fuss about it, anymore than at her going away. She has been so sweet about it, and it has been a great comfort to all of us to have her. I wonder if we've written to you about how chummy she and Alton are. Marian got some denim coveralls for her and I found warm things to put underneath so she goes out to the barn with Altie even on cold stormy days when she could not play outdoors. She loves the snow and has lots of fun in it and of course eats and sleeps better for the fun and exercise. My but she is a busy body and a chatterbox! And keen and quick as any youngster I ever knew.

254

Billy is growing up fast. I can't begin to tell you about him. And David is just about as sweet as is possible. He is having spots of eczema nearly all over his body just now. We think it may be due to teething and hope it will clear up soon. Ernestine is feeling better again.*

We received a notice one day last week that you were sending a subscription to Time for a Christmas present. That is a lovely gift and one which we will all enjoy if we take time to, I am sure, but you really should not have done it. We have the Post still coming on a three year subsc. Ellis and Kate have renewed our Digest again. Jan and John are giving us the B. Herald again. We just have to have the W. Times** and we have about a half dozen farm papers. If we only had time to absorb all the good information from them! But thanks for your gift. It was swell of you.

Dad and I sent in for the Reader's Digest for all of you boys and the Boonville Herald for Willis.

Did you get a Christmas package from home? Marian did the shopping, I added the eats. Teen packaged, wrapped and addressed it as only she can do. Please let her know you appreciate it as she feels that she has nothing to give. If she only keeps well, they have much to call riches, I think.

I've written quite a number of letters lately and forget what I have written so if I repeat, please forgive me.

Have we told you that Doris and Pete came home on an 18 day furlough? He wished he had realized sooner just where you were before you left Tyndall Field. Capt. Merrill Dewan and Elsie were home. We saw them in Boonville. Bill Healt came home and was married Christmas Day. You'll probably read about it in the Herald.

Yes, Willis writes quite cheerful, spirited letters. He always can find some fun in most everything. But I think he gets a bit homesick too. He called and talked to me on the phone the other night. No special news except that he had just heard from Burt for the first time. Guess he just wanted to hear a voice from home. It did me good to hear his anyhow. I miss the kid!

We had a letter from Bob written Dec. 8. There was not much news. He spoke of having been quite busy for a few days so he was too tired to

---

*Ernestine is expecting another baby.
**Watertown Daily Times.

do much – had just washed some clothes that had been soaking four days. He told of some improvements they were trying to make on their living quarters and spoke of trying to do a little gardening.

Burt probably has written you that he has hopes of getting into O.C.S. He could not qualify for infantry but hopes to get into quartermasters or maybe medical. Well, I hope he makes it.

Willis has applied for O.C.S. too but he is pretty young. They probably will shove him right over there to fight. They seem to want all the youngsters they can for cannon fodder.

Dad has taken four days off to work at home, part of the time having Benton to get out wood. He will have tomorrow too. I imagine if the work gets too much he will let Charley carry the mail and he will be home more of the time.

The war news looks like tough going* ahead of us, but we'll all plug along and keep a stiff upper lip. Maybe things will look better soon. Here's hoping.

Is there anything you've wanted for Christmas which you didn't get and we could still send you, maybe?

Love, Mom

---

*On December 16, German forces broke through American lines in the Ardennes Forest in an attempt to retake the Belgian port of Antwerp. The Battle of the Bulge continued until the end of January 1945.

1945

Winter 1945

The year begins as the Battle of the Bulge rages in Europe. The battle would end with a victory for the Allies at a cost of more than 185,000 casualties, including 19,000 American lives. The Markhams would lose another friend and neighbor in the battle.

In February, the Marines would endure huge losses on the island of Iwo Jima. April would see the struggle for Okinawa result in the biggest losses in the Pacific, more than 12,000 Americans dead. The war ended in Europe with Germany's surrender in May. But the war in the Pacific would go on for three more months, finally coming to an end In August.

Burt is still in Alabama, hoping to be sent to Quarter Master Officer Training Camp soon. In the meantime, he is experiencing some grueling training conditions, complete with live ammunition.

The photographs accompanying Burt's and Will's next few letters are from Ted's bivouac in San Angelo, Texas. They were chosen to represent experiences that both Burt and Will wrote about.

Sun. Jan 6 45

Dear Ted,

I guess it's been a dogs age since I wrote last but I've really been damned busy. We just got back from four days of bivouac last night and go out again Thurs. morning. It's plenty rugged and miserable weather. We came in soaked to the hide and I've got a cold that's the next thing to pneumonia.

Tomorrow we go out early again and run the infiltration course twice, once in the morning and once after dark. It's going to be muddy as hell when we crawl through with hot lead flying about 18 in. from the ground. Some fun!

We're awfully short of cadre around here and I've been moved up to platoon guide, so I get my ass run ragged. We don't have any platoon sergeant. The fellows cooperate well though.

I guess I told you that I put in for Q.M.O.C.S. Well, I made it but will have to wait for the quota to open. In the meantime I'm told that I'll probably stay on here, go to cadre school and be p.p. for a while. I understand their O.C.S. is at Camp Lee, Va. And a nice camp. I wouldn't mind getting my orders tomorrow.

Some of the fellows left Sat. for A.S.T.P.* (engineers). Most of them went to V.R.I.

Melrose left for Turin last Tues. I had a card from her saying trains were late so she had to spend two nights on the way. She plans to come back and bring Linda if I stay on here as I won't be getting a furlough.

I had a letter from Bob last week and he apparently didn't know your address. I sent it to him. The pictures enclosed are some he requested me to send on.

I've written Willie once since I knew where he was but as yet haven't heard from him.

When you get your wings and a furlough, would it be possible for you to come this way? I would appreciate seeing you. I may be able to get to see Willie in a couple of weeks as it's only about 100–150 miles away. Our platoon Lt. has told me he would fix me up with a pass. He's a great guy. Big as all outdoors – used to play end for Southern Cal. – played a damned good game, I understand.

Since we started our cycle we have had 3 C.O.'s and now we only have one sergeant that started with us. You can see how things are here. I hope Texas is warmer than it is here. We've had some snow and it's raw and muddy all the time. Great bivouac time. Well, if we're freezing in the mud, we're not fighting mosquitos, snakes, and chiggers.

We get a rough bivouac** here. The cycle has been cut two weeks and I guess they're trying to make it up. We get all night problems (no time off next day), forced hikes, etc. We did six miles Friday in one hr. & 5 min. A couple of weeks ago it was four miles in 41 min. My damned legs are lame every morning. I wonder if I'll ever get built up to this. Bones Gap is a rugged hill too. It's about two miles on each side and straight up. We came over it last night and it was pouring and damned slippery.

I guess I've slung about enough for once but you'll hear from me if I live through the battle of Morrisville this next week. We ride out and only hike back 12 rather than 25 mi.

As ever
Burt

---

*A.S.T.P. = Army Specialized Training Program.
**A bivouac is a temporary camp with little or no shelter.

Ted has a problem. Soldiers are only allowed to display one picture on their shelf, and he has four. His Christmas package included a portrait of Marian and Altie.

San Angelo Army Air Field
BOMBARDIER SCHOOL
SAN ANGELO, TEXAS

January 7, 1945

Dear Folks,

My letter writing has been poor because of the same old story – that about all of our free time is used to sleep. It seems as if all I do in free time is to write letters yet I have an awful stack of letters to answer and others to write.

The nice Christmas package came over a week ago. It was swell – especially so because I could see little things about the little details of the pkg. which gave me reason to know that everyone had a hand in fixing it up. I can't say how I know except that it is just a part of belonging to home. I didn't expect such an elaborate picture of Altie and Marian when I asked for one, but I am not going to complain. I must try to find a way to include my pictures in one frame because we are allowed to have only one on our shelf. I have four pictures now – Peggy's, Mom and Dad's, Marian and Altie's, and Billy's. Perhaps I should tell you to pack your pkgs. a little stronger for the last two were beaten up in the mail though not harmed especially.

Last week brought a letter from Bob saying that he was in the Admiralties and telling a bit about his doings. He sent me four pictures which you will get via Burt and Willie. I also have recent letters from Mel and Willie with news which they have probably written you. I'm sure happy with the possibility of Burt getting O.C.S. and that Willie may qualify. I guess its wishful thinking that they both can make it, but we can hope.

I've been wondering lately if Dad won't have his 30 years in next June and if he has a chance to retire then. It probably is more wishful thinking but something which I would like to hear more about.

Where will you be putting corn – in the north meadow or was it there this year? I'm afraid that I'm losing track. Do you have the new calves named yet, Altie?

Everyone write when you can.

Love,
Ted

Ted's Christmas gift from Marian

The next letter is from Willie, written to Shirley from a stairwell where the lights are still on. He has been seeing a lot of movies full of too many beauty queens. He wants to make sure his little sister is staying in shape.

CAMP WHEELER, GEORGIA

January 8, 1945

Dear Blondie,

Please excuse the pencil, it's a lot quicker and I have plenty of letters to get off. It's nine P.M. now and I'm writing this on the stairs because these lights don't go out till 12:00.

How is everything going with you at school? I imagine you are studying hard and getting good marks. I hope you are keeping right at your piano lessons. Keep it up because I wish that I had done it when I had the chance. If I had my pick of an instrument to play now I wouldn't hesitate in saying that it would be a piano. How is the baritone playing coming along?

I'm sorry I haven't answered your letter before but I have been so darn busy for the last two weeks some of the time I wondered if I was afoot or horseback. All the mail I've had (up until the last two days) for the last two weeks was one letter from Grandma & one from Burt and a package of cookies from Aunt Helen.

Macon, that is the town near camp, is quite a nice little town. It isn't so small because it is a lot larger than Lowville, it's about the size of Rome I'd say. There are about 6 U.S.O.s* in town. The Georgia peaches aren't so hot. Some of them are nice girls but most of the ones I've seen around town are bags. You can pick them up in any soda fountain, beer joint, restaurant or U.S.O. They have a good orchestra at the Recreation Center and there is a dance every night but Sun. On Sun. we can go to the Y.M.C.A. and go swimming if we want to. I haven't been as yet but am going before long.

How about it Blondie, are you keeping that girlish figure of yours? Boy you sure want to keep on the ball so it doesn't get away from you. If you should (by any chance) start to gain weight just let me know for I could give you instructions for some exercises that would put you in trim and make you look like Betty Grable.

I have seen quite a few good movies since I've been here. When we first got here a couple of my buddies and I went quite a lot but lately we haven't hardly had time to turn around. I've seen Hollywood Canteen, Winged Victory and a lot of other good ones but I can't remember them all. The theater is only about from home down to Sampson's** so you see we don't have to go far and it only costs $.15 so it isn't very hard on the pocket book.

Last week we were out on firing range and Thurs, Fri & Sat we had barracks orderlies from another company. Sat. night there were a lot of things missing from foot lockers. Hats, cigarettes, candy, socks and I had twenty bucks stolen on me. I don't know how they got it because my foot locker is padlocked all the time. Of course the fellow could have picked the lock. I'm just out twenty bucks because in the Army there is absolutely

---

*U.S.O. = United Service Organizations.
**The Sampsons were nearby neighbors on West Road.

no way to trace money. You can't prove anything just because some guy has some extra money on him. From now on my money goes where ever I do, even to bed. What I can't see though is why the fellow didn't take it all while he was at it. I had $45 in my pocketbook besides some other things, and there were plenty of things in my foot locker that would have been useful to anyone.

I didn't do so hot out on the firing range. The highest possible score was 220 and I only got 161. We had to have 140 to qualify. A hundred & forty to 165 is a marksman, 165–180 is sharpshooter & 180–220 is expert. I only missed sharpshooter by 4 points but you see 161 is no better than 140 as far as the tin we get to wear on our chest is concerned. I did a lot better on the carbine which I got 134 out of a possible 150. If you don't know what I'm talking about just ask Altie. The first of course is my score on the Garand* which is the infantryman's chief weapon. This week we fire the bazookas and the rifle grenade and the rifle grenade kicks like a mule does with both feet.

Thursday we go on a 15 mile hike. We start out at 7:30 P.M. and go out and set up bivouac, then we tear down our tents and roll up our packs and head back to the barracks. We are supposed to get back at 3:00

---

*The M1 was also called the Garand after the man who designed and developed it.

Roach, Ted's roommate from Tyndall Field (see page 207), and his M2 machine gun, also known as the Browning .50 cal. machine gun.

Marching with field packs

A.M. but it may be even later. We had one previous hike which was only 7 miles. We made the three miles back to barracks in just 1 hour and 15 minutes. The Army is supposed to travel at the rate of 2½ miles an hour but we practically ran all the way back and we were carrying full field packs at that. There are a couple of long legged Lts. here and they really set a pace that is darn tough on us short legged guys.

Well this is probably getting boring so I'll sign off for now till I can get some more time. Write when you can.

Love
Wills

Marian writes that Bob is in the Philippines. She is enjoying life at home.

Turin, NY
Jan 15, 1945

Dear Ted,

I guess I haven't written you in quite awhile. I've written Willis & Bob recently and Mel keeps Burt informed of the comings & goings around here.

Winter 1945

I'm glad you liked your Christmas package. We didn't have much chance to shop and it's hard to guess what you boys could use. Don't be flattered thinking I had that picture taken especially for you. Mom nagged me for ages for one so I relented last summer for her birthday. I had those miniatures made for you boys because I tho't they'd take up less room. I really meant to get one to you for your birthday but didn't get them till just before the packages went to Bob.

Willis got his package before Christmas. I took it that yours was real late. Mom sent the Digest to all you boys. Let us know if you get it.

Oh, the biggest news we have is a letter from Bob last week that was written Dec. 30 from the Philippines. He said he was surprised that it wasn't sooner. I'd guessed that it would be the Philippines. And he kept hinting that he didn't expect to stay in the Admiralties long enough to get much out of his garden.

Altie and Shirley are having a free for all and Mel & I are having trouble writing. It's really ridiculous. Altie reminds me of a bantam rooster and Shirley only laughs. Then once in awhile she picks him up and he can't do a thing and then he gets mad. They act like a brother & sister the way they pick at each other and fight. Linda gets mad at Shirley because she doesn't want anyone to hurt Altie. She thinks he's wonderful.

Oh tonight when Linda went to bed and said her prayer, Mel told her to ask to be a good girl. She said make Mamie* good girl too. Tonight we had ice cream for supper. Linda didn't eat what was on her plate so Mel sent her away from the table. She went out in the kitchen and got the big spoon that the ice cream was dished with and stood around wiping her finger on the spoon and licking it as loud as she could.

Mom and Shirley went to Rome & Utica with the Klossners last Wed. and then Mom went home with them and stayed until Sunday. Dad pretended that he nearly starved and we let the fires go out. We didn't do so hot with the furnace but did remember the kitchen fire. Dad raised the dickens all the while she was gone so we didn't think he fared too bad.

Saturday morning Altie went down to Dewan's and yesterday morning I went and we came home last night. Mother Dewan** is in bed and has been since Christmas. They are giving her dope but still she's in

---

*All of Marian's nieces and nephews called her "Mamie."
**Mother Dewan was Marian's ex-mother-in-law.

265

awful pain. It's awful to see her suffer so. She told me she didn't know whether she could stand the pain until Jerry comes home next weekend or not. When I went to say goodbye, she said, "Oh, I thot you were going to stay." So I promised her I'd come down in a few days. Tom went with us to the station and we had quite a visit. It pleases me that it seems to be a comfort to them to have me come. Almeta is home all the while. There isn't anything more that can be done for Mother (Dewan) but make the rest of her life as comfortable as can be.

Mel's letter from Burt today said it was rumored that there were vacancies in Quartermaster O.C.S. Here's hoping.

Everybody here is fine and so are the Klossners and O'Briens. When Teen asks David where Mamie is, he looks at the door and waves and says "bye". He's awfully cute and a rascal. You should see him get after Bill. He grabs hair, nose, ears or anything and then laughs and squeals. He looks more like Bob all the while.

We got two copies of Time last week. I know we'll enjoy it. I skimmed it but don't read the way I used to.

Next Monday is Willis' birthday. We are going to make some cookies to send I guess.

Guess I'd better get to bed.

Love,
Marian

I had a letter at Xmas from Peg. Says she's planning on coming up when you do.

Basic training is toughening Willie up, and he's learning to use the weapons of the infantry. He's waiting to be interviewed for Officer Candidate School.

January 16, 1945

Dear Ted,

Well we are in our seventh week now and we seem to be having it a little easier.

January 17, 1945

I didn't get a chance to finish this yesterday. We had it pretty easy yesterday. We had 8 hours of classes in Range Estimation.

Last Thurs. night we went on a fifteen mile hike which turned out to be 23 miles. We left at 7:00 P.M. and got back at 3:00 A.M. We went out and set up a bivouac and were there for two hours. Boy it was plenty cold out there just standing around but I went to sleep just the same. I was connecting file between our platoon & the one ahead. It sure was easier walking out there than back in the ranks. My feet were sore as hell, on the bottom, when we got back. Our sgt. said it was the toughest hike he had been on since he has been here and he was as tired as the rest of us. A p.f.c.* who went with us said it was the toughest hike he had ever been on (Pretty rough).

The night after the hike I had guard duty from 3:00 to 5:00 A.M. and boy I sure was tired Saturday.

We've fired the rifle grenade and it has quite a kick especially if you don't hold it tight against your shoulder. We fired three, two rifle

---

* p.f.c. = private first class.

267

grenades and one fragmentation grenade. I had three direct hits. The fragmentation grenade, you probably know, is fired with the rifle butt against the ground. I got a direct hit with it and the Major said it was a very good hit.

Sat. we fired the bazooka, two practice rounds and one high explosive. I got a good hit with the first practice round but missed with both the others.

Probably the last of this week or next week we will fire the B.A.R. We still have the light m.g. and 60mm. master to fire.

Our cycle has been cut to 15 weeks and the last two weeks are bivouac so we haven't too darn far to go. Maybe I told you I have made an application for O.C.S. I have had an interview with the capt. and I guess I'll have one with the Major this week or next. Then comes the interview before the board.

Burt, as you probably know, has been accepted for O.C.S. in the Quartermaster corps. If he is held over after he finishes his cycle he has been promised a pass to come up and see me. I guess he finishes this week.

Well we have a Bn. Parade* this afternoon so I guess I better quit and start getting ready.

Love,
Willie

*Bn. Parade = battalion parade.

Pitching tents on bivouac

Willie is frustrated with the delays and inconsistencies of the mail service. His first interview for O.C.S. was disappointing, but he has met some good-looking Georgia peaches after all.

Jan. 21, 1945

Dear Ted,

It sure has been a good thing that my mail hasn't been too strong because I haven't had too much time to answer. This last week has been fairly easy. We have had classes in Range Estimation and the principles of the B.A.R., which we fire sometime this week.

Of course I don't know if I did or didn't get all of your letters because I don't know how many you have written but I did get the one with $5 in it. It is evident that you haven't gotten all of mine because I thanked you for the present in one of my previous ones.

I can't understand why Burt hasn't heard from me because I have been writing pretty regularly. I had written to Bob before but I had sent

Digging slit trenches

them free* and Mom said it took two months for him to get some free ones from you and Burt. Since Mom told me I sent one air mail which he should get fairly quick.

If I do go to OTC it will be the Infantry, well we didn't have any other choice to have any chance at all. Also we had to have a secondary choice and I chose the engineers. Right now I have my doubts if I will make it or not. I have seen what the Captain wrote on my papers since my interview. He had "Lacking in leadership and initiative."

This makes me mad as hell because it shows the captain's ill judgement and inadequacy. The dirty rat couldn't be truthful and say that I lacked experience and age. How does he know that I lack leadership and initiative?

He had my character as excellent and also my service record as an interested man. I still have to be interviewed by the Major and The Board.

It certainly doesn't seem as though I'm going to be twenty tomorrow. I still feel like a little kid in many ways.

I guess the army life has done me some good. Before I came in I never weighed more than 140 and now I weigh 155 and I'm not gaining any around the waist. I don't know if I have grown any taller or not, I haven't measured myself since that day I raised my right hand.

We get our bivouac in our 13th & 14th weeks and I guess they are really tough. Infiltration course, street fighting technique with everything they got blazing over our heads. Barb wire obstacles will be nothing by the time bivouac is over.

Mom & Marian have been good about writing and I have heard from Blondie and Altie. Teen has been pretty good too but I haven't gotten any from Jan although I got a nice long letter from Johnnie. Sometimes I think I'm not getting all of my mail from home. Mom asked me some things and I answered them, then in the letter I got from her yesterday she asked me the same ones over. Mr. B has been very good about writing and I have had three or four from Janie and yesterday I got one from Mary W. I heard from Fred R. right along after he went home but he has been shipped across now and I probably won't hear from him for some time.

---

*Soldiers could send mail without using stamps by simply writing the word "Free" in the upper right-hand corner of the envelope.

Boy did we ever have a swell dance last Fri. night. It was just the 5th Bn. Nearly all the officers were there and they had as good a time as we did. We had a nice bunch of girls too and did I ever hook on to a nice one. She was really nice, pleasant to look at and had a very nice personality, and a darn good dancer. Our (C Co.) captain and the Major were feeling pretty high at the dance and the Capt. would recognize someone from C Co. and he would come over and shake our hand and say we were a darn good bunch. Captain Veatch is a very nice fellow and everyone likes him. He has been here at Wheeler just one day longer than I have.

I had a good laugh when a couple of girls wanted me to meet a Lt. It turned out to be our platoon leader and we really had a good laugh on them.

Well I guess I better quit and get some others off.

Love
Willie

Burt writes while waiting to make a phone call to Melrose. He has just received his shipping orders and will be shipped overseas in two short weeks.

Jan. 21, 1945

Dear Ted,

Well, I got my shipping orders today and it's as the phrase goes around here, "T.S., P.O.E."* done in the same cadence as the Lucky Strike slogan. I guess if the quota for O.C.S. opens up and I'm to go, that they'll tell me while I'm in a fox hole.

We go to Meade & have to report Feb.2. It will give me about five days at home. I'm afraid Mel isn't going to appreciate the news. I'm waiting to put a call in for her now, so am catching up a little on my letter writing.

It sure gives a fellow a funny feeling to think that he's going over. It hits you awfully quick and realize that it isn't a game that you've been playing for the past 15 weeks.

---

*T.S.P.O.E. = Top Secret Port of Embarkation.

We've been given a hell of a working over for the past three weeks. Bivouac was plenty rugged and we have a lot of fellows in the hospital at this point. Now we have to get plenty of good old chicken shit before we ship.

I guess I'll have to make this short as my call is due. I'll try to write as soon as I know my next station.

Burt

BOTTLENECKING VITAL WAR CALLS!

Telephone lines today are carrying a greater load of urgent war calls than ever before in history. Curtailment of vital materials and the continually growing manpower shortage prevent any increase in facilities at this time. To better enable existing equipment to carry the rising flood of calls, more party lines are being used. If you have party line service, you can prevent a jam-up of already overloaded telephone lines by showing more consideration and thoughtfulness for other subscribers who might be waiting to call, or to receive a call. Here are some suggestions worth observing:

- Keep your calls short. You might be delaying an important war call.
- Allow reasonable intervals between calls.
- Wait until the operator rings ten times before hanging up.
- Ask the children to co-operate.

Don't bottleneck the war effort ... think of the other party on your line.

UPSTATE TELEPHONE CORPORATION OF N.Y.

This notice from the Lowville Leader urges families to keep their phone calls short. (Image courtesy of New York State Historic Newspapers)

Ted hasn't received Burt's last letter, but he has gotten an urgent telegram from his parents asking him to come home while Burt is home on his Embarkation Leave. Even Burt's sudden deployment won't help Ted get a furlough to do that.

San Angelo Army Air Field

BOMBARDIER SCHOOL

SAN ANGELO, TEXAS

January 22, 1945

Dear Folks,

I just returned from sending the telegram saying that I couldn't get a furlough. You probably understand it anyway but it was worth a try. I don't know for sure of course, but it probably means that Burt is probably going overseas upon short notice – doesn't it? Enlisted men are often granted emergency furloughs for this reason but it is a different situation for cadets [Ted is an Aviation Cadet]. About the only reason they will grant us furloughs is because of illness in the immediate family or civilian business to be cleaned up. This field is very good about these things but it is probably best to keep me here. For me it would probably mean reverting to another class and delaying my training for four weeks or possibly shipping me to another field to join a class a couple of weeks behind ours. So you can see the disadvantage to the army as well as the disadvantage to me to have to change classes, training squadrons, and so forth. I sure want to see Burt as well as to get home, but I guess you can understand what the obstacles are.

I suppose this means that the need for men overseas has over-ruled his chances for O.C.S. now. It is sort of a bitter disappointment to all of us yet we have enough experience with the service to know that nothing is exactly predictable. However we do know that no matter what it is that in the end everything will come out for the best. In Burt's case it is probably

273

better that he be sent to Europe now rather than to have to wait and be sent the other way [to the Pacific] with the rest of us.

Hey Altie – I like the names of those calves. I see you do very well in following that naming system. Bess is Belle's heifer by Pedro which is fresh for the first – isn't she? Can you still grow the devil out of them? I'll bet you can! Are you going to have some nice big, healthy, growth calves when Bob and I get home next spring? Just feed them lots of good hay, grain, water at least twice a day, and keep them dry and healthy, and I'll bet you can.

I like Marian's and Shirley's accounts of the nephews and nieces. I guess they have plenty of admirers – probably too many!

I've been off post only one night in the past three weeks so you see we're moving pretty fast. Bombing is nearly over (as I've been saying for the past month) and navigation is coming up fast. My C.E. (circular error) stands pretty good now and I really believe that I could slap them in our pond from any altitude. I sure like to bomb with demolition bombs from a 17*, for the 17 is really built around the bombsight and the demolition bombs would be more uniform to drop. These AT-11's no longer satisfy most of us because our worst errors are faults of the ship which in turn gives us a poor level to level the vertical gyro. By the way have you seen pictures of the Norden** yet? It has been released and we've seen several in various publications. You won't see half of the knobs and switches, but perhaps it gives you a small idea of why we kid about and declare that a bombardier needs "four hands with eight fingers on each!"

I'd best quit now. I hope you can understand why our effort didn't work out but it was worth trying and no reason to not try in another case. I hope you could get Willie home.

Love,
Ted

---

*B-17 bomber.
**The Norden bombsight.

In the Philippines, the fight for control of the island of Luzon raged as Bob wrote his next letter. His squadron, VPB 137, was moved into an island area after the island was recaptured. The crews flew air patrols looking for submarines and maintaining air control. They were given missions to drop mines in harbors and channels and also had missions flying over Formosa to bomb alcohol factories and targets of opportunity. Bob flew the twin-engine (two 2000 hp Pratt and Whitney engines) PV1 Ventura, the fastest plane the Navy had. They were fitted with radar on their second tour (autumn 1944 to spring 1945). At the time Bob wrote the next letter to Ted, strict censorship rules kept him from sharing these details.*

Philippines
Jan. 25

Dear Ted,

Your letter came with a big bunch I got last week. Hadn't had any mail for about a month but a lot of people write around the holidays. It makes quite a lot of answering for me.

Sorry I haven't kept you better informed of what I was doing. Guess I just assumed that you knew somehow. Of course censorship regulations keep us from describing our work out here but I can answer a few of your questions. By the way, you can say anything you want to in your letters for mail coming to us is never censored. Our work is mostly the same as before and we are still flying the same old planes – I mean the same type of course for we do get replacements. I have only about 750 hrs. in these planes and only 1150 in all which really isn't a great deal for the time I have been at it but one doesn't build it up in these planes because of their speed and the jobs we do. Hour for hour it's pretty good time tho. I'm still flying as copilot part of the time also which doesn't please me particularly. It can't be helped however as we have a surplus of qualified persons and several of us are in the same boat. Have learned quite a bit from one of the senior pilots too.

In this area there are a lot of islands and a lot of mountains to either fly over or around and there has been a lot of pretty bad weather. Since we try to fly low all the time it's damned handy to have the instrument training we have had and to be sure of our navigation. Even this last time

*Special thanks to Joe Markham for this information.

back I had a complete course in celestial navigation including a night hop (without radio aide) and about twenty hours in the celestial trainer. That gives me three complete courses in navigation and I have also had those instrument courses plus extra Link hops, and if you'll permit me to brag a bit, I had the highest grades of anyone in the squadron last spring. I'm just trying to point out that we think a lot of training is important and you can never know all there is to know about the plane and the job. Our copilots are very well qualified too – most of them have 800 hrs. or more and even better training than we got. We have enlisted navigators who had about six weeks of nav. school and then we teach them all we can. The one in our crew is doing very well. I like to let every member of the crew learn any job he is interested in. It takes a lot of monotony out of the work. They take turns at the guns and get time in the co-pilots seat and get a big bang out of it. Howard and I sometimes go back and navigate or man the guns. We plan to teach another of the boys some navigation and one of them some radio. We feel we have a topnotch crew for they have gone there quite a bit but still enjoy this job and we manage to have a little fun among ourselves and best of all everyone works well with the rest. Yes, you guessed it. I am proud of them.

It was important for the crew to have some fun.
(Photo from Ted's album)

We don't live like kings out here but we are better off than any others we see and we move around enough to make the time go fast. To name the places I have seen this time – New Hebrides, Solomons, Admiralties, New Guinea, Monotai, and most of the Philippines. Of course there were several places we saw last year too and we certainly haven't stopped yet. I'd certainly like to get to Australia but doubt that that's possible.

I'll call this enough for now. We have a little club over here in a quonsett (sp?) hut and I think I'll go over for a beer and a song session the boys are having. Things are far from boring. We just had some darned good horseshoe games and some volley ball this afternoon.

Write again when you can.

As ever
Bob

It's fourteen below zero on the farm and Shirley writes that Burt and Melrose will be home for a few days before Burt is shipped overseas. John Klossner has been called for his physical.

January 26, 1945

Dear Ted,

We've had a very cold spell up this way lately. Yesterday morning & this morning it was 14 degree below 0, though it wasn't windy so we didn't mind it badly. The snow is squeaky under foot. We have a lot of snow now for the time.

Dad had only thought of getting Tom for a couple or more weeks to get some wood together. He seems pretty good help even if he doesn't know much. He is eager to do things the way Dad does, and seems to like it here. Mom told Dad he'd better ask him to stay & he said he would (Tom). Now he talks of haying next summer & getting wood in next fall before snow. (The snow is so deep over our big woodpile out on the north side of the house they can't buzz & have to saw by hand.) For three weeks he asked $25 and we think that's cheap enough.

Burt is coming home tomorrow as you probably know. He met Mel in Utica tonight & they're staying tonite. I don't know just how long he'll have. They're going out to Fillmore the last part of his furlo. We're kind of disappointed over his not being called for O.C.S. as they'd promised. He'll be shipped across now if things don't come different. Mel took it awfully hard & is very discouraged, but she isn't the first war wife.

Johnny was in 1-A & had his physical at Syracuse Wednesday & didn't get home until last nite at 5. I think & hope this was just to see how many men they could possibly call on if things are tight. There are certainly men around they could call before John. I shouldn't say that but there would be a good farm with a good farmer gone. John passed his physical.

We got a letter from Bob yesterday & he sent some Philippine & Jap money. He said the natives were fairly nice & quite smart, but he wished he could teach them a few things about cultivation & so on. That pleased Dad.

Linda's getting to be a little clip now. She's picking up saucy things Altie says & among them are "You don't say?", "You did, huh?", and "Oh, 'scuse me." She's beginning to know she's pretty cute. She says things frequently which are quite startling. She's as fat as a pig and weighs about 36 lbs. Her dresses keep needing greater length. They say David is getting to be quite a fellow too, but I haven't seen him since we had our Christmas.

We had a Latin Regents Monday and I only got 50 in it. I studied a lot, too, but we don't get much from our teacher. Yesterday and today we had the rest of our tests & the only one I know was social studies which I got 80 in.

The seniors had a dance last Friday night. I had a nice time until I got blistered heels from my new stiff shoes.

We got some very nice pictures of Willie last Friday. They look just like him.

I've got a sand-papery sore throat. I never would have gotten it if I had gone to bed when I should have.

Do you see many movies? Burt & Mel saw a lot & Willie does. Gee it must be swell to pay only $.15. Tom took Mother, Marian, & me to see "Frenchman's Creek." It was very good I thought.

We enjoy <u>Time</u> a lot. We all read it. There's so much you can get out of it in just a few minutes. I like it a lot. I'd never looked at it much altho we have it at school.

Linda is down again. We supposed she was asleep. She's been up there an hour or more. I was hustling her a little & she said, "You go write to Ted. I'll throw this (panda) at you."

I guess this is the end of the line. There isn't much more news.

Love,
Blondie

Willie writes to Shirley that he expects to be shipped out in five weeks. He is worn out from four hours of exercise including one hour of bayonet practice.

CAMP WHEELER, GEORGIA

January 31, 1945

Dear Blondie,

I got your nice letter quite a while ago but I just got around to answer. They have had my rear going first in one direction and then the other. If it isn't one thing it is sure to be something else. I have had enough extra duty in the last week to keep me for the rest of my stay here. Well I won't be here too much longer anyway. We only have five more weeks after this week is over. Two of those weeks we will be out on bivouac. Those two weeks will be tough and I don't mean maybe. It will probably be cold as the devil when we get out there. Some of the fellows who have been out on bivouac say they nearly starve you to death. Well I guess we can live through it. Our last week will probably be easy as the devil. Turning in our equipment and such things to get ready to ship out. We don't know whether we will get 10 days or 5 days at home.

The whole Bn. got restricted last night because the barracks didn't pass inspection yesterday. A Lt. Colonel did the inspecting and he was really strict.

Well I guess I better get ready to fall out right now. I just started this after I came back from dinner. Maybe you can see just how much time

This photo from the November 1944 edition of The National Geographic Magazine *illustrates the correct positioning of a bayonet. (Photo courtesy of National Geographic)*

we do have when we write letters whenever we get a few minutes. Well it's almost time for lights out now and I guess I'll have to hurry a little.

Our clean sheet came today you see we get one clean sheet a week and we are supposed to get a clean pillow case. I didn't get a clean pillow case so I had to take a dirty one and wash it. I'll be darned if I sleep on a pillow without a case for a week.

Boy I'm sure tired tonight. We had four hours of physical exercise this afternoon. One straight hour of bayonet practice and boy it sure is tough as h—l. You have to hold yourself in the most uncomfortable positions for so darn long you think your arms, legs, back or something else is going to break in two. I was so tired I thought my arms were going to drop off.

Everybody is feeling pretty good tonight because we got paid tonight. I pulled $43.50. I didn't expect to get that much because I expected to have my laundry taken out and some for some pictures we had taken. Our laundry is $1.50 a month but I haven't had any taken out yet. The picture was of our platoon and I'll send one home when they come.

Have you found out any more about swapping my Sax. for that clarinet?

Well I guess I'll quit for now, get a good shower and crawl in bed. I should write to Mr. B. but I'm too darn tired.

Write when you get time. Letters sure mean a lot to us Blondie and I have been getting darn few lately.

Love
Willie

Jan writes that the war has stripped the men from her home, but that helps her understand what other families are going through. She is proud of her parents' courage in the face of having four sons in the war. Evidently, there is only one pen in the household.

Jan. 31, 1945

Dear Ted,

I'm thru with the dishes early to-night and the men aren't in yet so realize this is probably as good a chance as any I'll get to write a letter.

The weather outside to-night is pretty blustery. Last night it snowed and blew some and all day long it has been blowing hard. Our driveway is plugged tight since noon. The banks were so high each side of the driveway before this storm that we couldn't see a car if it drove in 'til it got even with the dining room windows.

Johnnie has been plowing the driveway with his doodlebug all winter as usual 'til about a week ago when a piston went on the bum. There is only one other Jewett around that he knows of to get parts from and that is snowed under so that he can't get to it. It looks as if he and Pop will have plenty of shoveling to do from now on. I expect he'll make some kind of a plow for the tractor now but it has such a low speed it won't be able to compare with his doodlebug. (Enough of the snow & our troubles).

Sunday – perhaps you heard we all were over home for dinner. Burt arrived in Utica Fri. morn 2 a.m. and Mel was there to meet him. She waited about 5 hours. Sat. morning they arrived over home and so Sunday the O'Briens and we were there. Mother and Teen made him a cake after

281

dinner and Johnnie and I had made some ice cream the day before & stopped in town for more to take over, so we really did his birthday up pretty fine. Of course as kids usually are – Billy and Linda were all thrilled with the candles on Dad's cake & Mother had 2 other tall candles lit on the table. David sat at the table, too. Marian fed him a little ice cream & when Linda saw that she was right over and insisted she could do that. It was too comical for words watching her. She was just as serious as could be! I imagine you notice the biggest change in Linda than all the rest of us put together unless of course it's me. I suppose you've heard about my second front.* I naturally wanted to be the first to tell my own brothers but it has been apparent for such awhile that no doubt someone already has told you. Mother tickles me the way she mentions the subject. She speaks about the way my silhouette is changing. Very subtle, isn't she?

Had you heard that Johnnie was called last Wed. for his physical? As you probably know, all the farmers are being called up for physicals and if they are borderline deferments and 1A's they are taken in the draft. Johnnie, of course, is 1A, tho unless they take more than just the borderline farmers we don't expect we'll hear from the draft board for quite awhile.

The news from Europe** has been so good this past week we are all hoping that the turn for the good will soon be here and that it will mean that so many of you boys won't be shipping that way at least and perhaps they won't be taking so many of you and perhaps they won't be taking many from home anymore. Of course our home has been stripped from men but it makes us here that are left realize more and more what it means to other families.

It is needless to say we all miss you boys like the dickens here at home and I think probably it hits Dad & Mother much more than the rest tho I can't think of another couple who would stand up under the strain of having four sons in the service as well as they do.*** They are both so proud of all you boys! (but never whine or ask for sympathy because they have no sons at home).

---

*Jan is expecting her first baby.

**The Battle of the Bulge is over, and the Allies are fighting their way east to Berlin as the Soviets push westward.

***Both Ernest and Evelyn lost brothers in World War I: Robert Benjamin Markham (May 21,1895–April 15, 1918) and Walton Leslie Wasmuth (March 4,1900–August 7,1919). Walton died of meningitis while still in the service.

Did you hear about Bill and Marion's* wedding? Marion R. and I gave Marion a shower Fri. before Christmas and Xmas day they were married. Marion R. & I also decorated the church and of course Blondie had to get in on it. Never saw such a gal as Blondie to get in on everything possible. We had the house full up here with Fred & Rude's families both here and we had to eat before the wedding so I did some high scrambling that morning.

Glad you liked the candy and while Mother was up here she made a fruit cake which I meant to get off to you soon. If there is anything else we can send you let us know. Must close & give the pen over to Johnnie.

Love,
Jan

*Bill Regetz and Marion Long were married on Christmas Day.

Bob writes to Shirley next with good things to say about the natives. Then he compliments Shirley on her positive attitude toward other people. It's a good thing to have.

Philippines
Feb.3

Dear Shirley,

I hope you and Marian will forgive me for waiting a little longer to write to you. It just seems that the others are scattered around more by themselves and then of course you two get around and read everyone else's. That makes it harder to find something interesting to write about. Of course that doesn't mean that I don't enjoy hearing from all of you for everyone has something a little different to tell me about. T'was a big treat to hear from all of you just after the holidays.

We are having a beautiful morning so far. There is a heavy dew on the grass and everything is nice and green and fresh. The sun is shining part of the time but there are enough clouds to keep things cool. No doubt it will rain sometime today. Some of the people have their laundry out and most of us are just relaxing – reading, pitching horseshoes or something. I have

Bob's letter to Shirley was approved by the censor.

started a new book – <u>The Robe</u> by Lloyd Douglas. It is very good. After I write a couple of letters I'll probably go to work on it again.

I'm not much of a correspondent, as you know, but I think I write to as many different people as anyone in camp. Of course being a member of a large family is partly responsible. One of my team mates has written about 175 letters to his wife and most of them write to only about 3 or 4 people. I had mail from about twenty people in a little over a week so now I'm trying to catch up.

We have people in the squadron from nearly every state in the union and with all the other people I have met in the navy I will have a lot of traveling to do to visit them all after the war. I'm now rooming with fellows from Texas, California, Minnesota, and North Dakota. In the next tent there are fellows from Iowa, Kentucky, Missouri, Ohio, and California – it's quite an opportunity.

Wish you could have been here to meet the Filipino girls who picked up Dick's laundry this morning. One is fifteen and the other seventeen and both are in school. One of them said she was in the fourth grade and couldn't read very much English. They study many of the things we do but they don't have very good schools since the Japs came and many of

284

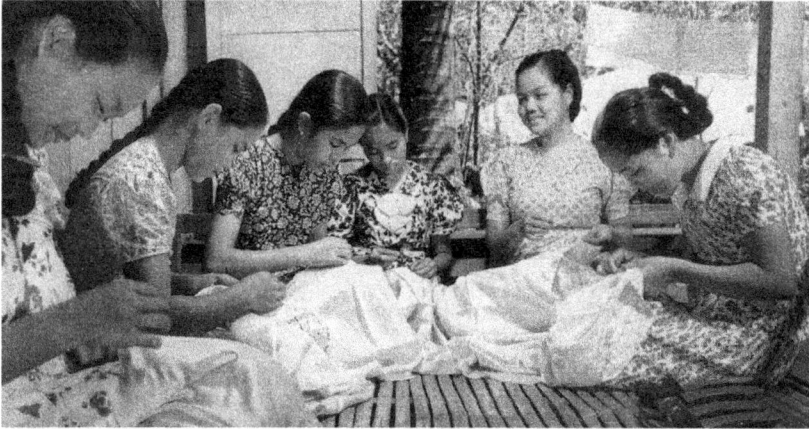

Girls from Binakayan "sit on a cushion and sew a fine seam." (Photo from the February 1942 issue of National Geographic)

them were closed. I wish these people could have some of our old books and other school supplies. They are very intelligent people and seem anxious to learn. They don't have a very large English vocabulary but their choice of words is usually good. I have had a few of the guerrillas sign my short snorter bills* or a bill they have given me and their penmanship puts me to shame.

Some of the fellows have Filipino houseboys to do their laundry and odd jobs around the tents. Nearly all of us hire them to do our laundry, cut our hair etc. They are earning quite a little money but don't have much to spend it on. Most of them would rather have us give them bits of clothing or mosquito nets than money but of course we don't carry many extras. Most of the women manage to dress quite well with the bits of cloth they pick up for most of them have sewing machines and a natural talent for sewing. Guess you can see I admire these people. I should have some fairly good pictures when I get home.

The things you said about Rita were very nice and I think she would be very happy to know how much you admire her. It never hurts to say

*A short snorter bill was a banknote carried by a pilot and signed by those he had served with. If he couldn't produce it after his mission had ended, he was obligated to buy a round of drinks. It also served as a record of where he had been. The name was derived from the term "short" (not a full measure) and "snort" (a quick drink).

nice things about people if you are sincere. Anyone who knows lots of people and likes lots of people is a more interesting person to talk to and to know. You will find that there are nice people everywhere. I wish you had the opportunities I have had to meet lots of different people because I know that you like nearly everyone and they like you.

Think I'll have to get you to teach me to play the piano when I get home. I have often wished I could and alas I wish I had my violin with me for now I have lots of time to practice and I'd enjoy it. It would be pretty hard to carry around tho and would annoy my friends so maybe it's better to spend my time reading.

Maybe we'll get some mail today. It has been a couple of weeks. A couple of the fellows expect that they are fathers and are anxious to hear.

This will be enough for now I guess. I'll try to find a picture or something to enclose.

Love
Bob

Ted wants to know who Tom is. He also has some comments about the Air Force and its unjust creation of glamorous pretty pictures.

San Angelo Army Air Field
BOMBARDIER SCHOOL
SAN ANGELO, TEXAS

February 4, 1945

Dear Folks,

I haven't much to write but had better get off a small note because it has been two weeks since I last wrote.

I imagine that by now Burt has reported at Camp Mead. I had a letter from him soon after I got your telegram. I sure hope he made the best of

286

his furlough and didn't have to "spare the horses" in doing everything he wanted to.

Blondie's nice letter came last week. I also got a nice card and note from Aunt Grace, but she didn't send her address – would you send it?

Sounds as if the snow is really piling up up there this winter. Must be quite widespread for we have reports of a lot all over the north. Peggy says that Wmsport has more snow than they've had in years.

Someone has been slipping up on news or something. Anyway I take it that you have a hired man when you speak of Tom. Tom who? Better try to keep him as long as you can because the extra help and care of the cattle and crops will more than equal it. I see that milk is bringing a pretty fancy price. I hope you're taking advantage of it and remember how to wring every last drop of milk out.

No, Blondie, I don't see many movies. The most movies I ever saw was while in Ft. Niagara, but I haven't been in many post theatres since. Post theatres have the best shows and change nearly every day. I just don't care much for shows unless they're extra good. Then I don't have much time for shows. Here it is practically impossible as it has been in some other busy places. Then shows are more of a thrill. I've only been to the theatre on this post once and that was to see "Winged Victory."* You had all better get to see "Winged Victory." It is quite a realistic show of the life of a cadet though it doesn't show much of that of a bombardier or navigator. It doesn't try to show the harder side of this living nor the foundation for our blues and gripes yet it doesn't try to over glamorize too much. That is an amazing accomplishment within this organization for the Air Force notoriously over glamorizes and creates unjustly a pretty picture. Another thing which makes the show good is because it was produced by amateurs or at least not our best professional producers. We like it because it tried to tell our story as truthfully as anything we've yet found.

Have I told you that our graduation is set for March 29 instead of March 24? So far no class has known definitely whether or not they would have leaves until the morning of graduation. However I'm going to count on it even if it is a disillusion.

I'm pretty sleepy right now. We flew two missions this afternoon.

Winged Victory was a 1944 production by 20th Century Fox and U.S. Army Air Forces.

The weather was poor last week and so it was pretty long when you have skipped a few days. Another thing which made it tiring was the fact that we flew through the lower part of a few clouds. That made it rough as the deuce and tough riding as well as tough bombing. We figured on finishing the bombing and being on navigation by now, but additional bombs and poorer weather have held us up. I only have 11 bombs left to drop now.

Slowly they are beginning to release information on the bombsight* now. We get a kick out of the write ups about it because few of us, though we've studied it thoroughly, can visualize just how complex its operation is. At times it seems so simple that we kick ourselves for not thinking it up, yet at others we realize how wonderful it is to incorporate so many coordinated features. Beyond its value in bombing it is also one of the best navigation and piloting instruments. I'd drive you mad if I went further so had better sleep now. Everyone write!

Love,

Ted

---

*The Norden bombsight was one of the most closely guarded secrets of WWII. It used an internal mechanical computer to calculate the trajectory of the bomb being dropped.

Ted poses in front of a B24, August 1945.

Will writes of more firearm training. He expects to be sent overseas soon and hopes to see Ted before he goes. He has a date and needs to keep the letter short.

Macon, Georgia
February 11, 1945

Dear Ted,

I guess I've been slipping lately, it's been quite a while since I have written to you. They seem to do a good job of keeping us busy lately.

Last week we fired the 30 cal m.g. I'm pretty good with it but certainly not an expert. I like the A4 a lot better than the A6f. The A6 creeps left on me and I can't seem to hold it in place. If I fire short bursts of 3 or 4 I can hold it but they want bursts of 6 or 8 and away she goes.

Saturday we walked about 5 miles with full field packs just to fire 30 rounds and that isn't much for a m.g. It was really hot and the five miles back went darn slow. I had on my long Johns because it was cold in the morning but I took off the top at noon, and I was still hot.

This week we take up our last weapon, the 60 mm mortar.

Just when do you graduate? Mom thinks it's the 31st of March. I hope so because I finish my cycle March 17th and we could see each other before I went back.

I was interviewed by the OCS Board last Fri. By my way of thinking I'll probably get my papers back in a couple of days. Well I don't know if I want to go now or not because there is no furlough after basic training.

Coming in from the range yesterday a cub plane flew around us for about 5 min. He came over a field beside the road about 30 feet above the ground and pulled up just over the telephone wires. The two fellows in the plane waved when they went over us. I don't know if they were rubbing it in or just waving.

Private Willis Markham

In two weeks we go out on bivouac. We have five weeks yet actually there are only two more besides bivouac.

We'll probably get a lot of bayonet training during the next two weeks. It is really rugged training too.

I guess I better quit for now. It's 6:00 and I have a date at 7:00. There is a girls college here in town and some pretty nice gals up there.

As ever,
Willie

Marian writes news of her nephews' antics and of canning Old Prim's liver. Best of all, the Markhams now have a hired man, Tom Dawley.

Feb. 18, '45

Dear Ted,

Time seems to slip by pretty fast as I don't get as much letter writing done as I plan to. Your nice letter came quite a few days ago – also Mr. B. sent me one you wrote him and one from Bob. Your letters are always nice and newsy and we always enjoy hearing about your bombsight and what you're doing. Sometimes we feel as if we didn't know anything about what you boys do. However, we haven't seen anything about the bombsight yet.

Before I forget – Pete may be sent to school in Texas in March. If he makes it before you come home, I'll let you know as there might be a chance to see him. The rumor is that he may go into B29 or B32's. Doris can't go to Texas with him. They have a dog, a cocker which complicates her coming home. We kidded Pete at Christmas time about his family. Teen and I ride him about the family question anyhow.

We haven't heard from Burt but once since he got to Meade. All but three of his group had been shipped. I presume he's on his way but Shirley has a "feeling" he's still here.

Willie writes quite often and such nice letters. Said he had his interview for O.C.S. but didn't figure he did so hot. I've still got my fingers crossed tho I've known from the first that he didn't have much chance because of his age. He seems to be determined to do as good a job as he can. He wrote Mom not to worry about him. He didn't plan to shut his eyes and pull the trigger like some of the guys. Says when he pulls the trigger there won't be as many to worry about. Good for him – any job well done is worth doing and he seems to realize it – and doesn't gripe. He seems to keep quite cheerful – tho he must have been god-awful homesick. Says he'll even be glad to farm it after the war. Guess I feel sorrier for him because he hasn't had a chance to do anything he wanted to and the rest of you boys did. But don't think I don't know it's tough for all of you.

We've all been getting letters from Bob. I got one Fri. Feb. 16 that was written Feb. 6, Teen's birthday. That was pretty quick for traveling half way round the world. He sent me some money and some propaganda sheets that they've been sending the Japs and Philippinos. He hasn't gotten his Christmas packages yet but we feel mail is going through better now and we may send a few trinkets we think he'd like. He says the natives like old clothes – the women most all have sewing machines and a national bent for sewing. Says the people are intelligent and he really likes them. He had some guerillas sign his sharp-shooter and they put his penmanship to shame.* He says a lot of fighting has been left to the

---

*Bob's challenging penmanship was the reason Marian interpreted "short snorter" as "sharp shooter."

guerrillas and they show no mercy. Mrs. Homer Markham sent him a picture of the "Fierce Foursome" and he thinks the enemy would fold up if they got a look – especially of that one with the blood thirsty look in his eye. But I don't think your dimples would scare them much. I sent Peg the clipping and she showed everyone. She doesn't know us very well yet, does she?

You didn't need to ask if she could come – we expected her anyhow – I'd written her that.

Well, we killed Old Prim [a cow] Saturday. She was quite fat and we hope we don't have to chew too hard. We fried her liver for supper last night and it was tender and delicious so we're having a feast. We will can some and freeze some. Teen is going to have what she wants. Mom and I decided we'll can hers too as we aren't overworked. Teen was quite indignant when I told her – guess she could do it herself but she won't get it till it's all canned.

Teen and Bob are going to have a few days' vacation and we are going to have the kids. David understands so much you say to him and tries to talk – he says, "Bad Boy." Stands up in his highchair and says "Bad Boy, Bad Boy." He creeps like mad and pulls himself up to things. Teen said he stood alone several times the other day.

But both Teen and I are of the opinion that he won't walk early because he doesn't care. He's so darned good natured. If he gets what he wants it's all right and it's all right if you take it away. One thing he goes for persistently is the goldfish. He caught one, one day. He isn't gaining very fast these days because he had eczema and all his food was taken away but milk, cereal and orange juice. But last Sunday he weighed 21 lb. 12 oz. Babies should triple their birth weight by the time they are a year old so he's pretty rugged. His eczema has cleared up good – it didn't get a bad start. So he'll start the trial and elimination method on food soon. Teen thinks it's green vegetables that he's allergic to.

A week ago Wednesday I brought Billy down on the bus. Then we went to school and rode home on Altie's bus. Some thrill. We went back on Sat. a.m. on the bus. But he didn't get everything done that he wanted to. Billy couldn't understand why Willis got tired on a 23 mile hike. He walks all day and he doesn't get tired.

You asked if we had a hired man. Yes, it's Tom Dawley. They live

in Mrs. Phillips' house. He's Willie's age and a 4F. We think we're very
fortunate. It helps things to run smoothly and Mom and I both tell Dad
to keep him as long as he can. He is a simple guy but seems to take an
interest in things and likes it here. He comes from a large family – the
father died in October from the results of an automobile accident.

Friday night our Home Bureau had a party at Charles Evans'. The
public was invited and I was on the entertainment committee (chairman)
and Mom was transportation committee for this road. We had sleigh rides
and everyone fell for the idea. Dad & Tom fixed up the rack on the sleigh
and found a lot of car seats and Tom got out all the bells on the farm.
Even Ben and Alice went and everyone seemed to have a good time. There
were over 80 there and we took a collection for our contribution to the
Red Cross. We had cards and games for the kids. But the kids went sliding
a little while. Altie tore the seats of his only knickers. But he doesn't care
these days what he wears – they went to church this morning. He ate
at Parquet's last summer in overalls and plaid shirt as poised as anyone
there.

He's determined that now that I'm home, he's going to tie me down.
He wants me to be a 4H leader for girls. I can't decide that I want to start
something that I may not be able to continue. Tho I did consent to take
on the job as a leader in Home Bureau for next year. I have the next lesson
at H.B. I went to a school on house plants last fall on my own hook and
they heard about it. Guess I'd better get busy and prepare my material. I'll
be some teacher, won't I?

I'm really enjoying the community life. I guess I missed it. And I've
been shoving Mom out as much as possible. She and Dad and Tom went
to a dance at C'ville with Shirley and had a good time. Mom was on
committee for Ladies' Aid dinner this week. It does her a lot of good to get
away from home. She's feeling a lot better than she did in the fall and is in
good spirits. We all have to hand it to Mom the way she can take it.

And not only Altie would like to tie me down at home. Mom has big
plans about what we can do. Someday I may decide I need to work but it
seems to be a comfort and a lift to Mom for me to be here. I guess one of
my biggest faults always has been that I'm easily satisfied with the little I
have.

Bob says both his older sisters are long-winded. You don't think so,
do you?

Did anyone tell you that Lincoln was killed in Belgium in Jan.?* He hadn't even gotten mail since he went over and no Christmas packages.

We had a nice letter from Harry Mathis lately. I guess he's still in England. Said one advantage he had was no foxholes.

I must get to bed. Guess we'll have a full week. Will try to write sooner next time so you won't get tired out reading my writing. Bob says it's worse than his.

Love,
Marian

---

*Lincoln Ackerman, June 14, 1921–January 16, 1945. Lincoln enlisted in February 1944 and was killed in the Battle of the Bulge eleven months later. Lincoln left his wife, Doris, and daughter, Claire, behind.

Ted writes that he has been doing some wishful thinking, that it might be possible to see Bob and Will if they can get leaves at the same time. Spring may be in the air in Texas.

ARMY AIR FORCES

February 18, 1945

Dear Folks,

I hardly know what to write about for I haven't much to say. It has been two weeks since I wrote though.

I have quite recent letters from both Bob and Willie. Bob didn't have much news but rather devoted his letter to mostly "shop talk" regarding his work. He sort of figured that he may even go beyond the Philippines though I don't quite see how. Willie had a lot of spirit in his letter, but I know that his routine is darn tough. I've had some wishful thinking lately. It might be possible that Bob, Willie, and I might be getting leaves at nearly the same time.

Burt hasn't written since he returned but I guess it is my fault for owing him a letter. Maybe I'd better send it through you folks to have it forwarded.

The Boonville Herald brought me the tough news about Link Ackerman. That makes Link and Harley Abbey* of the bunch whom I grew up with.

We are doing navigation in the air now. So far as bombing for record goes we have finished that phase, but we still have about 15 miscellaneous bombs to more or less experiment with. I feel pretty good about my bombing and hope that navigating turns out as well. Soon we'll be navigating to various places and then picking out special buildings on which to synchronize and "mock-bomb." We take pictures of these synchronizations so perhaps I can get one to send you. Our navigation missions involve a triangle about 100 miles on a side on which we do our work. The crew is made up of those students which rotate on each leg and one always doing one of three types of navigation – that is dead reckoning, pilotage, and follow the pilot methods. The other day I caught a faint glimpse of Camp Swift where Clyde is. It was probably about 30 miles distant though. I also navigated night over camp Bowie where Brian Kent is stationed.

The weather here seems to be turning a bit now even though it is unusually nasty and cold today. Last week we had some unusually warm days when the temperature got up to 80°. It was enough to start the grass just a slight bit. However the air up a few thousand feet is getting warmer so perhaps the season is turning. I have had hopes of seeing some snow this winter but the chances are running slim here. You'd better save some for April or else have spring break unusually fast.

I saw my first close up view of a B-29 the other day Altie. It is massive – all wing and fuselage. Measure out about 145 feet and then you can

---

*PFC Harland Robert Abbey, a member of Ted's graduating class, was killed in action in Luxembourg on September 20, 1944.

imagine its length from wing tip to wing tip. We of course couldn't climb around in it because of its radar and gun sights. The bombardier sits between the pilots' seats like a king on a throne.

Everyone write and how about telling me about how well you're growing those calves Altie.

Love,
Ted

P.S. We have 39 days to go.

Evelyn has been busy with community events, and she writes to Ted of all her "gaddings." Tom is a huge help and a welcome addition to the family.

MRS. ERNEST L. MARKHAM

BOX 143

TURIN, NEW YORK

Feb. 19, '45

Dear Ted,

Marian wrote last night so I want to add a bit now.

It is always so nice to hear what you are doing or interested in. We've realized you must be busier than ever, lately.

I've been rather negligent lately, partly because I thought the others were writing oftener; and partly because I have been a sort of "gadder." I've been getting out a bit. Marian and I have gone out to Home Bureau and served on some committees, etc. I spent one day last week over at Turin visiting Aunt Clara and W.B. and helping get dinner at the church. We fed 81 people. Would you ever believe so many would get out in such a snowy time, in <u>Turin</u>?

One evening, Dad and I went, as other parents, to sponsor a dance put on at school by Shirley's class. Had a swell time.

A week ago Sunday, Dad, Altie and I were invited over to Miller's to dinner. The girls were down at Ernestine's. Mary & Albert were alone.

You see things are getting sort of easier since we've had Tom. You asked about him. I thought we had told you. He is Tom Dawley, a 4F, twenty-one, lives in the D. Phillips house, and has been here since Jan. 1st except for a few days when he helped put ice at the milk station. He's good-natured, farm-bred, – tries hard to please all of us, so we try to treat him as a son and brother. I hope we can keep him.

That's a <u>fine</u> snap shot you sent. I have it where I can look often at your old <u>grin</u>!   Heaps of love,

Mom

Aunt Grace's address is: 112 East Liberty St. Rome

Ted writes that he has a new appreciation for Lewis County weather. He is looking forward to graduation when he will become a commissioned officer after which he wants to show Peggy either the famous Lewis County snow or a northern springtime rupture of the earth.

UNITED ✪ STATES

ARMY AIR FORCES

March 10, 1945

Dear Folks,

I guess that I've been slipping a bit too much on my letter writing. I believe it is three weeks since I last wrote.

It hasn't been because I was too busy because bad weather has given up some extra time lately. However in good weather they have pushed us extra hard. It must be a characteristic of country bordering the gulf to have poor weather at this time of year. You'll remember about the rain

Ted in his new officer's uniform

and mud in the southeast a year ago. It doesn't rain here but it is pretty cloudy at times. A couple of weeks ago we awoke to find it white – I did finally see the ground white here! It was from a freezing rain and hail but was soon melted away. You have no idea how much more spirit and hilarity the fellows had that morning. It was a wonderful feeling because the nasty weather reminded us of home. Clear sunny days are pleasant, but you have no idea what a blessing our variable climate is. It adds so much more spirit, initiative, and general well being to our lives. No, I'm not crazy but just trying to say that you may call me such if I ever complain about our weather.

It seems to feel as if things are on the down hill jump now. Anyhow it feels mighty good, even if we are sweating even harder. It stirs up a wonderful feeling down inside to think that three weeks from tonight I should be on the way. We have two big obstacles yet – a final comprehensive in all phases of our ground school and a phase check on everything given us on the flight line. Navigation has been going very well and I only have five required missions left. After that we'll drop a few more bombs for practice and be done. We are getting our papers and records in shape for the big discharge from enlisted to officer status. I still don't know whether I'll get 2nd Lt. or Flight Officer, but that makes no difference. I have all but a few odds and ends of my uniforms bought. I'm only getting the bare essentials for some things are impossible to get here and others aren't the best. I have hopes of picking up some of my uniforms in the north, for I have a notion that I can do better at some place like the PX at the Rome Air Depot.

My plans for a leave aren't complete or definite, but I'll tell you what I plan on. Graduation is Mar. 29. I plan to be leaving Ft. Worth on the 11:20 train that night. I'll be going through Wmsport to pick Peggy up first and hope to get in there sometime Saturday night. It won't be before Monday when we leave for Turin. It is going to be hard to do everything I wish, but I'm sure going to try my best. It's going to be wonderful to have a couple of weeks of freedom after a year of captivity! I'm sure going to make the best of it!!!

Please keep a lot of snow for me or else have spring breaking fast. Peggy has never had a ride in a sleigh and has her heart set on it. As for me I am not particular so long as there is some snow to see or else a northern springtime rupturing the trees and earth.

It sounded as if a pretty close member of the family left when you butchered Old Prim. Somehow I have to feel rather indignant because you "butchered" her. I guess that my idealism always called for a natural death for her and a place to rest with Old Weatha. Sometimes animals' characters can be so strong as to be nearly human.

I'm on OD tonight in case you wondered why I was taking so much time. It gets sort of monotonous sitting around like this. We'll be flying tomorrow so I'll be pretty tired. How about a note?

Love,
Ted

Evelyn writes of receiving a letter from Burt written on February 22 as he was on his way to combat in Germany.

MRS. ERNEST L. MARKHAM
BOX 143
TURIN, NEW YORK

Turin, N.Y.

March 11

Dear Ted,

We seem not to write very often, but there is not much here to write about.

The day before yesterday, we had a V letter* from Burt, written on ship. We guessed that it was mailed after he landed. It was dated Feb. 22nd; postmarked Mar. 7th. He said he did not mind the trip, a few were a little sick. Had no idea where he would land.

Clyde Dewan has gone too. They don't tell his mother. She is too far gone. Has to be kept doped. Jerry has come home to care for her.

The Millers hear often from Ray. A recent letter came in a week. They usually take about two. He says he is having a fairly good time. Has been near Saarbourg.

Bob's letters come in about 10 da. All of us have been hearing from him lately. He gets more time to write and to read books. Says his work is easier. Thinks the war situation is going much better, hopes to get home before too many weeks but I am afraid not while you are here. How we wish you could all be here together though! Willis probably will come in a little over a week. I suppose he will have to go over across. I try not to think of it, but keep hopeful.

I'm reading Ernie Pyle's "Here Is Your War."** It is a great book; good for anyone's morale, and I think him a great master at describing things vividly and in simple words. He surely gives us the human side of

---

*A Victory letter was written by a soldier overseas, censored and copied to a standardized paper, photographed, microfilmed, and shipped to the States via airplane. Next it was printed to 60% of its original size and mailed to the soldier. One mail bag of microfilm was equal to 37 bags of paper letters.

**In 1944 Ernie Pyle earned the Pulitzer Prize for distinguished correspondence. On April 18, 1945, he was killed by enemy fire on the island of Ie Shima in the Pacific.

the war. And I wonder if you see the "Up Front With Mauldrin" cartoons. Mauldrin is comparatively a kid, used to be at Pine Camp, is well known by the Times in Watertown.

Dad tore out the chimney in the girls' room, patched plaster in several places, is making a closet on the west side of the girls' room now. We hope to get quite a bit of painting and papering done soon, before spring's work comes on.

That won't be long now, at the rate the snow is going. It surely seems good to see the snowbanks shrinking. They have been so high for so long. Streams are opening and the blackbirds have come.

Our folks are very happy about the little calves. There has been just one bull so far. The heifer, Betty, had a nice calf the other day. We'll keep her, you can bet. Geo. Higby bought two lately, and wants some more.

Tom is with us still and seems to be planning to stay right along. He talks of spring's work and haying.

We probably wrote that Pete expected to go to Texas. He doesn't have to after all. He will go to school right where he is.

You said something awhile ago about having Peggy come. Of course we will like to have her. I am quite sure I told her so, in a letter some time ago.

Paul Freeman has had scarlet fever, but they are out of quarantine now. He hasn't been very sick.

Erwin Wendt is out after a tedious time with some infection in his eyes, a tonsil operation and various things.

You get the Boonville Herald so you must have seen the picture of Gary Healt and Verne Frank in Belgium, also other pictures and items of interest.

The Ackerman's latest news from Len tells that he has had an operation for kidney stone. I hope they will send him home soon. Mrs. A. isn't giving up hope that it might be a mistake about Linc.

Everybody else is in bed and I'd better go too. Remember, we are always thinking of you. Keep your faith and courage high.

Love,
Mother

Ted: Just a line to tell you that Billy is planning on having you & Peg at his birthday party. I've got my fingers crossed that you'll see Willis. He finishes this Sat.

Bob writes of moving to a new camp with better facilities and bug-free nights.

Philippines
Mar. 12

Dear Ted,

This is going to be a quick one because it's getting late and I've got to hit the sack pretty soon. Have a big day coming up tomorrow. I'm sending this home because probably you'll be there when this gets there. Probably this should be addressed to Lieut. Markham or F. O.* Which will it be? Can't remember that you have said for sure.

Willie expected to be home about now and said you two might make it together. Hope you do. It'll be a few months yet for me.

We have just moved into a new camp and are having a big time getting settled again. I have been cutting bamboo to prop up the sides of the tent and to make a rack to raise some of my gear up off the ground. Built a set of shelves out of a big heavy cardboard box our mattresses were shipped in. Four shelves about 3 ft. wide and nearly as deep so it's big enough for both Shafer and me. Tents are about the same as before with four men but we have all new equipment – metal bunks, mattresses, sheets and blankets. The blankets are essential here too for it gets quite cool at night and there is a good breeze and these new bunks are really OK.

These cool nights are a real treat, and <u>no bugs</u> or mosquitos. We can really sleep tho there is a little anxiety about what goes on some places around here. We are in a pretty flat and dry section for a change – almost like the place we were based in California last year. It is dry and dusty but if there were much rain we might be nearly flooded out for it's an old rice paddy.

The work here should be fairly interesting and we will see some new scenery so all in all it is a pleasant change. I should get some good pictures from this area for there certainly is a lot to see. We should be able to get around more on the ground too. The people seem to be even more intelligent here and somewhat cleaner, and they have better facilities in general. It's a little hard to tell who you can trust, however tho although they all seem friendly and no trouble has arisen worth mentioning.

*Flight Officer.

Ted, if you expect to come out this way I'll write and try to give you suggestions on what to bring and how to live out here. That goes for Willie too of course tho undoubtedly he won't be able to have much extra gear around. That's one of the rough things about the ground army. They have to carry nearly everything on their backs. I have a pretty nice little home here and other places have been satisfactory too. Wish everyone could do as well.

Must turn in. The old pad will feel good too for a little over six hrs. Good luck to you – keep me informed.

Bob

The family is expecting Ted home soon for the long-awaited furlough. Wartime shortages have limited the availability of such things as cigarettes. Marian has resorted to smoking her pipe.

March 19

Dear Ted,

I happened to think the other day that I better write you and remind you that I'm expecting some silver wings. You know I've got a dress with silver buckles and need some silver decorations to go with them. Just didn't want you to forget.

Also it would be very nice if you could bring us some cigarettes. They're pretty tight around here and it's pretty hard if you can't get to the store often. George gave me a pack last night and it's the first I've had in ten days. I've been smoking my pipe – much to the disgust of the whole family. It works pretty good tho.

That's all I want except for you to get home fast. I'm still in hopes that you may be able to see Willie. He wrote that he finished Saturday night and could probably leave before Wednesday. So if he's late you may be able to connect. I've still got my fingers crossed.

Tom is looking at our family snapshots and I'm not getting much written.

I wrote a note to Peg. Mom wrote to invite her formally or finally or something. We won't be able to give her a sleigh ride even up in the lot on the manure boat. Our snow is going so fast. At one time, or rather since before Christmas we walked straight in on the back porch and the path finally got about even with the top of the pump. And we couldn't see up the road for a long time. Now it's most gone on the walk. There weren't any thaws this winter and the snow is just disappearing now. The roads on the hill are getting open so Dad can go up there.

Blondie went up to Jan's tonight and the house seems rather empty and quiet. She puts in her hour of piano practice every night. She's doing real well. She gets awfully disgusted at my pounding. She's finally hid the "Army Air Corps" song on me. I ought to find it and get practiced up for your arrival. Maybe somebody else could find a tin pan and we could have an orchestra.

I've got to get to bed I'm so sleepy I can't think of anything to write. I'm painting the woodwork in the living room and have plenty to do before you get here with Peg. Shirley's and my room is torn up too and we're sleeping in the front room. So if we don't hurry there won't be any place for you to sleep.

See you soon. Hope you can see Pete.

Love,
Marian

After two years of training and relocations to ten different places, Ted is finally graduating from the Army Air Forces Bombardier School in San Angelo, Texas, with the rank of 2nd Lieutenant. Evelyn writes to tell her son how proud the whole family is of him.

There has been no word from Burt for nearly a month.

The Army Air Forces

Bombardier School

of

San Angelo, Texas

announces the graduation of

Class 45-6-B

Thursday morning, March twenty-ninth

Nineteen hundred and forty-five

Theodore W. Markham

LIEUTENANT, AIR CORPS
ARMY OF THE UNITED STATES

United States Army Air Forces

MRS. ERNEST L. MARKHAM
BOX 143
TURIN, NEW YORK

March 19, 1945

Dear Ted,

I've just written to Peggy to say that we'd like to have her come with you tho I am sure she knew it anyhow.

I am afraid we won't be able to hang on to "Old Man Winter" as you requested. Spring came suddenly, just as winter did. The roads are bare, snowbanks shrinking, robins and blackbirds are here and "sugaring" is in progress. But this still is March, we never know what may come. We might get a big snowstorm yet. Anyhow, there is pretty sure to be snow enough somewhere for warm sugar. Tom is boiling some now.

We are hourly expecting word that Willis is on his way home. Too bad he couldn't be a little later, so he could stay until you come! And Bob won't come for some weeks later than you, we think. His latest letters sound very optimistic. It sounds as tho he is due for a big rest and change. Maybe he is getting about all the flying he can stand. We'll just pray that he will be able to, "hold 'er steady," until then.

Mel and I each had a V letter from Burt written Feb. 22nd on ship and probably mailed on landing. And she wrote that she had one written sitting in a crowded boxcar, going east, in France. Well, this is war and probably we are just beginning to realize it.

You have felt held back and slowed up, but maybe it is all for the best. You know the old story about how one summer is long enough to grow a squash but it takes a hundred years to grow an oak tree. And I feel that you are going to be as strong and sturdy as an oak.

We went to see "Winged Victory" last week because you spoke of it. It is a great story. We imagined you in it. "Thirty Seconds over Tokyo" is on now, but I hardly think we will get to see it.

Thanks for the fine, long letter we had from you the other day. Last night I took it over to read to W.B. and Aunt Clara. They are always anxious to hear from all of you, and surely appreciate hearing the letters.

Ted, second from right, and some of his buddies on graduation day.

We are in quite a torn up state here in the house just now. We just had to get some of the big jobs done before the men get too busy with outside work. Some plastering, carpentering, painting and papering. Oh, yes, even a little electric wiring, we hope to have it finished before you come.

I have Pete's address for you. They have just got it from Doris. Ethel and all of us hope you'll meet.

We are all well here, and we hope to see all of you soon. How we wish we could come to see you graduate! We are a proud family!

Love,
Mom

307

Spring 1945

Following Burt's departure for the war, Melrose and Linda returned to Melrose's family home in Fillmore, NY. On a morning in late March, Melrose was out running errands when a family member brought her the telegram pictured below.

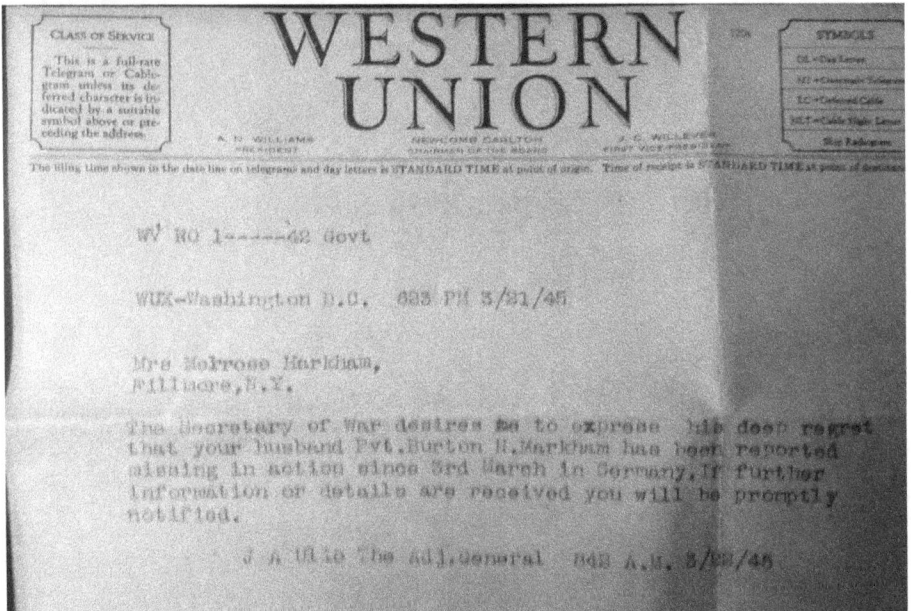

WV NO. 1-----'42Govt

WUX-Washington D.C. 623 PM 3/21/45

Mrs. Melrose Markham
Fillmore, N.Y.

The Secretary of War desires me to express his deep regret that your husband Pvt. Burton H. Markham has been reported missing in action since 3rd March in Germany. If further information or details are received you will be promptly notified.

J A Ulio   The Adj. General   842 A.M. 3/22/45

Burt had been missing in action for nearly three weeks before the telegram arrived. There are no letters from the time of this telegram until Ted's letter to the family on April 29. It is likely that the family communicated the urgent news via telegram. The telephone was used sparingly, but it is certain that phone calls were made.

Mrs. Karl Benedict, correspondent for *The Journal and Republican* in Lowville, contributed the following story on April 5, 1945.

TURIN
MRS. KARL BENEDICT
Correspondent

Theodore W. Markham, 23, son of Mr. and Mrs. Ernest L. Markham, March 29 received his wings as a bombardier and was commissioned a second lieutenant in the Army–Air Forces, at the Army Airfield at San Angelo, Texas. He is now home on leave. Lieut. Markham enlisted in the Army Reserve Corps and was a junior in Cornell University when he entered the service in March 1943. For a time he was stationed at Fort Niagara, then he began training for a bombardier. He was stationed at Miami, Fla.; Williamsport, Pa.; Nashville, Tenn.; Columbus, Miss.; Maxwell Field, Ala.; Decatur, Ala.; Valdosta, Ga.; and Tyndall Field, Fla., before going to San Angelo, where he completed his training. He attended grade school in Turin and was graduated from Constableville Central High School. Mr. and Mrs. Markham have three other sons in the armed forces: Lt. (j.g.) Robert W. Markham, U.S.N.R., now in the Philippines; Pvt. Burton H. Markham with an infantry division in Europe, who has been reported missing in action in Germany since March 7; and Pvt. Willis H. Markham, who has completed infantry training at Camp Wheeler, Ga., and is now home on furlough.

[Story courtesy of New York State Historic Newspapers]

Almost a month after Burt was reported missing, Melrose received another telegram.

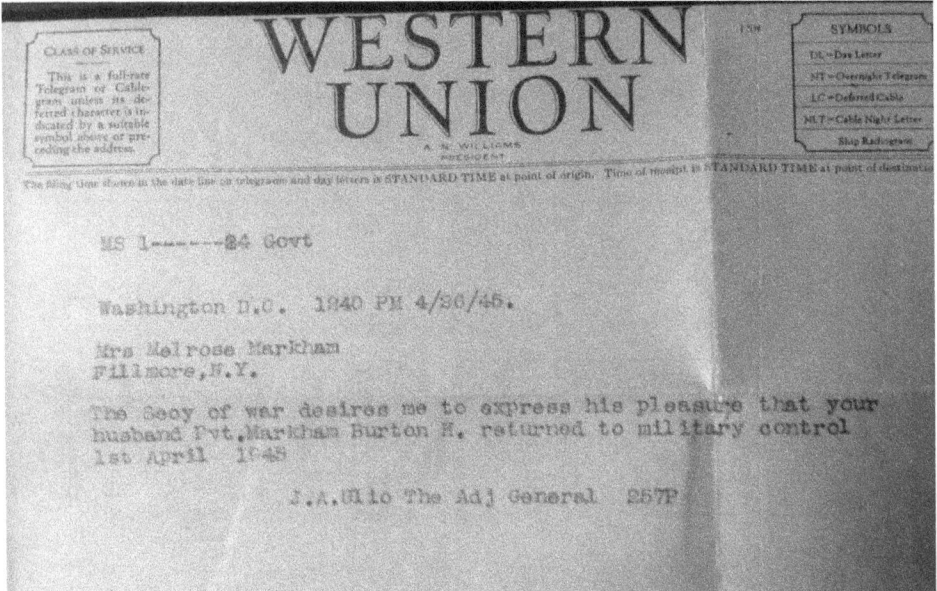

MS 1 ------ 24 Govt

Washington D.C.   1240 PM 4/26/45.

Mrs. Melrose Markham
Fillmore, N.Y.

The Secy. of war desires me to express his pleasure that your husband Pvt. Markham Burton H. returned to military control 1st April 1945.

J.A. Ulio The Adj. General 257P

Burt had been safe for almost a month before Melrose received the good news. After his liberation from a German POW camp, he was hospitalized in France for another month. One of the first things he did after his liberation was to write the following Victory letter to Melrose.

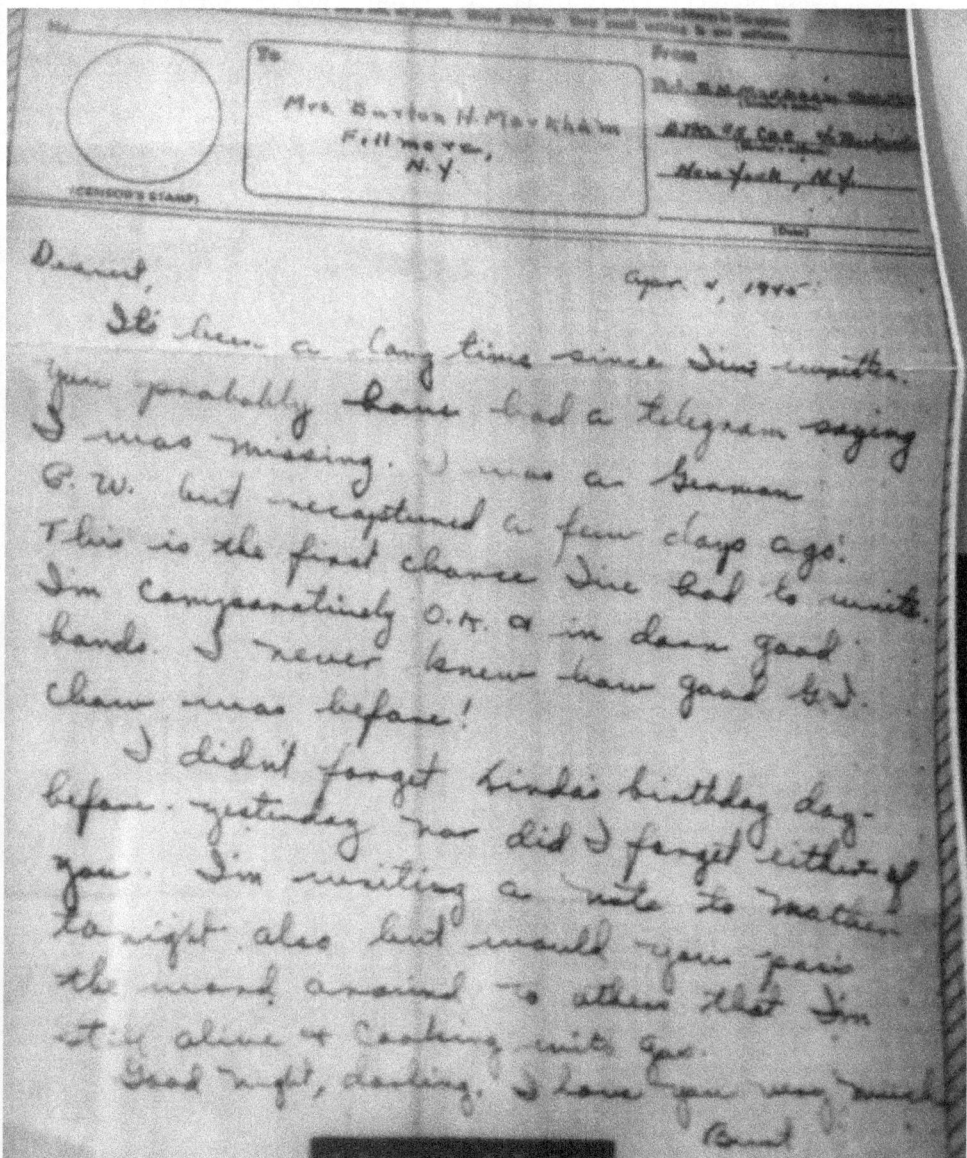

April 4, 1945

Dearest,

It's been a long time since I have written. You probably have had a telegram saying I was missing. I was a German P.W. but recaptured a few days ago. This is the first chance I've had to write. I'm comparatively O.K. and in darn good hands. I never knew how great GI chow was before!

I didn't forget Linda's birthday – day before yesterday. Nor did I forget either of you. I'm writing a note to Mother tonight also but would you pass the word around that I'm still alive and cooking with gas.

Good night darling. I love you very much.

Burt

Private Burt Markham

Following his graduation and subsequent furlough, Ted was shipped to Langley Field in Virginia. He writes that he is relieved to hear about Burt, but we learn that Willie is now on his way to the war in Europe. Ted's experience in the service has given him a profound appreciation of "the most wonderful sort of place called home."

U. S. ARMY AIR FORCE

April 29, 1945

Dear Folks,

I just happened to think that Jan is 22 today. Quite an old woman – huh?

It was great to hear the good news from Burt. Peggy gave me the news when I called her the first night I got in here. I'll return Burt's letter. Everyone from Peg's folks to my buddies have read it.

It's been so long and I've so much to say that I hope I can remember it all this time. I don't remember that I gave you my address the other night. The one which you got first was only a shipping order. I was disappointed not to have been able to see Willie the other night but should have realized how quickly they are moved through Mead. I saw his shipping orders which shipped him to Camp Shanks on the 9th. (Camp Shanks is about 40 miles up the Hudson from N.Y.) Everything looked as if he would be going to Europe and had probably shipped within a week after arriving at Shanks.

Luck was still with me though because I got to spend nearly two days with Peggy. It was quite a break to have had those three days before starting school tomorrow. I also got to Washington [D.C.] last week and so I've been getting right around lately. (Nearly 8,000 miles on trains and busses within a month.) Washington is a great sight. One could spend weeks looking at the nice things it offers. Things will tighten down now that we start class.

Gosh folks, I can never express the good which the short leave did me. At times I have worried a lot about the changes and tension which the

Altie and Billie playing ball in Evelyn's yard

service brings onto a fellow, but at least a part of that worry is over now. Everything seemed so natural and relaxing when I struck home that acting and feeling my old self came fairly natural. It was such a relief – even to the point where I was sort of disorganized and made confusion for you. It seemed that I didn't do a lot of things like helping out as I planned nor to see everyone, but my selfish self felt satisfied with it all. Mom, home seemed so natural and wonderful that it is every dream which we have of it while away and feeling lonesome for it. I'm so glad that so many could be there and especially the short time with Willie. It was great to have Teen and the children all of the time and especially to see them romp and play as Altie and Bill did. It seems that each time I go home I think Dad has the best bunch of cows he ever did. It is even a bigger feeling this time and especially because he has them looking and milking so good. How can it be helped when those daughters of Pedro are so easily mistaken and when we probably never, unless Weatha, had a better looking heifer than that Betty? It is quite a feeling of pride to see how well Altie's calves are doing too. They are about as good as we've ever had. All in all it just means a good warm feeling to know that tucked back in the hills of Lewis Co. there is a place which is a bit confused at times but still where

314

a small group of people work hard, play hard and love hard. It's just the most wonderful sort of place called home no matter what strife has been required to build it.

There are of course some favors which I want to ask of you too. In a couple of weeks I want to send all of my woolen uniforms home rather than to try to pack them whenever I move or let moths get after them. I plan to have them all pretty dirty by then so could you have them all cleaned and then put them away for me? You tell me what the cleaning bill is please.

Next could you send me my <u>old</u> radio? I hate to take it away from Mom, but I want her to use my other one which shouldn't look so horrible. I think it should ship all right if you just stick it in a cardboard box with my address on it. Perhaps if you insured it for a slight sum it would surely ship all right, but irregardless it owes me nothing. Komis and I have a room now so may as well add the comfort of my "poor old $2.00 radio."

Training will start tomorrow and last for about 10 weeks. After that it is likely that we'll get a delay en route and be sent right across to join crews over there [the Pacific]. This training will be in 17's or 24's which we'll probably always fly in thereafter.

Langley doesn't seem nearly as bad as previous reports we had had of it. That has been generally true of most previous camps. Our quarters are about the same as enlisted quarters we have had before. Chow is the biggest problem. We have an officer's mess in our area but it is so rotten that most of us refuse to eat there. However, there is an officer's mess over on the main base which is fair and only costs us 75 cents a day. Mess at the officer's club is good but costs about $2.00 a day. Langley is an old permanent base and is real nice on the base. However we live away from that in temporary buildings in an area called "Shellbank." Lots of things go on here to make it like a "mad mess", but things seem to get done. We're right in here with a mad mess of navy establishments. When I get a chance there seems to be lots to see about here. Right now they claim the carrier, Midway, lies over in the bay. By the way, if I should call you from here, don't be alarmed if I reverse the charges. I'll send you the money. It is because we have no pay phone here and have to reverse charges on long distance calls.

It's good to hear that Tom is back. He is worth all you pay him in order to keep the farm work up and some strain off from Dad & Mom.

Everyone write and pass my address about.

Love,

Ted

P.S. I asked Peggy if she would send the pictures which we took up there. I like the one of Dad & Mom with their grandchildren.

On the following day, April 30, Hitler committed suicide just four days after the Russians finally entered Berlin.

Burt writes from the hospital in France where he has been recuperating for a month.

May 1, 1945

Dear Ted,

I guess it's about time I got around to congratulating you on that nice new shiny bar. I realize how hard you've worked for it and how well you deserve it. I'm proud as hell of you and want you to know it.

I've given up any idea I ever had about getting a commission. I'm just going to take life easy and remain a pvt. Or maybe a pfc. The only ambition I have in this job is to go home. I may even make that. They say I'm going back to the States & have a 30 day furlough & I'm led to believe that I will be stationed there but you know the army.

I had my first mail since I left the States just day before yesterday and I've nearly read them to pieces already. Mother's first letter came today. It's great to be getting mail again.

I don't have any big news, I guess. You've read enough in the papers to know what things were like back there. I didn't fare badly compared with most but I still lost about 20 lbs, mainly because of dysentery. I guess I'm pretty well over the dysentery & gaining weight. I put in a requisition today for a Purple Heart. I got a little shrapnel on the side of the thinker. The only ill effect was the loss of a good head of hair, my fountain pen, & even my cigarettes I had on me.

I've sure got a lot of respect for those boys that fly the P.47's.* I've seen them work up close (too close a couple of times). I'll tell you about it some time.**

I've got to close and write Mother & Mel yet tonight. Best of luck and maybe we'll be able to get together if & when I hit the States.

As always
Burt

---

*The P.47 Thunderbolt was a short- to medium-range fighter/bomber.
**A story that Ted told long after the war was over was that a train Burt was being transported on was attacked by the American P.47's. Burt and some other prisoners were able to signal the pilots that the train was a PW train by waving their white undershirts as flags.

Melrose writes to Shirley while waiting for a telephone call that will tell her that Burt is in the States. She and Shirley both have secrets.

May 4, 1945

Dear Blondie,

Your letter came so long ago & I'm just getting around to answer it. I've all sorts of excuses & the biggest one is that I've been writing like mad to answer all the letters I had when Burt was missing. Now everybody is answering those letters & I have just as big a stack as ever. Linda is helping me so there may be no head or tail to the letter now that I'm actually writing.

It seems wonderful to be getting letters from Burt all the time again. He never got any of the letters I wrote before, but he should have letters sent to the hospital by now. I don't know if I had the War Dept. telegram when I wrote to Mother last or not saying that he was freed on Apr.1 – Easter Sun. I also got a nice early birthday gift for Linda. Now I just listen for the telephone to ring saying he is here. 2000 liberated Yanks came into Staten Is. last Sat & it seems as tho' Burt should be with the next bunch. He has been mighty impatient in the last few letters I've received.

Mel's birthday card to Shirley in 1945

Linda broke out with a rash last nite. The Dr. came this A.M. & thinks she has nothing. She feels fine – no temp. or anything. She has been so comparatively good all week that I've suspected she must be sick! She is very happy that her Daddy is coming home & calls him up on her telephone every few minutes.

Now a whole day has passed since I started this letter. I went to see "A Tree Grows in Brooklyn" last nite.* I enjoyed it very much. It was quite a novelty to go to a show for I hadn't been in two months.

So you have a secret, Blondie! That's the most natural thing in the world – it isn't awful or disgraceful. It's the way we're made. There seems to be no "cure", but an interest in things besides boys keeps a gal "balanced" you know. Just be a good girl, Blondie, & have a lot of good clean healthy fun & you'll be O.K. I'm not worried about you. I've no doubts but what the boy & boys will like you too. People will kid you when they find out you've discovered boys exist but that's all part of growing up I guess.

How is Latin? I don't have anybody to talk to me anymore when I write letters. They don't seem to go much faster either 'cause I just sit & think.

I have a secret too but you'll have to wait till you see me to find out.**

---

*Based on the novel, *A Tree Grows in Brooklyn*, by Betty Green.
**Hugh Markham, Melrose's secret, was born on October 25, 1945.

Ruth Clinton writes sometimes & she always wants me to say hello to you.

I'd like to see your room all fixed. I'd like to come up but will wait till Burt comes. Jan wrote & asked me up there. Linda & I went from Mt. Morris to Wayland, all of 25 mi. or so, on the train & she mopped up all the dirt possible, insisted on getting off at every stop & in general made me glad we weren't going any farther. I took her to S.S. last Sun. & she had a wonderful time trotting around. I sometimes wonder if she'll ever hold still!

Happy birthday & I wish I were around to spank you. I'm a good spanker – have lots of practice.

Love

Mel

P.S. This picture of Burt belongs to someone beside me. I had it in with my things.

On May 7, Hitler's Third Reich came to an end when Germany surrendered to the Supreme Commander of the Allied Forces in Europe, General Dwight D. Eisenhower. It was also Shirley's birthday. Bob writes the next day, his birthday, that he is waiting to hear President Truman announce that the war in Europe is over. It's doubtful that he has heard of Burt's release yet.

Philippines

May 8

Dear Shirley,

Yes it's my birthday here but back there you are a little behind so it's still your birthday.* The news sounds as tho we will have more to celebrate than our birthdays. They tell us that President Truman is to speak tonite and rumor has it that the war is over in Europe.**

---

*Shirley's birthday, May 7.

**In a radio broadcast on May 8, President Harry Truman announced the unconditional surrender of Germany but also mourned our casualties and reminded Americans that the war in the Pacific still remained to be won.

Spring 1945

It has been a rather uneventful day so far, otherwise. We haven't been doing much for several days now. We rather expect to go back to work again for a short time, tho unless something unexpected happens. It will be a relief really for we have been bored with so little to do. We are thinking too much about getting home too. There have been a few people we knew who left after we did and are saying good-bye to us these last few days so that makes it worse. Certainly I'm not complaining for most of these fellows deserve a rest more than we do. We have had a pretty easy time of it really.

I hope everything looks as good around home now as it did three years and a couple of days ago. I'm sure it will still look good in a couple of months – not a bit worried.

There isn't very much to write about, Shirley. I'll have to save most of it until a little later. Mostly I hope that you folks have had other good news from Europe and that Jan's birthday and her big event, your birthday, and Mother's Day are all that they should be. I should be home for the next birthday excluding David's and his prospective sister. I'm not sure I know when to expect the latter.

I'm going to have to stop about here. There are too many interruptions. Hope you keep the news coming the rest of this month. See you soon.

Love
Bob

Ted has sent Melrose a set of his newly earned silver wings. She writes that she is happy to accept them, and that she's quite ready to hear the telephone ring.

May 8, 1945

Dear Ted,

VE day* & quite a historical day, no doubt, tho' I was wondering this A.M. what Linda will say in 15 years if we ask her what VE day is.

*Victory in Europe Day, May 8, 1945.

She stood up & sang with the Nat. Anthem after the Pres. speech & I hoped there will never have to be a VE day in her day. I'm very thankful that I can be thankful for VE day for the meaning of Partial victory was completely dependent on one person.

That person should be arriving soon. He has known from the first that he was coming home & has been getting quite impatient. The papers say the freed Yanks are being sent home as fast as possible but for Burt, able to be about & idle, it isn't fast enough. I've learned to be patient but I'm quite ready to hear the telephone ring for me. I'm glad he wanted to come back to be Linda's father so much for I'm sure that was a big factor in his safety. For his short absence I guess we've gone thru enough so I hope he doesn't have to go the other way.*

I had no idea of not accepting your wings. Burt will think it is nice for me to have them & I think it was very thoughtful to send them. Linda likes them & I'll let her wear them too. I'll bet she'd know you if she saw you because she never forgot you. Sometimes I get kisses for all her uncles plus her Daddy when she goes to bed.

Glad you like your new training. I've never had an opportunity to congratulate you for your shiny new bars. I'm sure they were worth waiting for. Thanks for the announcement of your graduation.

Burt's never had any mail since he left, up to Apr. 26. He was hoping in the letter I had to-day that he'd get some for some of the boys had. It was Feb. 14 that I saw him last & that's a long time to wonder about your wife & daughter. I hope all the letters I wrote weren't in vain.

Say hello to Peggy for me. You're no doubt glad to be near enough to take advantage of those 3 day passes!

As always
Mel

P.S. I tho't Va. pretty when I went thru. Is it pretty where you are?

---

*I.e., to the Pacific.

Evelyn has been staying at the Klossners' and keeping house while Jan is hospitalized in Utica awaiting the birth of her baby. Evelyn writes her first letter to Ted after learning of Burt's release. She has much to be grateful for despite a May snowstorm that has dropped six inches of snow on the wet, plowed fields.

MRS. ERNEST L. MARKHAM
BOX 143
TURIN, NEW YORK

At Klossner's
May 16

Dear Ted,

These have been busy and rather exciting days. We've not been very good about writing letters.

It was nice to get yours recently. It would be a great treat to Dad and me if we could come to Virginia, but just now, at least, we can't see our way clear. Mr. Hathaway recently got an injury which keeps him laid up, and it appears that Bob will not be coming home as soon as he had hoped.

Yesterday, Dad called me on the phone and read a letter from him which had just come dated May 3rd. They are still in the Philippines but have just moved to a new camp, not done much flying as yet. They can have no lights except at the movies, so they go there or sit in the moonlight, or pitch horseshoes evenings. It is 120 degrees there and very humid. Says he hopes to come in time to celebrate <u>my</u> birthday.* Wants us to send all of you boys' addresses, and any news of Burt. I wrote so the letter was mailed this morning and Dad is forwarding your letter which was home.** Bob also said he might write to you boys and send the letters home, so we could forward them.

Last Friday, a lovely letter came to me from Burt in which he was remembering Janice's, Shirley's, and Bob's birthdays and Mother's Day. He had just received a letter from me that day and one from Melrose the day before. The first mail he had had, I take it. "I've already written to Ted

*Evelyn's birthday - July 10.
**The family frequently forwarded letters to one another.

322

and Willie," he said, but hoped to be home soon and see Bob here. No doubt you've received his letter and I do not need to tell you more.

The same day, and dated the same, May1st, a V-mail letter came to Janice from Willie. He had seen Le Havre, France, and was going through farming country by "40 or 8" (boxcar) which he said was "something though." Said the voyage over was quite rough but he wasn't seasick. The sea was beautiful when the sun shone. He "enjoyed it as much as he could under the circumstances." Willie would. He mentioned the neat little farms of France and friendly people who waved and called out to them, the kids crowding round to get gum or candy. He got an amazing long letter on the tiny sheet and he seemed, on the whole, quite cheerful. It is the only word any of us have had from him.

You probably have heard the news from others of the family. VE Day was a great day for us. About 6 in the morning the call came for John to go to Utica so the day wore on slowly for us here in spite of the music and speeches and excitement in the air. Late in the evening, John called on the phone to say, "It's a boy!", and he came later. A birthday present for Bob, so he is named Robert John. I went to see them at St. Elizabeth Hospital, on Thursday. We found Janice quite bright and got a look through a window at the nice big boy (8lbs). Shirley went with Clara and John Sunday, and on Monday Marian was down to see about Alton's glasses so she visited Jan. Today John has gone alone and probably soon he and I will go and bring them home. I am having a pleasant time keeping house for her and I guess the folks get along without me very well. I go home every Saturday and stay till Monday morning because Clara is here.

Since you went back we've had very cold, rainy, dark weather, several frosts and last Thursday, a real snowstorm. It was the day John and I were in Utica. It snowed from noon till sometime in the night. There was fully six inches of it here and the plow had to go up on Mohawk Hill to open drifts of four or five feet. We could have given Peggy a sleigh ride if she had been here.

Tom finished our plowing quite awhile ago and did some dragging. Most land is so wet nothing is being done. Mr. K. is about sick over it. The land they plowed last fall is getting very green. Grass grows well and some cows are out. We and Klossners have heifers out. Apple trees have been almost in bloom for 2 or 3 weeks.

Last but not least, I want to thank you for the lovely gift and card you sent me. I didn't need any gifts to make it a happy Mother's Day. Having men in the family as we have, the girls nearby, and the little ones to love and enjoy is enough. God bless you all!

Mom

Wed. evening,

John has returned from seeing Janice. He found her all fine and we are to go after them Friday.

Shirley reports that Kate got 3 letters from Willis today all written aboard ship.

Aunt Mary, Helen and Paul came to see us Sun. P.M. We all think Paul is someone we will like a lot. Helen came home just in time to help care for a new niece, Susan Marie, May 1. They had a letter from Ray, of Apr. 29 written in Paris on his way to Eng. for a rest. He had been flying lately, on observation work. He has a bronze star,* as you probably know.

---

*The Bronze Star Medal is awarded to U.S. Armed Forces personnel for bravery, acts of merit, or meritorious service.

Ted writes next from Virginia. He expects that in a little over seven weeks, he will take a "boat ride," meaning that he will finally be shipped to combat in the Pacific, where the war is far from over.

The island of Okinawa in the Pacific was secured in April to serve as a staging ground for the planned invasion of Japan. The cost: 12,000 Americans dead and 60,000 wounded; 100,000 Okinawan civilians were lost, along with 92,000 Japanese soldiers – the largest losses of the Pacific War. The battle served as a terrifying sample of the carnage, both civilian and military, that would come with an invasion of the mainland.

Spring 1945

May 20, 1945

Dear Folks,

Mom's nice letter came last Friday. By the way, letters mailed on one morning get to me the afternoon of the next day. Of course that is if the mail isn't held up here at the post.

Seems as if May 8 was quite a day for the Markhams. Perhaps Robert John should have been born two days after this defeat of Germany. I'll be darned if it isn't getting a bit monotonous to have nephews all of the time – you may tell Teen that!

May 8 was quite a mild day around here. We had a parade and speech by the Colonel but otherwise it was a normal day. There are a good number of returnees here from Europe but apparently they sided with the rest of us who figure that our war is yet to be won.

I wondered what became of Bob. In a way I should have told you not to have forwarded that letter which I sent him at home. It probably didn't contain any great secrets, but still I shouldn't have sent what I did in that one beyond the limits of this field. I hope you stuck on an air mail stamp because he fussed about my "Free" postage once.*

It is good that you have heard from Willie. He was probably late for the excitement. I hope he can stay in Europe with the Army of Occupation for awhile.

I had a letter from Burt last week, also one from Mel. I doubt if there was any news which you already haven't heard.

I want to thank whoever it was who renewed the Boonville Herald for me. I imagine it was Dad. I was beginning to miss it.

Do you suppose someone could pack up my old radio and alarm clock and send them? I of course don't want the clock if it doesn't work nor if you are using it because I can get along. However they would both be pretty handy if you could send them soon. You see we don't have anyone to blow a bugle or toot a whistle for us anymore. Don't be fussy about wrapping the radio because it is pretty sturdy and isn't liable to be hurt in the mail.

It seems that I was going to but never did tell you what we expect after this. The way it looks we will finish training in about seven more

---

*Ted usually used his "Free" postal privileges.

weeks. After that it seems that we'll get a short delay en route and then take our boat ride. That is likely if we get sent to lead ships (17's & 24's) and join the lead crews over there. There are other possibilities of getting further radar training and staying on a bit longer or if we get assigned to B29's or 32's that we train with those crews in this country. Those are just possibilities.

I'd best quit now. Let's hear from you. I missed Marian's letter with Mom's.

Love,
Ted

Bob is writing a letter while trapping rats for a little recreation while his buddies are off to a USO show. He has some advice for Ted about what to bring to the South Pacific. Another piece of advice: "It's good life insurance to be happy and keep your mind on the job."

Philippines
May 23

Dear Ted,

Since I haven't heard from you recently or gotten your address I'll have to send this home and have it forwarded. Thought probably I'd hear from you after your graduation to let me know what you are doing and how the leave went. The folks told me you were home about a week and that Peggy was with you. They also added that they didn't see much of you. That gal must have quite a hold on you. Well! Gals are pretty nice to have around sometimes, but they're no damned good to a guy when he's out here.

Had expected to be home on leave by this time as I told you, but the admiral had other plans. It won't be long now tho and if the trip doesn't take too long, I might make it for Mom's birthday. This cruise has been a little long and we have covered a lot of territory, but time has passed rather easily and for the most part it hasn't been too rough. I'm glad I didn't miss it and glad it's about over. Have a little "livin" to catch up on and should be able to get a start with some shore duty.

We have had some work lately that is a little different and rather exciting, but alas a little more strain on the nerves at times. It has turned out well and has furnished me with some pretty good pictures that I may be able to show you sometime. Have logged about forty five missions this trip and with the twenty or so last time I guess I'm almost an old timer at it. Most of it has been fairly easy tho as the sea and air opposition is pretty light these days. There is still a hell of a lot of ground to cover tho and I don't envy the boys on the ground a bit. Things should move fairly fast when more men and equipment get out here too.

Chances are you will be seeing this place one of these days. I might suggest a few things you should try to bring. We always say, "It costs but little more to travel first class," and it really helps to be as comfortable as possible and have something to do. There will be lots of leisure time so bring some good books, make sure you will have a radio and record player available. Bring a few electrical connections so you can make extension cords etc. (bulbs and wire are usually plentiful), not too many clothes for you can make out with 8 or 10 suits of underwear and 4 or 5 shirts and trousers. Some fairly heavy socks are good to wear in field shoes. I like white wool athletic socks, a fellow has to keep clean next to the skin or he is in for a lot of fungus etc. so figure on changing underwear and socks every day if you can. Usually you can get soap, tooth paste and brushes etc. so there is no point in lugging it around. Stationery is sometimes scarce but can be found usually. Make sure your outfit is going to have some athletic equipment. We play a lot of volleyball, some soft ball, horseshoes, and badminton. It helps to get a little exercise and it makes it easier for the fellows to get along together. That's darned important. Bring along some liquor. It has a good punching power and good to calm the nerves after a rough job. Above all be prepared to have a good time with the gang. You leave the girls and family behind and there is no point in getting homesick or lonesome. It's good life insurance to be happy and have your mind on the job. It's a good experience so be prepared to get the most out of it and enjoy yourself.

Tonite the movie is one most of us have seen. Some of the fellows went over to an army camp to see a USO show, but there wasn't enough transportation for all of us so Charlie and I are sitting at home waiting. We are out of beer at the moment or we'd have a couple on the table. The rats have been pretty numerous and bold lately so tonite I have a trap and have caught two in the hour or so we have been sitting around here.

The folks wrote the other day that Burt is OK and that was certainly a big relief. Of course I hadn't heard anything until about the time he was recaptured, but I had to wait just as long to learn that everything had turned out all right. I am about convinced that we Markhams can get through about as much as the rest of them. I take it Willie went over to Europe about the time it was over. At least the folks said they expected to hear from him from overseas and I thought it was probably that direction. Hope he has a little more time to get ready for the job than Burt had. You should be pretty sharp at your job by now so I won't worry much about you.

It's time to hit the sack so I'll sign off. Be sure to let the folks know where you are all the time. I'll get in touch with them as soon as I can and by some freak chance we might get together in a month or so. Don't know where I'll be going after leave but I'll let you know. I'm really looking forward to the next four months.

Take it easy.

As ever,
Bob

Marian writes about her new-found social life, family events, and of hoping to make her errand-running legal. She enjoyed her unexpected overnight in Rome.

Peabody, Major Burton W.
2814 Linden Lane
Forest Glen, Maryland

May 27

Dear Ted,

I was just filling out an address book for Willie and came across Burton Peabody's* address in Mom's book. I had meant to send it to you before so you could look him up if possible.

I'm sorry I hadn't written you lately – I got the hint you dropped. Mom was up to Klossner's and it wasn't very convenient to add a note.

I've been on a tear lately. Mom has been at Jan's for three weeks and a lot of the time a couple of weeks before that. And my social life has me in a whirl – in between times I am a chief cook and bottle washer.

As you probably know by now, I've finally got to driving and have been kept busy running errands. I take my driving test tomorrow. Here's hoping I pass it. I've been going all over without a driver but there's a lot of checking right now because licenses are running out.

I've also stuck my neck out and am attempting to be a 4H leader for girls. Hope I can really accomplish something. I have a rather young group (8 to 15 yrs.) and two Gibbs'.

I've had two all day meetings in Lowville for Home Bureau. One was week before last and we spent the day learning to make lamp shades.

Monday of that week I spent in Utica getting Alton's eyes examined. He broke his frames and as they were too small and as his eyes needed checking, it was a have to. His right eye is normal and has a plain lens. He has overcome the tendency of being cross-eyed entirely. And he only has to wear his glasses to read. It looks funny to see him without them.

And ever so often I wait on table at church suppers etc. So you see everyone is most helpful finding jobs for me. In fact so much so I can't

---

*Major Burton Peabody was the soldier who accompanied the body of Robert Markham home from Kelly Field, Texas, in 1918. Robert was Ernest's brother, a flight instructor, and was killed in a training accident. Burt was named after Major Peabody.

find time to do my mending to say nothing of attempting some badly needed sewing.

And of course there's housecleaning, gardening etc. besides the regular work at home. And the family all seem to be going in opposite directions at once

So you don't have to wonder why I don't write. I write George once a week and usually have a date on the weekend.* He didn't show up last night as I expected nor tonight so I've got a little extra time.

The housecoat you sent Mom was swell. She's got to shorten it and then I think it will fit me. (Now I was only kidding.) She said how nice it would be to put in a suitcase. I said that sounded like me. Folks have got so they laugh at my buying things that pack well. After you live in a suitcase for awhile, you learn to outlaw big things and things that muss.

Mom says to tell you we sent the radio. I took the alarm clock to Lowville yesterday. Mom thinks it needs cleaning or something. Well they wouldn't take it. Now I don't know whether to try some other place or to send it as is. Mom says it has hardly been used since you used it and probably is just gummed up from standing.

Aunt Grace, Gladys, Ray and their children Mary and Billy were here tonight. Billy was a year old in March and walks all over. Aunt Grace is still bemoaning the fact that she couldn't get those uniforms for you. Said she had a pass to see the major and everything.

Did anyone tell you we all went (including Tom & Aunt Ethel) to open house at the Rome Air Depot three weeks ago? I went with George and the folks were supposed to meet me at Aunt Grace's. Well Dad got a bit weary of the traffic so he legged it on home and never came after me so I stayed with Aunt Grace and enjoyed it a lot. She has a 2 room apt. I got home by bus next nite. There were 185,000 at the Depot that day. A few too many to get around well. Altie took off by himself and I guess he saw everything. He wore his soldier suit but took off the insignia so he wouldn't get in trouble. The day we went to Utica he got two salutes.

He also got a model of a rocket plane in Utica and has it all made. There's rockets (10 cents a piece) and a gun to shoot them. He has recently finished the Condor glider model and has that on the wall of his room – no room on the ceiling.

---

*George Waters was Marian's gentleman friend.

David took two steps on his birthday. Yesterday morning he got off his pot-chair and took a couple to get to Mom. He now can say "up" to add to his vocabulary of "hot". He can say "outdoors". He's crazy about the "Zizzey" but the Plymouth is all he's interested in. When he sees it he starts teasing me to "Zizzey". Mother's Day they were down and he knew the difference between the Dodge and the Plymouth and only was interested in the Plymouth.

Now he goes around the living room at home saying "hi" to all the pictures. He got interested in yours first and calls it Ted. Then "Dad" and "Gum" and "Mamie and Aldie". He's learned Burt lately but the picture of Bob puzzled him. He'd talk and walk too if there really was any necessity. You should see him push his pen all over the dining room. And he's found out the register is nice to poke things down. Teen heard a noise the other day and here he had a drawer in the buffet open and her best spoons out and he was right beside the register. They were all there.

The weather has been putrid. It's been so cold and rainy. I've had the worst luck washing. If there was a nice day I wasn't home. This week we had a bad thunder storm with wind. It took two quilts I'd washed across the lawn. The juice went off so I had to wring them by hand after rinsing them over – also a bed pad. Then I went to town and got some clothesline and put it on the porch and I'm going to leave it all summer I think.

Tom got the oats in this week and the ground is about ready for corn. Lots of farmers haven't even that much done. Johnny thinks he'll have to plow over some he did last fall the ground is so bad. The week you were here is quite typical of what we've had since. We've even had a couple bad snow storms since the leaves were on the trees.

Mr. B. pops in about once a week. He's been going to Dr. Germann. Last week he looked and acted bad. Could just about put one foot after the other. He has to stop to get the news on you boys.

Guess I'd better ring off now and get to bed so I'll be fresh for tomorrow. I'll have to tear to get to my appointment for my test. Shirley is at Jan's and maybe Mom won't go up in the morning. Then I won't have to get lunch and supper ready before I go. Hope this doesn't tire you out.

Love,
Marian

Guess Bob's right – I'm longwinded and worse writer than he is.

Willie writes from Germany, where he is guarding POWs. He seems disappointed that he didn't see action but is relieved not to be in the South Pacific.

Germany
May 30, 1945

Dear Ted,

I got your letter yesterday and also one from Burt. I had had only one other letter (from Marian) since I got off the boat.

I didn't get a chance to see much of Washington. I wasn't there long enough to do anything.

You would like a snapshot of me? Well the only ones I have with me are the one I had taken with my buck and one in my baseball suit the year we won the championship. You could probably get one from home. Kate has three I had taken with my turtle neck sweater. Maybe you could talk her out of one of them. Yes you can send any snapshots you want to. I don't recon I'd have to ask for them because they would be sent in a letter.

Yes, I figure I got a pretty lucky break by coming this way [Europe]. We are guarding P.W.'s here. We can't get out of camp though, to see any of the country or do anything. It is a hell of a lot better than being in the Pacific and having a lot of bullets flying around. It gets monotonous as hell but as I said before it's better than being in CBI.* Of course I still may be sent there. We are attached to the 106th Div.

I didn't get to see any action at all. We were on the way to Germany when peace was signed.

Well I guess I'd better quit as I have to go on guard in a few minutes.

As ever
Willie

---

*CBI: the China–Burma–India theater.

It wasn't until June 4 that Melrose finally received the following telegraph announcing that Burt was really on his way home.

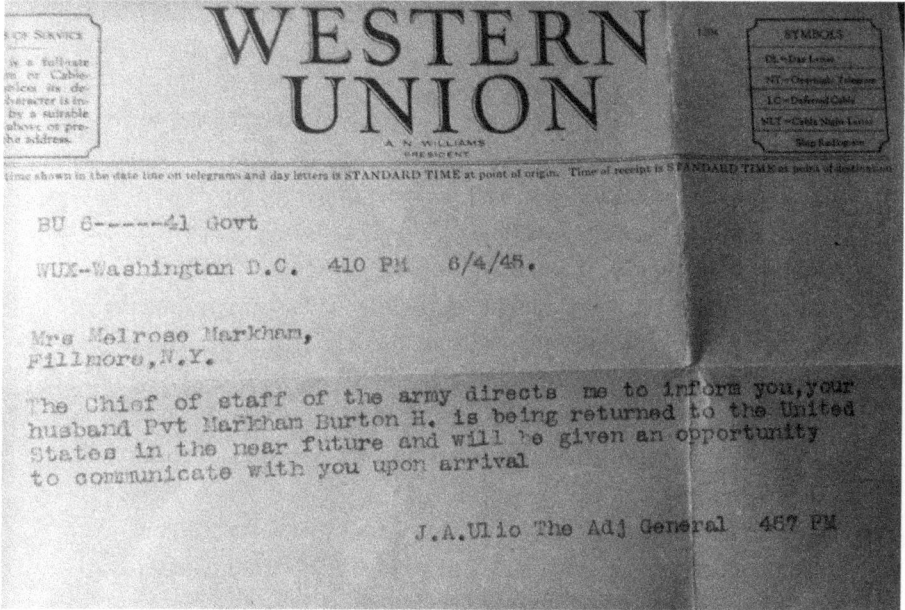

BU6---41 Govt

WUX – Washington D.C. 410 PM   6/4/45.

Mrs. Melrose Markham,
Fillmore, N.Y.

The Chief of staff of the army directs me to inform you, your husband Pvt Markham Burton H. is being returned to the United States in the near future and will be given an opportunity to communicate with you upon arrival.

J. A. Ulio   The Adj. General   457 PM

Marian writes that the family expects a visit from the Burt Markhams soon. Burt will get a sixty-day leave and will then spend time in Lake Placid for rehab and reclassification. Alton writes a note at the bottom of her letter.

June 17

Dear Ted,

Altie wrote a few days ago and I meant to write a real letter to go with it. However I'm on a tear today so this will only be a note while I eat lunch. Dad has gone fishing and we'll have dinner tonight.

In regard to the radio – your good one that Altie broke. The case was broken and he mended it and then I took it to be repaired. He didn't tell you he was sorry but Mom said he felt awfully bad. It sure ruined the looks of it and we haven't the verdict yet on the repairs. We want to make it good and Altie will buy it if you'll sell.

We expect the Burton Markham's on Wed. No recent news from the other boys. Burt reports to Lake Placid Aug. 14. Says he's kinda soft. I just hope his painting arm works.

Mom and I just papered the pantry. Today I've had a spell on organizing drawers etc. and can I throw out stuff! Guess I'd better keep going while my mind is good.

Love,   Marian

Went to Schoffs to see Irene [Freeman] the other night. I think Jerry looks like Herb.

We have your alarm clock fixed and will send soon.

Turin, N.Y.
June 17, 1945

Dear Ted,

I broke your radio a week or two ago. I sent it in to be fixed. Could I buy it from you. Burt got home at 10:00 Friday morning. He gets 60 days furlough and then goes to Lake Placid.

Mr. Baxter is in the Ithaca hospital. He's at 109 now.* It's his heart but he's feeling better and hopes to get back to camp [Marian's writing].

---

*109 E. Upland Rd., Mr. B's new address in Ithaca.

Dad went out to the sale at Syracuse Saturday. A cow sold for $1,500. The Luchsingers were the honory family. We got the calves and heifers out all but one.

Cindy got hurt Friday night her pad and hind leg were hurt.

Love Alton

Ted writes that it's hot in Virginia, and that he would like to find a furry friend. A recent mission has taken him over some brightly lit cities.

June 15, 1945

Dear Folks,

I didn't mean to wait nearly three weeks before writing. During that time I've gotten a nice letter from Marian and then her card telling of Burt's arrival.

Last weekend was a big one for Peggy had four days of vacation and came down. She came Sat. morning and left Tuesday noon. I found her a nice room at a private home which was extra nice for short notice. It was lucky for me because I had quite a light schedule. It was sweltering hot but a nice weekend.

I have a recent letter from Willie. He says that he has only had three

Peggy in 1945

letters – one from Burt, Marian, and me. In case he hasn't told you, he is guarding PWs in a guard company with the 106th Division.

I also have a recent letter from Bob saying that he hopes to help Mom celebrate her birthday. We thought perhaps it might be possible for Burt and me too.

We finish here about that time but I have no idea whether or not we can get a delay en route. We can hope but have no certainty.

I didn't want you to go to the trouble of getting my old alarm clock fixed. I thought that if it still ran it would be useful. You needn't bother to send it now if you have gotten it fixed, but I may need it after leaving here. The old radio was very welcome. Did Mom get the other radio to take its place? I want her to use it.

It has been terribly hot here recently. It seems to be a heat wave for before a week ago it was quite cool. Yesterday it was 96. It is quite humid here.

You don't know where there are some cocker pups for sale do you? Komis and I are wishing that we had one. We need a pooch whether it is a mongrel or cocker but we both like cockers.

I'm glad that Marian writes so well even though I don't write directly to her. I wish that Teen and Jan could do that too. It is pretty difficult to get letters to everyone and I often wish that my letters home would cover everyone there – such as Jan and Teen.

I've grown to like this post about as well as I could like the Army anywhere. It was a good break to be sent here. It is a good field and a good location for one in the south.

I haven't gotten to fly north but once. Most of our missions have been south. Twice I was scheduled for missions over Williamsport, and then the flights cancelled. The other night my mission north was over Philadelphia and New York. It is quite a glitter of lights to see. The radar is coming well and we're getting used to "playing Buck Rogers." We are called "Mickey's" if I haven't told you. I'd like to get a mission over Ithaca but haven't much of a chance for that route.

It's time to quit for this time. Let's hear from you. How about it Dad?

Love,
Ted

P.S. I didn't forget Father's Day, Dad, but didn't have the chance to do much about it.

Summer 1945

Ted writes that he is sending some of his dirty uniforms home for dry cleaning. One of his shirts has a special bar for Altie. Ted would like to get home to spend some time with Bob and Burt.

June 21, 1945

Dear Folks,

I'm sending a box with my winter clothes. There are three shirts, two trousers, and a cap. I'm not sending my blouse and cap because I'm going to send them to Peggy where I hope to get a picture taken sometime. Photo studios are no good here so guess the best bet is to try and get it done in Williamsport. She has my short coat which I left on the way back from the leave. I've also stuck in a few packages of gum and some maps. Perhaps Dad would like to look at the maps and then put them where every visitor can't see them. They are classified restricted material so don't wave them about too much. Do you suppose you could have the clothes cleaned and then put them away from the moths? Everything needs cleaning except for the pink shirt made of 100% wool and with scalloped pockets. It is the nicest shirt of the three so I guess you can identify it. Here is some money for it.

The letter from Altie and Marian came yesterday.

No Altie you can't buy the radio nor should you worry about breaking it. After all, it didn't cost me much money in the first place, and I'm sure it has paid its worth to everyone who has enjoyed it. I want Mom to use it anyway. You tell me how much it cost to be fixed and then have Mom take the money from my bank account.

Say Altie, I left a bar on one of the shirts for you. I got to thinking that Merrill couldn't outdo me by giving you a silver railroad track nor should Billy and Linda flash wings about occasionally when you have neither a pair of wings, nor gold bar.* Rub the bar with cloth and don't touch it with your sweaty fingers, and it should stay shiny. Perhaps you could

---

*A gold bar is the military insignia of a 2nd Lt. A double silver bar, or "railroad track," is that of an Army Air Force Captain.

wheedle a small silver bar from Bob or by that time maybe a small silver railroad track! (A navy Lt.(jg) wears a small silver bar and a full Lt. wears the small silver railroad track which is equivalent to our captain.)

You'd better be sure that Cindy's foot heals up alright, Altie. You want to make sure the young calves on pasture get enough grain to supplement the less nourishing grass too.

Don't bother to send the alarm clock right now. Wait a bit.

So Marian you think that Jerry Freeman looks like Herb – huh? Didn't I suggest that nearly a year ago? I agree anyway.

I imagine that Burt, Mel, and Linda are there by now. Maybe I can get to call Burt sometime soon.

I wish I knew whether or not it is going to be possible to try and get home with Burt and Bob. You see we finish in two weeks but know nothing of the disposition of the class. We seem to have three alternatives: 1. To stay here and be crew up in low altitude bombardment in 24's; or 2.&3. To be sent to a field like Boca Raton, Fla. or Phoenix, Ariz. for 29's. To stay here would mean a leave but to the other fields it would mean a leave after we finish instead of now when we're nearer home. I have a notion to ask for 24's, but have long known it best not to stick one's neck out. It might be possible to get a few hours home if I could get a hop to Rome and then fly to Arizona but can only guess now. Maybe I can come but probably not.

Everyone write!

Love,
Ted

Evelyn updates Ted on Bob's whereabouts and his upcoming leave. Burt, Melrose, and Linda are with her, and Shirley has just worn a formal gown for the first time.

Mrs. Ernest L. Markham
BOX 143
TURIN, NEW YORK

June 26

Dear Ted,

Marian isn't here just now and I realize I've not done much writing lately, though there are several things I have wanted to tell you.

We had finally sent your clock before we got your letter. It had not been running since soon after it came here. It took Mr. Ornstedt long enough to fix it. I hope you get it and can still get some use of it.

Marian got your radio fixed up. It has been needing it for a long time. I think perhaps Burt will see about setting it up better than it has been.

Yes, Burt, Mel and Linda are here, since last Wednesday night – nearly a week now. He looks and seems just like his old self tho still has some of the intestinal trouble. He eats just as usual though and can lie down anywhere and go right to sleep just as he used to. He works around quite a bit but gets tired sooner. You probably know that he (and Melrose) will go to Lake Placid Aug. 14th where he will be processed and reclassified. I suppose, also have a nice vacation for a week or so. Of course he doesn't know what he will do afterward. Anyhow it seems wonderful that he is really here and able to enjoy living. He has seen plenty.

A letter from Bob, from Hawaii June 17th says he and crew flew that far, arriving the day before, I take it. He would stay in a beautiful rest home on the beach, get his clothes cleaned, etc., and try to get to something like normal. He said he had had the first hot water shower in 8 mo., some green vegetables and even a glass of milk! He would be waiting for transportation and can hardly wait to get home, yet wishes he could see more of the islands; it is so lovely there and he will probably never see them again. Thinks he will get to the coast about July 1st, send us a telegram and be home soon after that. I think we'd better telegraph you as soon as we know.

We still get letters from Willis quite often but ours do not seem to catch up with him very well. He mentions one from you and one from Burt at the same time written from the hospital in Verdun. We have sent off a couple of packages to him – things he has requested and a few other things, such as cigarettes, tobacco, a roller, his pipe, fountain pen, coffee, air mail stamps and stationery, figs, maple sugar, cookies, some photos of the family he had left at home. We hope he gets them soon. He sounds homesick. It must be a rather boresome existence but safer than some other things he might be doing so we are glad he is there.

Last night Dad and I went with Shirley to the recital of Miss Hoffman's piano pupils. Shirley wore a formal for the first time, and surely did herself proud. She has worked hard on her music and made good progress.

Marian has gone to work for some people who needed help quite badly. She thinks she will not stay very long though.

I asked Marian to thank you for the Mother's Day gift. It was swell of you, but I didn't need a gift to make me happy. I have many reasons for being a proud and happy mother.

All here are well, crops, etc. doing fairly.

Love from all, Mom

Rec'd the $5.00 you sent for cleaning. Clothes haven't come as yet.

Ted is still struggling with the stifling Virginia heat. Meat shortages have caused some friction between the civilians and the soldiers.

June 28, 1945

Dear Folks,

By this time I imagine that haying is well underway and that home is just bustling with business. It makes me wish that I could be there. I believe it is five years since I've done much haying – a long time! I think it would be a much easier and nicer way to keep cool than in some stuffy ground school class here.

It is unusually hot now. Today has been about the worst yet. My roommate, Jim Komis, and I have blankets on which we are laying outside in early evening. We have nothing on except undershorts but it is still uncomfortable. It seems the only way that we can try to escape this heat. I flew last night and early morning so had a heck of a time trying to get my rest this afternoon. It's a humid heat without any breeze in here.

It seems as if I expressed optimism over getting home after we finish here. It doesn't seem as if we will now. We are supposed to finish next week and will then be shipped probably to Arizona for a two week familiarization of the radar set in B-29's. I do have a chance to stay here for further training in low altitude work, but I am not sure that I'd want it. We are pretty certain of a leave after the two weeks in Arizona or after OTU in Nebraska or Texas. Gosh I sure hope that it will be possible to get home to see Burt while he is there.

I am afraid that I can't get any cigarettes for Willie. I've been looking about but can't find a way to get more than a couple of extra packs occasionally. We are allowed six packages a week so haven't much of a chance to get extra unless we know a civilian!

Lately we've been doing quite a little flying on our northern routes. It has been quite interesting when we've had observer missions. However as a Mickey we never see the ground except through the radar returns. It is quite interesting to see country like Pa. and the cities in the east from the air. I've flown over Williamsport a couple of times lately – once at night when the pilot blinked the landing lights and another time during the day when he raised the wings for me but it was probably too high to be seen or heard. Over Lancaster county and other regions of Pa. where they strip crop it is interesting to see the contour and strip patterns. If one studies and looks the land over closely he can see where the wheat is being harvested, corn is leafing out, and some haying. Today I was noticing the super-highway in Pa., how straight it is, and how it tunnels through two mountain ranges. There is a lot to see on a mission like that if you can keep your work caught up enough to look around and can then know how to pick out features of terrain, cultivation, culture etc. It is difficult to be able to distinguish anything at first, from high altitude, but after you study it a bit there are more interesting things that you can get a chance to see.

They're having an awful time with meat down here. The civilians around here are having an awful time about it all. They're getting sick of fish and take pains to throw it in our faces as often as they can. I really feel awfully sorry for them!! We don't get much but hot dogs and stew instead of better meat, but the boys don't gripe over much except for poor cooking. If the poor civilians can't work without steaks each day than I wonder if they could do better on K Rations. We just get a little sick of hearing about what soldiers get and they don't.

It is time to quit. Let's have a note when it's possible.

Love,
Ted

P.S. Thanks for the clock.

Willie writes from Germany that there's not much to do; sometimes he gets homesick . . . and that's a good thing.

Germany
July 16, 1945

Dear Ted,

I got your letter a couple of days ago but just got around to answer. I guess I'm slipping a little on my letter writing. Your letter took nearly a month to come it was dated June 15.

We have moved twice from Kreuznach, the first time to a little town about 4 miles from B.K., Biebelsheim was the town. We were guarding P.W's. there also. It was a larger cage than A-3 but was emptied about 7-8 days after we got there.

Two weeks ago we went on a 10 day field problem up near Kohling. We could have done everything in two days that we spent 7 days doing. One problem was to take a pill box on the top of a big hill. I guess we took it but we didn't see the pill box. It was about a half a mile from us on the other side of the hill when we finished. Oh well, as long as the officers were satisfied I guess I am. I sure would like to go to C.B.I.* with them, we would never come anywhere near the battle lines. What got our goat was

---

*The China–Burma–India theater.

342

that we were nearly on top of it once (about 500 yds.) when the 2nd. Lt. (no insult) took us down the hill way around the other side and up again. Then we just fired our ammo. into the side of the hill (away from the pill box) strategy huh! It sure would be a good way to keep your men from being killed and still take the pill box.

When we came in from the problem we shipped up here. I'm sending you a card showing an aerial view of the town and also the name of it. How it is pronounced is beyond me. Your guess is as good as mine and the next guys. I'm sleeping in the top floor of the school house. It isn't bad, sleeping on cots, at least a lot better than the wooden bunks we had at Kreuznach and the floor. I put an X on the school house roof but in case it comes off it is the largest building down on the bottom right in the middle of the card. This town is down near Heidelberg and Mannheim. I have seen quite a bit of country now, all of the Rhine Valley from Mannheim to Kohleng and it is quite a nice country through there, although some of it is blown up considerable.

Grunwettersbach bei Durlach v. Flugzeug aus. Willie's X can be seen on the large building in the foreground.

Here we are doing nothing at all. No P.W.'s or D.P.'s*, just a small training program. I don't expect to be here long, maybe not even all of this week. All of the low point men are shipping out, where to I don't know. Maybe home, maybe C.B.I., occupation nobody knows. At least we are getting out of the chicken s_ _t 106th div. Some of the fellows I came over here with were transferred to the 28th and 35th divs. and may be on their way home by now. At least they will be home by August.

We came up here to do M.P.O.** duty but don't know just when it will start. Probably I won't be here to get in on any of it.

While I was in Biebelsheim 12 applications came to our company for courses in two colleges, one in France and one in England. There were about 40 fellows interested and I wasn't one of the lucky ones to get an application but it wouldn't matter now as I'm being trans. to another outfit and the app. would be cancelled anyway. I will get another chance anyway. These colleges offered some real good courses in Science and Agriculture.

Boy it was good news to hear that Burt got home and 60 days plus 2 weeks rest at Lake Placid. I got a letter from Jan & John the same day as yours and it also had the news about Burt.

Although it is past Mom's birthday I hope you and Bob could be home together then, at least I hope Bob could get to see you if you didn't get a delay en route.

No, Ted, I haven't a snapshot of me since I've been in. The only small pictures I had taken were the ones in my turtle necked sweater and Kate has them. I looked more like a lumber jack than I did a soldier of the U.S. I'll write and ask her if she would give one of them up so you could have one. I can't see why she wanted them in the first place, there was nothing to brag bout in the pictures.

I thought I was fat when I was home but now I've got that topped. When I was home I was hard but now I'm soft and flabby. I don't know how much I weigh but I'd guess about 165.

Well Ted I guess I'd better quit before I write a whole book. Don't ever worry about me. I find things to keep occupied and nothing in this army is going to change my way of thinking or the things I have always

---

*D.P. = Displaced Person.
**M.P.O. = Military Police Officer.

wanted to do. I'm with a darn good bunch of fellows and things go along pretty good. Sometimes I get pretty homesick but I guess everyone does. If we didn't what the hell would our home mean to us if we didn't miss it and the people we hold dear to us.

As ever,
Willie

Ernestine writes from the hospital, where she has just had another big event! Richy is the newest arrival, and Ernestine is happy to have another "little man."

July 21, 1945

Dear Ted,

There have been so many times I've had your address and not written. Now – at last – I'm writing and have no address.

If I'd had my choice I would have waited a while before I came to the hospital. I saw so little of you and Peggy. We had looked forward to really seeing you for a good visit this leave, and to a little entertaining for you, too. I'm sorry to miss so much of the fun but glad to get this over with. It has been awfully hot here for a few days.

Your newest nephew is Richard Francis but I hope not Dickie. Bob's mother gave him his name but I reserve the right to insist on Richy or Ricky.

He is a nice baby – strong and plump and good. Already he has gained three ounces, which is unusually good. I hope Bob isn't too disappointed in another son. I really can't be – I like little men.

Shirley is still at home with the boys. Billy is having a wonderful time sleeping in the tent and building the dam in the gully. It is always such a thrill (I hate that word but it really fits in this situation) for him to go down home when you boys are there. He'll have lots to tell me.

Compared to most of my letters this is a pretty short one, isn't it? My energy has run out, though, so I must rest.

Love,
Ernestine

On August 6, the first atomic bomb was dropped on the Japanese city of Hiroshima. Three days later, a second bomb was dropped on Nagasaki, resulting in a combined total of over 200,000 fatalities. On August 14, Japan agreed to an unconditional surrender to the Allies, and the war was over.

Ted writes that hearing the news was an unforgettable event, but it came with some mixed feelings. After two years of what seemed like interminable training, his burning desire to serve his country would not happen. Nonetheless, the war's end couldn't be called a disappointment.

August 19, 1945

Dear Folks,

Your nice card [birthday] came last Monday. I also got nice cards from Teen, Marian, Jan, Shirley, Billy, Peggy and her folks.

The great news was heralded with a lot of happiness and celebration around here. Most of us who had our ear next to the radio last Tuesday evening will remember that news as vividly as we do that Sunday afternoon* nearly four years ago. Some of us didn't quite know how to think when we heard the news because we had prepared our thoughts toward helping win this war and contributing some points to get out sooner though it is hardly a disappointment with the more important news.

You probably wonder how this good news is going to affect us. Well, we would like to know too. Things are, of course, in too much of a turmoil for anyone to know. About all we know is that it caught the Army, as well as we who have our individual thought, by quite a surprise. It is only logical to believe that I will be with the forces of occupation or held in active reserve until all danger is past. Most of us in my category figure that we will be very lucky to get out of the service within a year. A good lot of us would like to plan to resume our school work in the fall of 1946, but that may be far too optimistic. It is hard to imagine what capacity we will be filling. We are primarily specialists trained for the primary purpose of waging war, though our training and qualifications are broad enough to fill quite a variety of tasks.

---

*The day of the Japanese attack on Pearl Harbor, Sunday, December 7, 1941.

Our training has been in a turmoil and still is. On Wednesday and Thursday all training was shut down while on Friday and Saturday it started up enough to resume some ground school. No flying has been done since Tuesday morning but next week it seems as if some of the flying training will be resumed. Tomorrow night our crew will fly an eight hour navigation mission, but as yet no bombing missions have been scheduled. Most anything is likely to happen.

I've been wondering if Bob has gone back or if he may have gotten an extension. Since he thought he might come this way or have me meet him somewhere I have more or less been expecting a message.

It seems likely that both Burt and Bob should be able to get out quite soon, but I doubt if Willie and I will be so fortunate. It is only fair, I guess.

I want to hear of Willie's whereabouts as quickly as possible if and when he gets in from Europe. I sure hope that he got close to these shores before they decided to keep such low point men in Europe.

Everyone drop a line.

Love,
Ted

Burt has been stationed near Ted in Virginia and is hoping for a desk job. He writes that Willie is on his way home for a furlough from Ft. Dix. Burt wants to get together with Ted.

Fri, Aug 24

Dear Ted,

Well, I guess I'm a neighbor of yours now. I don't know how long for but we're about 20 miles from Richmond.

I thought that I'd call you tonight but I'm too damned tired to dress & find a phone. I got in here about 1:00 P.M. & have been on the run since.

They've put me in limited service now because of my eyes and as yet I'm not assigned to any branch of the service. I guess they are going to make me a clerk but you never know.

I called up Mel from New York. I hung over there a day & could have gone home if I'd known. She's up at Turin for a few days. She was at

Placid with me. She says that Willie had called from Dix and was on his way home. They expected him last nite.

Ted, why don't we try to get together? Perhaps I could meet you in Richmond or maybe you could get over here. I may try to get a pass so I can go up & see Willie. Do you think you might? Give me a call will you?

As ever

Burt

Ernestine writes next, first thanking Ted for a gift of summer shorts. Shirley has been helping out with the new baby but has returned home to Turin. They both have some heartfelt words of appreciation for Ted.

---

44 Lanpher St.

[August '45]

Dear Ted,

Really our gratitude is better than our manners. Both of us were so glad to get the shorts. I say both because I was beginning to wonder if I could make shorts from G.L.F.* bags. Thank you an extra amount. It was very thoughtful of you.

This has to be a very short letter, though there's so much I want to write. There's one thing I do want to say. Shirley and I have decided we want to let you know how much we respect and admire and love you for the way you have taken your part in winning this war and for the way you take the ribbing you get from the fighting members of the family.

Of course we know you're caught between the Navy and the Infantry. Second lieutenants catch it from everyone and the Air Corps from the "Joes" and the Army from the Navy. Don't feel you're outnumbered, tho, when the other fellows ride you because we girls think you have been wonderful all through your training.

I do know you have been homesick and bored and poor and disgusted. You have doubtless felt useless and scared and neglected. But you have done what you had to do with such splendid spirit and learned well what you had to learn. You have worked harder than any of the rest

---

*G.L.F. bags = feed bags.

to save money, planning ahead always. And always you have been so wonderfully considerate and thoughtful of Mother and Dad.

I'm ashamed that I need to say this now. I should have let you know by letters for months and months back. Probably your morale doesn't need so much boosting now as it has many, many times before. But I want you to know I'm proud of you.

There's lots of news but I must close. Will is home, of course, for thirty days. Bob is in S. Carolina. Burt had a weekend pass last week end. Melrose met him in Fillmore. Peter & Doris are honorably discharged & home. Helen [Miller] Seipe is home & expecting Paul any day. He is discharged, too. Altie made forty dollars at the fair with his calves.

The O'Briens are all well and very happy. David's beginning to be curious about his powers of speech. Billy did not start kindergarten and Richard grows like a healthy weed. I prove to be much tougher than the doctor thought and work like a horse but miss the other half of the team – Shirley! Bob [O'Brien] has had it easy for a few days but will begin threshing etc. tomorrow.

Now I must close. I'm happy to know you owe me a letter!

Love,
Ernestine

Bob writes from Beaufort, South Carolina, where he will finish out his time in the Navy as an advanced instructor. He'd like to find a way to have Rita there with him.

Box 2
NAS Beaufort, S.C.
Sunday Aug. 26

Dear Ted,

Meant to get in touch with you sooner and possibly stop and see you. As you might guess tho I stayed home as long as I could and then had to push along pretty hard to make it in time. Maybe we can find a way to get together more if you are going to be around awhile. I should be able to fly up to Norfolk or perhaps you can come down here.

I have about what I expected to get for duty. Mac could have fixed me up with duty in Miami flying B26's for training targets or at St. Simon Ga. flying Beeche's for radar training but I decided to come here with the rest of the old gang. We will be advanced instructors in PVs. The crews come here pretty well trained so we don't have to give them any bounce drill, but just help them with the first touches in navigation, gunnery, rockets, and bombing.

Don't know how much longer I'll be in the navy. I only have 34 points and if our awards don't come then it might be quite awhile. If they do come thru tho I think I'll get out as fast as I can. I'm guessing that I'll be on my way home in a couple of months.

Guess you know I had a pretty wonderful time while I was home. Probably the folks have told you that George and I went out to Luchsingers and bought another bull and we got 7 or 8 loads of hay from Ackermans etc. Alton took Eleanor and Elsie to the fair and did fairly well. I think it did both he and Dad a lot of good. Farrington has a very nice heifer by Duke and Starings have a very good one but we could have done very well with a herd.

Rita and I certainly had a wonderful time together. I don't know what can come of it, but I'm certainly wishing she could be down here with me. We certainly could have a wonderful time because I can't see that the navy is going to work me very hard now that the war is over and it looks as tho there will be a lot of sitting around while I'm in the process of getting out.

Must write to the folks and let them know where I am so I better call this enough for now.

As ever
Bob

Will was on a ship headed for the States, a furlough, and then on to the Pacific when the war suddenly ended. He writes the next letter from home but will soon be on his way to New York City for Military Police duty. He is pleased that he will be so close to home.

Summer 1945

Turin, New York
August 29, 1945

Dear Ted,

Well I should have written before but didn't get around to it. I got into New York the 20th and got home Sat. night the 25th. Jan, John & Kate met me in Utica and brought me home.

The trip across was quite uneventful except that the Japs surrendered while we were coming home. What a day that was on the boat! We came back on a Liberty Ship, "James Hoban", and it took us 14 days to make the trip. About half way across we ran into a four day storm and the waves were really rolling up high.

We left the E.T.O.* as replacements headed for the Pacific, going through the States for a 30 day furlough and more training. We have all been split up now, some going in the Air Corps and some of us are going to be M.P.'s. I have to report back to Whithall St., New York City for the M.P. duty. I think it is a pretty good deal being so close to home. Possibly I'll be able to get home now and then from there.

A week ago yesterday while we were in Camp Shanks we were given passes into New York. I saw quite a bit of New York but of course there was a lot I didn't get to see. I was with two other fellows. We saw a show at Radio City Music Hall and it sure is some place. Saw the damage to the Empire State building,** Rockefeller Center and a radio show.

Yesterday Dad, Altie & I got in a load of oats & a load of second cutting. I found out I'm pretty soft, got blisters on my hands and am lame today. I guess I'll get used to it after awhile.

Must quit and write to Bob and Burt.

Love
Willie

P.S. I'll send you some snapshots soon

---

*E.T.O. = European Theater of Operations.
**On July 28, 1945, a B-25 Mitchell bomber on a routine personnel transport mission crashed into the Empire State Building, killing 14 people (the three crewmen and 11 people in the building). The freak accident was caused by heavy fog.

Burt writes that he's looking for another pass to go home again. He hasn't been feeling well and hopes that he won't be hospitalized.

Tues. nite, Sept.4

Dear Ted,

I guess you and I haven't had such good luck getting together. I've called twice but I guess you beat me out each time. Did you get the message I left?

I'm rather up in the air right now. Our C.O. promises us passes from Thurs morning until Mon. morning but it would be my luck to pull K.P. or Guard. If not I'm going home again, I may even be able to get out Wed. afternoon.

I was to Fillmore this weekend & thought I might see you get on the train at Wmsport but if you did I missed you. I only had 2 nights & Sunday at home but it was worth it. Mel & Linda are fine but mother Marriott has been in the hospital having X Ray treatments. They believe she has a tumor in one lung & hope to halt the growth with X Rays.

I called up home Fri morning and talked with Dad & Willie for a minute. Willie has until Sep. 26 & then reports to N.Y.C. for M.P. duty. It looks as if he might have a decent break. I should write to Bob but left his address at home.

I've been hitting the sick book & they are sending me over to the clinic in the morning. I hope they don't stick me in the hospital but maybe it would be best.

I guess I'll sign off. Why don't you try to get over next week? If I go home I'll be broke for the rest of the month. I'll be seeing you.

Burt

Ernestine's husband, Bob O'Brien, writes to thank Ted for the gift of shorts. He has been having some fun with the neighbors.

Sept. 4, 1945

Dear Ted –

My hand is so unaccustomed to the pen that I doubt if you will be able to make very much of this out. If this were a pitch fork instead I probably could do a much better job.

I received the three pairs of shorts you sent me and I thank you for them. They were exactly the right size and I don't know of anything I needed more. There wasn't a pair to be had in Lowville & I doubt if there were any in Watertown. I will reimburse you for them when I see you.

I suppose you are experiencing warmish weather down where you are. Our days have been quite cool & I suppose before long, the frost will be on the "punkin." Willie & Kate were down the other night & Willie said he had been pitching grain that day. Our grain is all reaped & the thresher arrives to-morrow. Oats are small & light this year but plenty of straw. One of our neighbors said he weighed a bag of his oats this year & it was 40 lbs. We didn't raise any corn this year & I guess it is just as well because that promises to be rather light too. We have taken up archery in our neighborhood. Clint Alexander has borrowed one of Will's bows and sent for a bunch of arrows & a target. He spent 2 or 3 days on making a support for the target and has it set up between our house & theirs. So that is where we spend our spare time. I can almost hit the target all ready. Madeline is the expert. She has hit the bull's eye. Don't work too hard making this hen scratching out, Ted. Bring it with you when you come & I'll de-code it for you.

Sincerely
Bob O'Brien

Shirley writes with details of the new school year, her senior year. She is taking typing and is worried that Ted might not like typed letters. Willie won't accept them.

September 9

Dear Ted,

I'm too lazy to run upstairs to get some writing paper as you see so grabbed first thing I found. At that, I'm doing better than usual, aren't I? The writing bug has left me I guess. Every bit of time I get I usually have to practice my music or have to read for a book report. I could be doing either now. Maybe I'll get to write more letters this winter for practice, if you don't mind getting type-written letters. Willie said he wouldn't accept one. I'm taking typing this year and the more I type the better and I could just as well write letters.

Other than typing I am taking English, Social Studies, Physics, Intermediate, and Health. It sounds like kind of a full schedule but won't be so tough as last year I hope I really want all these (except health). This schedule will be satisfactory for admittance to Cornell. Mr. Kaskela advised me to write and tell them what I'd had, what I'm going to take, and all the draw-backs. He said if it wasn't satisfactory, he'd go down to Ithaca and have a talk with someone explaining my circumstances. They sent me a bulletin and a circular which answered all my questions. The requirements have changed a lot Mel said. Only a foreign language is given as required not 3 years. Mel, Irene, and Rita figure my chances are pretty good if I retake Chemistry this January and raise my mark, etc. The more I think about it I think I want to major in foods with all the science I can include. I've done quite a bit of talking with Mel, Rita, and Irene about different things. I feel pretty well set, and more confident. I'm going to try to try harder, providing there aren't too many things outside of school to do. That was my drawback last year. All my teachers are very good this year except Social Studies and I wouldn't call her much good. She's too lazy and slack about it. In English, Mrs. Kornmeyer, a new teacher appears to really know her stuff and isn't going to work us so hard for homework. She doesn't believe in homework. Hurray.

I came home [from Ernestine's] 2 weeks ago today (when Will came). On Thursday morning, Irene, Rita, and Jerry and I went to take Mel and

Shirley at the start of her senior year

Linda back. Rita and I, the maiden aunts, as Irene and Mel called us, had fun carrying on some good old confabs as Irene and Mel talked about their husbands and marriage problems (they were very often interrupted by their greater problems). Jerry sure is an individualist and masculine. Linda wanted to kiss him and he'd give her a shove, then she'd say, "Jerry – you stop! Stop that, Jerry." And she'd try again. He quite took to me on the way back & we had a great time. I stayed at Schoff's* Fri. nite. I think it was the nicest trip I ever took. On the way back we stopped at Avon at the coppersmith shop & pottery & wooden shop. My they are nice places. We had lots of fun.

Marian tho't you'd be home this week-end. Hope you'll be able to come sometime soon.

Uncle Ellis mite come soon.

Love,
Blondie

---

*Rita and Irene's family.

The final letter in the collection is from Evelyn. She writes that Will is happily doing farmwork – he's cutting wood and fishing with his father. She writes about picking blackberries and about a newborn calf. There is a birthday celebration to tell Ted about, and Altie has won some money at the fair. The oats went in fine, the old barn is pretty full, and it *is* just the most wonderful sort of place that Ted calls home.

MRS. ERNEST L. MARKHAM
BOX 143
TURIN, NEW YORK

Turin, N.Y.
Sept. 9, 1945

Dear Ted,

I surely have been pretty negligent about writing to anyone. But it surely is nice to get your letters.

Your last one made us feel that perhaps you would be home this week-end. All of us would be glad to have you. We suppose Burton spent last weekend in Fillmore. He called us on the phone Friday to see whether Mel and Linda were still here. Irene, Rita, Shirley and Jerry had gone with them to Fillmore. On reaching there, they found Mrs. Marriott in a bad way in the hospital – tumor in the lung and it is inoperable. She won't stand it long, I fear.

Willis has written you, I know. He is a tickled kid to be home. He seems so well and full of pep. His leg and arm muscles were hard but some muscles got lame and sore when he started pitching hay and grain. His hands were all blisters. Now he is working on the farm harvesting gang and getting quite farmerish. He and Dad have drawn down some wood too. Last Sunday they went fishing and brought home nine nice trout. They both had a great time. Labor Day we five went over the river looking for blackberries. We didn't get very many berries but we all had fun, anyhow. Willis takes Kate out frequently in the old truck. Today they have gone up to Mr. Baxter's. Friday evening we had her over to supper and had a birthday cake with eighteen candles for her.

I've just been to the barn on Alton's invitation to see a newcomer [a calf]. He and Dad brought it in from the hill last night, after milking. It is Ellen's – rather small but spry and smooth and pretty as can be. Altie says her name is Elizabeth. He explained to me that she is a full sister to his Eleanor, sired by Pedro; and Elsie, Ellen's last year's calf was sired by Duke, because we alternate the bulls. I just wish you could have been around to see Alton at the fair with Eleanor and Elsie. Bob & Burt had coached and encouraged him so he got a great lift to his interest in stock and in everything about the farm. He helps a lot lately. He took $40 in premium money and his first investment was a $50 bond. Then, adding some other money, he bought clothes for school. The oats went in fine. The old barn is pretty full.

We have searched quite a bit for the book you want, but so far, no luck. Sorry. I shall look a little further among Bob's books.

You probably know that Pete is home, discharged. He goes Nov. 1st to Cornell for some engineering course, I imagine electrical. Fine! Maybe you'll be there soon.

Grandma has word that Ellis and family may come soon.

School has started. Alton is going to C-ville. Likes it fine.

Must close now and write to the other boys.

Love,
Mom

Epilogue

World War II ended leaving the Markham family with little more damage than the loss of a good head of hair, a fountain pen, and a pack of cigarettes. Sixty-one other Lewis County families weren't as fortunate, though, and did not see their soldier sons or brothers again. Cornell University's losses totaled 500 alumni and students, while New York State's fatalities numbered more than 43,000. The death total for the country exceeded 400,000. Estimates for the number of war deaths worldwide vary from forty to fifty-five million, including the victims of the Holocaust.

The Markhams were able to resume their pre-war lives after the war's end. Ernestine and Bob O'Brien welcomed four more sons and two daughters into their Lowville home, where they resided for the duration of their 46-year marriage. Bob eventually left the family farm to work with a construction business in the village. Ernestine continued to teach in Lowville, retiring as a reading specialist after 30 years of service. A scholarship in her honor is awarded yearly to a future educator from the Lowville Academy. A commemorative stone stands next to the one-room museum on the school grounds.

Marian eventually moved to Rochester where she worked as a supervisor for Monroe Community Hospital. She and her friend, George Waters, never married but dated for the rest of her life. "Mamie" never failed to share her humor and warm spirit with her many nieces and nephews. She became a grandmother to two granddaughters following Altie's marriage to Jeanne Horne in 1960. Alton retired from the Eastman Kodak Company where he worked as an engineer.

Bob left the navy with a Distinguished Flying Cross and an Air Medal with four gold stars. Shortly after the war ended, he purchased the family homestead from Ernest and Evelyn. He and Rita were married in August

1946, and a very large family of eleven sons and four daughters followed, supported by an excellent herd of Holstein cows. In 1974, they sold the farm to a son, Scott. Bob was an active public servant, serving on the town board as well as serving twenty years on the school board where he frequently officiated as president.

Burt was safely discharged from the army with a Purple Heart and resumed his career with Farm Credit. He, Melrose, and Linda welcomed Hugh into the family shortly after the war's end and two more daughters followed. Melrose's housekeeping skills were legendary, and the family lived in a house full of beautiful antiques in Phelps. They then moved to New Hartford where they both were active in the First United Methodist Church. Burt retired from Agway in 1981.

Ted was able to resume classes at Cornell in January 1946. He and Peggy were married the next month, and after graduation Ted began his long career with the Cornell Cooperative Extension Service. They raised their three daughters and two sons in the village of Bath, where Ted was active in a long list of Extension-related activities and public service projects. The Ted Markham Nature Center at the Mossy Bank Village Park in Bath is a testimony to his love of teaching and his commitment to nature.

Jan and John raised a family of four sons on their High Market Road farm near Constableville, where they farmed for another thirty-nine years. Jan was known for her excellent cooking skills, putting them to use often as she fed numerous hungry hay crews. She was a warm hostess to her visiting nieces and nephews, and is also remembered for her love of garden flowers. She was active in St. Paul's Episcopal Church in Constableville, where she served on the Ladies' Guild and taught Sunday school. Jan and John moved to a home in the village following John's retirement.

Willie was discharged from the army in 1946 with the rank of Sergeant and went to work for Bob on the farm. In September of 1948, he married Jeanne Jones and worked as a self-employed carpenter. The couple welcomed three sons into their home on the East Road in Turin. Both Will and Jeanne retired from the South Lewis Central School District where they worked for more than twenty years as custodians. Will was active in the High Market Fish and Game Club and was head of the construction crew that built a school-owned nature center on Smith Road in the town of High Market.

Shirley earned a Bachelor's Degree in Education from the Plattsburgh

State Teachers' College following her high school graduation. She lived in Utica where she made her career teaching elementary school. Active in the New Harford Presbyterian Church, she served as a Deacon. She was able to pursue her life-long love of music by singing with the church choir and with the Utica Chorale. Shirley never failed to remember her many nieces' and nephews' birthdays and was always quick to welcome them to her home for a visit.

Ernest was able to retire not long after the War's end with more than thirty years of service in the Post Office. After selling the farm to Bob, he and Evelyn moved to a charming Carpenter Gothic farmhouse further down West Road, closer to Turin. There, in his retirement, Ernest practiced his woodworking skills, and Evelyn pursued her interests in horticulture and gardening. It was that home that a throng of grandchildren came to know as Grandma's house.

Her house is still there, but Ernest and Evelyn, their children, and their memories of World War II have slipped into the last century now. But for their grandchildren, memories live on – of Jersey cows and calves, Ernest's well-used woodshop, a resident cocker or collie, Evelyn's homemade bread, a stunning perennial garden – all part of the home and family that we will forever hold dear to us.

The Markham home as photographed by Ted in 1956.

Ernest and Evelyn at work in their garden.

Evelyn, Ernestine, Ernest, and Marian in 1916.

Ted's high school graduation class, 1939.
Front row: Noreen Roser, Marion Long, Marion Regetz, Eileen Gillette, Eileen Mackey.
Back row: Theodore Markham, Harland Freeman, Harland Abbey*, Robert Kraeger*,
Donald McGovern, Mr. William Kaskela (*died in the war).
(Image courtesy of Peter Hayes, Constableville Historian)

Acknowledgments

It has only been with the help of my family, my friends, and my colleagues that what began as a collection of letters and a photo album became this book. Special thanks go to my book designer, Veronica Seyd, who after retiring from the University of Washington Press, became my neighbor and friend. There is no question that without her professional skill, her proximity, and most of all her patience, this book would not have happened. Another friend and neighbor, June Layton, has been my unofficial consultant, always willing to share her professional opinions and advice.

Members of the Union Springs High School staff were also contributors. Special thanks go to Stephanie Berry, High School Librarian; Donna Brier, Library Assistant; Susan Haag, Global History teacher; and Heather Doyle, American History teacher.

Many of my Markham cousins were helpful. Judy Markham and Betsy O'Brien provided details of their mothers' lives. Hugh Markham contributed his knowledge of the Markham genealogy. Linda Markham Macklin lent me the telegrams from her father's war experience. Ed Markham solved the mystery of the short snorter, and Joe Markham shared details of Bob's tours of duty in the Pacific. Ron Klossner and my sister, Leigh Markham Peck, contributed more letters for the collection. Mary Hebblethwaite helped with some questions I had concerning her grandmother, Marian Dewan.

More thanks go to Peter Hayes, Constableville Historian, Glenn Gaston, photo illustrator, Jill Van Housen and Lisa Carr from the Watertown *Daily Times*, and John Hammond from the New York State Historic Newspapers Project, administered by the Northern New York Library Network. Conversations with Kate Ackerman and Brian Klossner were also helpful, as were some suggestions from my daughter, Anne O'Hara.

Thank you, all.

Notes

Introduction

Gould Paper Company
Lyons Falls History Association. Retrieved from http://www.lyonsfallshistory.org/post.php?pid=7.

Adirondacks Tug Hill Region
Visit Adirondacks New York U.S.A. Retrieved from http://visitadirondacks.com/regions/adirondacks-tughill.

1942–43

Attack on Pearl Harbor
Danzer, G., Klor de Alva, J., Krieger, L., Wilson, L., Woloch, N. (2007). *The Americans*. Evanstown, IL: McDougal Littell; pp. 760–761.

Japanese Aggression in the Pacific
Danzer, G., Klor de Alva, J., Krieger, L., Wilson, L., Woloch, N. (2007). *The Americans*. Evanstown, IL: McDougal Littell, p. 785.

Blackouts on the Pacific Coast
The Impact of WWII on the California Coast. *Mobile Ranger*. Retrieved from http://www.mobileranger.com/blog/the-impact-of-wwii-on-the-california-coast.

Schneider Index
Schneider Index. Merriam Webster. Retrieved from https://www.merriam-webster.com/medical/Schneider%20index.

Sahara
Sahara. Barnes and Noble. Retrieved from https://www.barnesandnoble.com/w/dvd-sahara-humphrey-bogart/3626475.

Turin Man
Turin Man Wins Navy "Wings." *The Boonville Herald* (1943, February 4).

Notes

PBY Catalina, PBY-2, B24 Liberator, Ventura, PB 2y, TBY, Stearman PT-17 Lockheed PV-2 Harpoon/Ventura. Warbird Alley. Retrieved from http://www. warbirdalley.com/pv2.htm.

(2016/05/12) Staff Writer Consolidated Voltee TBY Sea Wolf Torpedo Bomber. Military Factory. Retrieved from http://www.militaryfactory.com/aircraft/detail. asp?aircraft_id=1221.

Grant, R.G. (2002). *Flight –100 Years of Aviation*, D.K. Publishing, Inc., New York

Lowell Thomas
The Editors of Encyclopedia Britannica. (2017, March 17) Lowell Thomas/ American journalist. *Encyclopedia Britannica*. Retrieved from http://www.britannica.com/biography/Lowell-Thomas.

Fierce Fighting on All Fronts

Africa
Hastings, Sir Max. (2004) *The Second World War/The World in Flames*. Great Britain/Osprey Publishing, p.22.

Total War in the Pacific. Spark Notes World War II (1939–1945). Retrieved from http://www.sparknotes.com/history/european/ww2/section8/page/2/.

Russia
The Invasion of Russia. Spark Notes World War II (1939–1945). Retrieved from http://www.sparknotes.com/history/european/ww2/section8/page/2/.

Battle of the Bismarck Sea
Hastings, Sir Max. (2004) *The Second World War/The World in Flames*. Great Britain/Osprey Publishing, pp. 22, 257.

OPA
Danzer, G., Klor de Alva, J, Krieger, L., Wilson, L., Woloch, N. (2007). *The Americans*. Evanstown, IL: McDougal Littell; p. 773.

2nd War Loan
Brief History of World War Two Advertising Campaigns War Loans and Bonds. Duke University Libraries. Retrieved from http://library.duke.edu/ digitalcollections/adaccess/guide/wwii/bonds.

The 2nd War Loan Starts April 12. *The Black River Democrat* (1943 April). Retrieved from http://nyshistoricnewspapers.org/lccn/sn86033360/2007-12-29/ ed-1/seq-1/.

Notes

A.A.F.T.T.C. , W.A.A.C.
Abbreviations, Acronyms, Codewords, Terms. *Hyper War Glossary of Abbreviations and Code Words.* Retrieved from http://ibiblio.org/hyperwar/Glossary/V.html.

The Morrill Act of 1862 (Land Grant Colleges)
The Morrill Acts of 1862 and 1890. The 1890 Land Grant Universities. Retrieved from http://www.1890universities.org/history.

Pine Camp
Forts/Pine Camp. New York State Military Museum and Veteran's Research Center. Retrieved from https://dmna.ny.gov/forts/fortsM_P/pineCamp.htm.

Invasion of Italy
Hastings, Sir Max (2004). *The Second World War/The World in Flames.* Great Britain/Osprey Publishing, p. 22.

Dean Ladd
Clarke, John W., Editor in Chief; *The 1937 Cornellian*, copyright by the Cornell Annuals, Inc.; Ithaca, NY.

Jan's Engagement
Engaged. *The Boonville Herald* (September 1943).

Italy's surrender
Timeline of World War II 1943. THE WAR. Retrieved from https://www.pbs.org/thewar/at_war_timeline_1943.htm.+

Wake Island
Hastings, Sir Max (2004). *The Second World War/The World in Flames.* Great Britain/Osprey Publishing. p.248.

Food Rationing/Blue Points/Red Points
OPA Rationing Token Information. Retrieved from http://www.usmilitariaforum.com/forums/index.php?/topic/104233-opa-rationing-token-information/.

Barrage Balloons
Barrage balloons. World War II. Retrieved from http://www.worldwar-two.net/weapons/barrage_balloons/.

Enola Gay
Sherman, Stephen (2011, June 29). Paul Tibbets and the Enola Gay. Retrieved from http://acepilots.com/usaaf_tibbets.html.

Wedding Write-Up
"Miss Janice E. Markham to Wed." *The Watertown DailyTimes* (1943, October 30).

Notes

Undulant Fever
Medical definition of undulant fever. Retrieved from http://www.medicinenet.com/script/main/art.asp?articlekey=9306.

Dr. Stanley W. Warren
Professor of Merit. Retrieved from https://cals.cornell.edu/academics/awards/professor-of-merit.

Cecil Brown
Woolbert, Robert Gale. Suez to Singapore. *Foreign Affairs*. Retrieved from https://www.foreignaffairs.com/reviews/capsule-review/1943-04-01/suez-singapore.

Ernie Pyle
Journalist Ernie Pyle Killed. *This Day in History 1945*. Retrieved from http://www.history.com/this-day-in-history/journalist-ernie-pyle-killed.

1944

Monte Cassino, D Day, Saipan, Market Garden, Hurtgen Forest, Leyte Gulf, Battle of the Bulge
Timeline of World War II. 1944. *The War*. Retrieved from https://www.pbs.org/thewar/at_war_timeline_1944.htm.

Ploesti
Zubrin, Robert (2013, August 3). Remembering Ploesti. *National Review*. Retrieved from http://www.nationalreview.com/article/355074/remembering-ploesti-robert-zubrin.

The Draft
1940 United States Imposes the Draft. *This Day in History*. Retrieved from http://www.history.com/this-day-in-history/united-states-imposes-the-draft.

Selective Service Classifications. Retrieved from http://www.cufon.org/CRG/memo/74911231.html.

Tennessee Valley Authority
Danzer, G., Klor de Alva, J., Krieger, L., Wilson, L., Woloch, N. (2007). *The Americans*. Evanstown, IL : McDougal Littel, pp. 726–727.

Normandy Invasion Casualties
(June 6, 2014). Fact Sheet: Normandy Landings . The White House Office of the Press Secretary. Retrieved from https://obamawhitehouse.archives.gov/the-press-office/2014/06/06/fact-sheet-normandy-landings.

Notes

General George Patton
George S. Patton. *H History*. Retrieved from http://www.history.com/topics/
world-war-ii/george-smith-patton.

Photograph of Pilot Solo
(1943, November) Pocket Carriers Fight the Submarines. *The National Geographic
Magazine*, p. 555.

France, Belgium, Luxembourg
Danzer, G.; Klor de Alva, J; Krieger, L.; Wilson, L.; Woloch, N. (2007). *The Americans*. Evanstown, IL: McDougal Littell, p. 780.

Claron (Pete) Markham/Distinguished Flying Cross
"Lewis Lives for Liberty". *The Lowville Leader* (1944, February 10). Retrieved from
http://nyshistoricnewspapers.org/lccn/sn92061742/1944-02-10/ed-1/seq-1/.

The Siegfried Line
Editors of Encyclopedia Brittanica. Siegfried Line. *Encyclopedia Brittanica*.
Retrieved from https://www.britannica.com/topic/Siegfried-

M I /Garand
Moss, Mathew. (2016, December 30). "The Legendary Rifle That Fought World
War II." *Popular Mechanics*.com. Retrieved from http://www.popularmechanics.
com/military/weapons/a24537/m1-garand-world-war-two/ics.com.

B.A.R.
(2017, 07/14). Staff Writer. Browning M1918 BAR (Browning Automatic Rifle)
Light Machine Gun LMG/Squad Support Weapon. Military Factory.com.
Retrieved from http://www.militaryfactory.com/smallarms/detail-page-2.
asp?smallarms_id=58.

News Story
"Family's Four Sons in Service." *The Watertown Daily Times* (1944, November 27).

1945

Battle of the Bulge
Timeline of World War II 1945. *The War*. Retrieved from https://www.pbs.org/
thewar/at_war_timeline_1945.htm.

(2011, Dec. 1) Will. 10 Bloodiest Battles of World War II. *Military Education*.
Retrieved from http://www.militaryeducation.
org/10-bloodiest-battles-of-world-war-ii/.

Notes

Photograph
Wilbur, Brigadier General W.H. (1944, November). Infantrymen – The Fighters of War. *The National Geographic Magazine*, p. 516.

Phone Calls Short
"Bottlenecking Vital War Calls." *The Lowville Leader* (1944, November 9). Retrieved from http://nyshistoricnewspapers.org/lccn/sn86033360/2007-12-29/ed-1/seq-1/.

Short Snorter
Famous Short Snorters. *History Detectives Special Investigations*. Retrieved from http://www.pbs.org/opb/historydetectives/feature/famous-short-snorters/.

Luzon
Will. (2001, December 1). "10 Bloodiest Battles of World War II." *Military Education*. Retrieved from http://www.militaryeducation.org/10-bloodiest-battles-of-world-war-ii/.

Photograph
Simpich, Frederick (1942, February). "Facts About the Philippines." *The National Geographic Magazine*, p. 201. J. Baylor Roberts/National Geographic Creative.

Norden Bombsite
(2007, September 25). World War II Norden Bombsite. *Hill Air Force Base.* Retrieved from http://www.hill.af.mil/About-Us/Fact-Sheets/Display/Article/397308/world-war-ii-norden-bombsight.

Victory Letter/V-Mail
Resizing Lifelines Victory Mail. Smithsonian National Postal Museum. Retrieved from https://postalmuseum.si.edu/VictoryMail/.

P-47 Thunderbolt
Hickman, Kennedy. (2016, November 8). World War II Republic P-47 Thunderbolt. *ThoughtCo*. Retrieved from http://militaryhistory.about.com/od/worldwariiaircraft/p/p47.htm.

Victory in Europe Day
Harry S. Truman: "The President's News Conference on V-E Day," May 8, 1945. Online by Gerhard Peters and John T. Woolley, *The American Presidency Project*. Retrieved from http://www.presidency.ucsb.edu/ws/?pid=12248.

Bronze Star
Bronze Star Medal. *USAMM.COM*. Retrieved from https://www.usamilitarymedals.com/products/bronze-star-medal.

Notes

Hiroshima/Nagasaki Casualties
Timeline of World War II 1945. *The War*. Retrieved from https://www.pbs.org/
thewar/at_war_timeline_1945.htm.

Empire State Building
1945. "Plane Crashes into the Empire State Building." *H History*
Retrieved from http://www.history.com/this-day-in-history/
plane-crashes-into-empire-state-building.

Epilogue

61 Lewis County Dead
WW II Army Casualties: New York. National Archives. Retrieved from https://
www.archives.gov/research/military/ww2/army-casualties/new-york.html.

Lewis County: retrieved from https://nara-media-001.s3.amazonaws.com/a.

Cornell Casualties
Cornell University Veteran's Memorial. Retrieved from http://veteransmemorials.
cornell.edu/files/2013/11/Cornell-Veterans-Memorials-Tour-2ll0y6m.pdf.

American Casualties
Murray, Lorraine. National World War II Memorial. *Encyclopedia
Britannica*. Retrieved from https://www.britannica.com/topic/
National-World-War-II-Memorial.

World Casualties
Royde-Smith, John (2017, 07/18). World War II. *Encyclopedia Britannica*.
Retrieved from https://www.britannica.com/event/World-War-II.

Hastings, Sir Max (2004). *The Second World War/ The War in Flames*. Great
Britain/Osprey Publishing, p. 463.

Will. (2011, December 1). "10 Bloodiest Battles of World War II."
Military Education. Retrieved from http://www.militaryeducation.
org/10-bloodiest-battles-of-world-war-ii/.

Genealogy
Hartwig, Nancy Markham; Hartwig, Curtis Paul (July 2000). Descendants of
Deacon Daniel Markham.

Markham, Hugh. Descendants of Evelyn Lucinda Wasmuth.

www.ingramcontent.com/pod-product-compliance
Lightning Source LLC
LaVergne TN
LVHW091212080426
835509LV00009B/962